DISASTER AT THE COLORADO

BEALE'S WAGON ROAD AND THE FIRST EMIGRANT PARTY

DISASTER AT THE COLORADO

BEALE'S WAGON ROAD AND THE FIRST EMIGRANT PARTY

Charles W. Baley

UTAH STATE UNIVERSITY PRESS
LOGAN, UTAH

Utah State University Press
Logan, Utah

Manufactured in the United States of America
Printed on acid-free paper

Cover illustration: *Mitchell's Pass*, by William H. Jackson
Cover design: Richard Howe

09 08 07 06 05 04 03 02   1 2 3 4 5 6 7

Library of Congress Cataloging-in-Publication Data

Baley, Charles W., 1922–
    Disaster at the Colorado : Beale's wagon road and the first emigrant party
/ by Charles W. Baley.
        p. cm.
Includes bibliographical references and index
    ISBN 0-87421-437-8 (pbk. : alk. paper) — ISBN 0-87421-438-6 (Cloth :
alk. paper)
    1. Beale Road—History. 2. Southwest, New—Description and travel.
3. Arizona—History—To 1912. 4. Mohave Indians—Arizona—History—
19th century. 5. Mohave Indians—Wars. 6. Beale, Edward Fitzgerald,
1822–1893. I. Title.
    F786.B23 2002
    979.1'304—dc21

                            2002003862

Contents

PREFACE

Volume after volume has been written about the Oregon-California Trail and other overland routes to California, but comparatively little has been written about Beale's Wagon Road. The reason is simple: The disaster suffered by the first emigrant parties who attempted this route discouraged its use. In later years as Route 66, and more recently as Interstate 40, it would become a major east-west highway, but it took the development of the automobile to bring this about. The first wagon train to attempt Beale's Wagon Road was the Rose-Baley wagon train in 1858. The hardships and suffering endured by these hardy and courageous pioneers have seldom been equaled in the annals of our nation's westward frontier movement; yet their story remains largely untold. The purpose of this narrative is to tell their story.

My great grandparents, William Right Baley and Nancy Baley, their children, and my great-great uncle, Gillum Baley, his wife Permelia, and their children, were members of this unfortunate wagon train. As a child I heard a few tales about their overland trip from my father and his relatives, but over time, many of the details of their ill-fated adventure had been forgotten. While researching my genealogy, I came upon bits of information about their harrowing journey across the western plains. This piqued my interest and motivated me to learn more.

An undertaking of this nature could not have been accomplished without the aid of many generous and cooperative individuals to whom I am deeply indebted. Many went out of their way to lend a helping hand. Some, who had no knowledge of their own to contribute, nevertheless made a valuable contribution by providing me with the names of persons who were knowledgeable. Much valuable information was gained in this manner. And, as with any project, there were those who promised much but delivered little.

A survey of the literature revealed only one known journal kept by a member of this emigrant party. That was the journal keep by John Udell. Without this little book, many of the details of the Rose-Baley wagon train would probably never be known. I wish he could have been a little more informative about the interrelationships between the various members of the group; nevertheless, the facts given by this old Baptist preacher were of great value in my research. Udell provided the names of those families who comprised this emigrant party and he provided information on where each family departed from, thus furnishing a starting point for locating descendants. Udell provided the basic framework; my task was to fill in the details.

One of the first descendants that I was able to locate was Dr. Joel W. Hedgpeth of Santa Rosa, California. Dr. Hedgpeth, an oceanographer of considerable fame, is a great grandson of Joel and Jane Hedgpeth, who were in this wagon train. Dr. Hedgpeth was very helpful in providing details about the Hedgpeth family as well as providing documents and photographs. He was also kind enough to give me the name of another researcher of the Rose-Baley wagon train, Mark S. Simpson Jr., of Pittsburg, California. I discovered that Mark was a great grandson of William Right Baley and a distant cousin of mine. Mark had done some preliminary research on the Rose-Baley wagon train, but ill health forced him to discontinue. He kindly lent me the results of his research and urged me to continue the work. Unfortunately, Mark passed away before I completed the project. To Mark S. Simpson Jr., I will always be grateful.

My next step was to pay a visit to the areas where much of the story took place: Arizona and New Mexico. In Kingman, Arizona, my wife and I visited the Mojave Museum of History and Arts. Here we learned that a man by the name of Jack Beale Smith of Flagstaff, Arizona, (not related to Edward F. Beale) was a student of Beale's Wagon Road and had discovered and mapped most of the original road between Zuni, New Mexico, and the Colorado River. He has written several booklets on Beale's Wagon Road and related subjects. We spent two days with Jack in his jeep going over sections of the road which can only be reached by travel in a four-wheel drive vehicle. Finding Jack was a real stroke of luck.

From Bob White, sheriff of the Garden of the Sun Corral, Westerners International, I received several helpful suggestions for which I am grateful. Bob is a native of Arizona and a student of Arizona history.

Another researcher to whom I am deeply grateful is Dennis G. Casebier of Goffs, (near Needles) California. Dennis's field of expertise is the Mojave Road. He is the author of a book by that name in addition to several other books dealing with the early-day history of the American presence along the lower Colorado River. The Mojave Road was an extension of Beale's Wagon Road from the Colorado River to San Bernardino and Los Angeles. Dennis is very knowledgeable about Beale's Wagon Road and the Rose-Baley wagon train. He gave me much information and encouragement. He also read my manuscript and offered valuable advice which resulted in many improvements.

To Willetta Pokorny of Clovis, California, I am deeply indebted for much of the information on the Gillum Baley family, including photographs, newspaper clippings, scrapbooks, and other documents. Willetta is a great granddaughter of Gillum Baley.

Much of the information on the Brown family and Sallie Fox came from Gloria Kidder and Shawn Lum from the staff of the Harbison House and the Nut Tree in Vacaville, California. Leona Crownover, a direct descendant of Sallie Fox Allen, also provided me with much useful material and photographs. From Dorthy Kupcha Leland, the author of *Sallie Fox: The Story of a Pioneer Girl,* I received moral support as well as some excellent photographs. From Dr. Genevieve Thompson, a descendant of Sophia Frances (Franc) Fox, I received photographs and genealogical material on this branch of the family. To all of these individuals, I give my deepest thanks.

For details on the life of John Udell, I am indebted to C. Melvin Bliven, a descendant of John and Emily Udell. He provided me with a photograph of John and Emily as well as a genealogy of the Udell family. In researching the Daly and Holland families, I was most fortunate in finding the late Hart Ralph Tambs, a descendant and unofficial historian of these families. I also received much help in collecting data and photographs on these families from Dorothy Wilbur of Waterford, California. Ever try finding a person by the name of Smith? This can be a daunting task, especially when the only bits of information available were the subject's initials and the general area in which he probably settled. Thanks to Dorothy DeDontney of the Santa Clara County

Historical and Genealogical Society, this task was made simple. She found a recent obituary of a descendant of E. O. Smith which listed the names of next of kin. From this list she provided me the name and address of Terry Feist, a great-great grandson of E.O. Smith. Terry kindly provided me with a copy of a memorial sketch of E. O. Smith which was published in the *San Jose Mercury* on March 12, 1892. The sketch proved to be a valuable source of information on the life of E. O. Smith.

The following historical societies played an important part in my research: Arizona Historical Society, Tucson, Arizona; Fresno City and County Historical Society, Fresno, California; Mohave County Historical Society, Kingman, Arizona; Santa Clara County Historical and Genealogical Society; State Historical Society of Iowa; Tulare County Historical Society; and the Van Buren County, Iowa, Historical Society.

Libraries, museums, and archives were also important sources of information. The Huntington Library and Art Gallery in San Marino, California, played a major role in my research. My special thanks to Peter J. Blodgett, Assistant Curator, Western Historical Manuscripts, for his help. While on the subject of the Huntington Library, I would like to thank John E. Osborne, former sheriff of the Garden of the Sun Corral, Westerners International, of Fresno, California, for his assistance in helping me in obtaining a reader's card at the Huntington Library. His assistance made access much easier.

Other individuals and institutions that I wish to thank are: The Bancroft Library, University of California, Berkeley, California; The California State Library, Sacramento, California; The Church of Jesus Christ of Latter-day Saints, Family History Department, Salt Lake City, Utah; The Church of Jesus Christ of Latter-day Saints, Fresno Stake, Family History Library, Fresno, California; Fresno County Library, Fresno, California; Henry Madden Library, California State University, Fresno, California; General Commission on Archives and History, The United Methodist Church, Madison, New Jersey; Ruth Ann Hager, Genealogical Researcher, Florissant, Missouri; Holt-Atherton Department of Special Collections, University of the Pacific Libraries, University of the Pacific, Stockton, California; the Library of Congress, Washington, D.C.; Missouri West Conference Archives, Central Methodist College, Fayette, Missouri; National Archives, Washington, D.C.; Rose Ann Tompkins, Chandler, Arizona; Tulare City

Library, Tulare, California; Tulare County Recorder, Visalia, California. For helping me to master my fear of the computer, I am indebted to Gayle E. Jordan. Without her calm assurance I don't believe that I would ever have conquered the beast!

For the tedious work of proofreading I am indebted to Bobbye Sisk Temple, Doris Hall, and Dorothy Cufaude. They wore out several red pencils while performing the task.

Last, but by no means the least, my wife, Mary, who accompanied me on field trips, corrected my grammar, and offered suggestions for improvement. Without her patience and encouragement this work would have been impossible.

If I have omitted anyone, the omission was not intentional, but simply an oversight by the author.

Chapter I

The Roster

"I thought it was preposterous to start on so long a journey with so many women and helpless children, and so many dangers attending the attempt."

This is how John Udell described the decision of his fellow travelers to leave the old established road and follow a new and completely untested and unproven route that promised to get them to California a few days sooner. But the lure of shorter routes and cutoffs often proved irresistible to emigrants, as it did with Udell's companions.

Udell and his wife, Emily, were members of a California-bound wagon train from Iowa and Missouri that had arrived at Albuquerque, New Mexico, in June of 1858. Here, they heard about a newly surveyed road (Beale's Wagon Road) that would run from Fort Smith, Arkansas, to San Bernardino, California. The proposed road at that time was little more than a survey trail, traveled previously only by a few experienced and well-equipped explorers. Some day it would become a major east-west highway. But the time was not yet.

Udell's fellow travelers were a diverse group with little in common other than a desire to establish new homes for themselves and their families in California. Emigrant trains crossing the western plains were usually named after the largest or the wealthiest property owner, or owners, in the group. That is probably why this emigrant party would become known as the Rose-Baley wagon train, after its two wealthiest members, Leonard John Rose and Gillum Baley, although some of its members might have objected to this name. The two companies, the Roses and the Baleys, did not start the journey together but joined along the way, a common practice as there was greater safety in large numbers.

Leonard John Rose, better known as L. J. Rose, was by far the wealthiest member of this group. He was thirty years of age, and a resident of Van Buren County, Iowa. Traveling with him was his wife, Amanda, age twenty-five, and their two children, Nina Elizabeth and Annie Wilhelmina, ages four and one. Also traveling with the Rose family were Mrs. Rose's father and mother, Ezra M. Jones, age fifty-five, and Elizabeth Burgett Jones, age fifty-four, and the Joneses' eighteen-year-old son, Edward C. Jones. All were from Van Buren County.

L. J. Rose was born in Rottenburg, Germany, on May 1, 1827. When he was eight years old, he immigrated to the United States with his mother and sister. The father had come to this country sometime previously and was operating a small store in New Orleans. After a short stay in New Orleans the family moved to Waterloo, Illinois, where they purchased another store. The younger Rose finished school in Waterloo and attended one year at Shurtleff College in Alton, Illinois. He then returned to Waterloo and went into business with his father.

Father and son did not get along well together in business; the elder Rose was slow in becoming Americanized and held onto his old country ways, while the son, with an American education, had a better understanding of American merchandising methods. The two quarreled frequently until, finally, the younger Rose could take no more and left the business to strike out on his own. He invested his share of the money from the partnership in apples, which he packed in barrels and freighted down the Mississippi River to New Orleans, where he quickly sold the consignment at a favorable price. Looking around for an opportunity to reinvest his money, he observed that there was an oversupply of draft animals in Louisiana, and they were selling at a much lower price than what they would have sold for on the Illinois market. He bought all the horses and mules his funds would allow, then shipped them up the Mississippi River to his home in Illinois, where he sold the animals for a substantial profit. He repeated this process until he had saved enough money to open a small store of his own.[1]

In 1841, at the age of twenty-one, Rose moved to Keosauqua, Iowa, where he purchased a general store. Here, he met Amanda Markel Jones whom he married in 1851. By 1857, through hard work, good luck, and excellent management, the young man accumulated a sizable bank account. With things going so well for him, one might wonder why he wanted to pull up stakes and move himself and his family halfway across the continent to a place he knew nothing about. Rose supplied the answer to this question in an article he wrote in 1892 for a magazine, *The Californian*:

> In 1858 some miners who had just returned from California, so fired my imagination with descriptions of its glorious climate, wealth of flowers and luscious fruits, that I was inspired with an irresistible desire to experience in person the delights to be found in the land of plenty.[2]

After selling most of his property and settling his debts, Rose had a net worth of more than $30,000, a small fortune in those days. With this substantial sum of money he was able to put together one of the best-equipped outfits ever to travel the western plains. He purchased a herd of 200 of the best cattle on the market, mostly thoroughbred Red Durhams.[3] He knew he could sell these animals in California for a hefty profit. For driving the loose stock, and for scouting and hunting, he purchased twenty of the finest horses that he could find in Iowa and Missouri, including a Morgan stallion, Black Morrill, valued at $2,500, and two matched Morgan fillies valued at $350 each. To manage this huge herd of livestock, and to perform the myriad duties of camp life, he obtained the services of seventeen young single men. For the most part these young men were grubstakers, receiving no salary or other compensation for their services other than their board. This was a common method of getting to California and other Western states for young single men who lacked the funds for purchasing and fitting out teams and wagons of their own.

To oversee this extensive outfit, Rose hired a man by the name of Alpha Brown, a forty-five-year-old fellow Van Buren County resident. Brown was to act as general manager and to have charge of the day-to-day affairs, while Rose would act as chairman of the board and take care of the more serious matters. Alpha Brown was well qualified for the job, having been to California during the gold rush in 1849. Dame Fortune, as she had with so many other forty-niners, failed to smile upon him, and he returned to his family in Iowa a poorer but a wiser person. Brown was a man of sterling character, greatly respected by all who knew him. He possessed considerable experience in the handling of horses and cattle, a skill of great value for managing a California-bound wagon train. Rose considered himself fortunate in having secured the services of such a competent and experienced individual.

Brown planned to bring along his family, consisting of his wife, Mary Baldwin Fox Brown, age thirty-five; their seven-year-old daughter, Julia; their five-year-old son, Orrin; and Brown's invalid daughter, Relief (Liefy), age thirteen, from his previous marriage. Mrs. Brown also had two daughters from her previous marriage, Sophia Frances (Franc) Fox, age fifteen, and Sarah (Sallie) Estelle Fox, age thirteen.

For carrying the passengers and the necessary supplies and equipment needed for such an extended trip, Rose purchased four large prairie schooner-type wagons, each with high sideboards and covered by a heavy painted canvas. Two barrels of water were secured to one side while feedboxes for feeding the animals were attached to the other side and to the rear. Three yoke of oxen (six animals) were required to pull these stout but ponderous vehicles. Oxen, although slower than horses or mules, were the preferred power source for pulling the heavy wagons because they had greater endurance and stamina and required less care than either horses or mules. Three of these prairie schooners were used for carrying equipment and supplies, while the fourth was used by the Alpha Brown family. The driver, sometimes referred to as a bullwhacker, usually controlled the oxen by walking at their left side rather than riding in the wagon as did stagecoach drivers. For transporting his own family and his in-laws, Rose purchased an old ambulance pulled by two mules. It was light but fast and was jokingly called the "avalanche" by one of the young wags in the party. It was usually in the lead when the procession got underway each morning.[4]

Emigrants traveling to California or Oregon from the Midwest usually went by way of the Oregon-California Trail since this was the shortest route for them. In 1858, however, the United States was having a problem with the Mormons in Utah that threatened to lead to hostilities. This was the so-called Mormon, or Utah, war of 1857–58.[5] Fearing possible conflict with the Mormons, many emigrants that year were fearful of traveling this route. Some chose to avoid Mormon territory by taking the Santa Fe Trail to Santa Fe, New Mexico, and from there traveling the Southern Route through the southern part of the New

Mexico Territory to California. There were several variants of this route, but they all came together before crossing the Colorado River into California at Fort Yuma. This road was considerably longer than the Oregon-California Trail, but many emigrants in 1858, including the Rose company, believed that this was the safest overland route to California.

The Rose company left Van Buren County, Iowa, in early April of 1858. They set their course for Westport (present-day Kansas City, Missouri), where they crossed the Missouri River by steamboat. Shortly before arriving at Westport they were joined by another family by the name of Bentner. This family consisted of seven people: a husband and wife, a daughter of about eighteen, another daughter about fifteen, a son about twelve, and two younger children whose gender and ages are unrecorded. Like Rose, the Bentners were also German immigrants. Although well-Anglicized, they were usually referred to as the Dutch Family by other members of the wagon train.[6] Little is known about this family. Even their first names are not recorded in any known accounts of the journey. German immigrants in those days were frequently lumped together with the Dutch, probably because of the similarities of the languages and the fact that the German word for themselves is Deutsch, which sounded like Dutch to the American ear. The Bentner family was traveling light; their outfit consisted of a single small wagon pulled by a team of mules. They were driving no loose livestock, not even an extra pair of mules.

In Putnam County, Missouri, just across the Iowa-Missouri state line, John and Emily Udell were also making plans for an overland journey to California. At ages sixty-two and sixty-four, they were considerably older than most emigrants on the trail. They were the parents of eight grown children. Two of their sons, Oliver and Henry, were living in Solano County, California. Feeling the twinges of old age, and not having accumulated much in the way of worldly goods, the Udells wanted to be near their two sons in California, who they hoped might be able to assist their parents during their twilight years. John Udell had tried earning a living in several different fields including mining, farming, bookselling, and preaching (he was a lay Baptist minister), but with little success in any of these endeavors.

For John Udell, this trip would not be a new experience, for he had been to California three times, the first in 1850 during the height of the gold rush. The big nuggets had eluded him, but this didn't discourage him from trying his luck twice more with equally poor results.

Thanks to John Udell, many of the details of the Rose-Baley wagon train have been preserved for posterity. He faithfully kept a journal in which he recorded each day's activities for nearly the entire journey.[7] Others in the group might also have kept diaries or journals, but if so, they have not come to light. Udell kept journals during his previous trips to California, and in 1856 he was successful in having one published under the title, *Incidents of Travel Across the Great Plains.* The book was not a big financial success, but it did bring him some favorable attention. He very likely had publication in mind when he started his journal at the beginning of the Rose-Baley trip. As a published author, and having made three prior trips to California, Udell considered himself quite an authority on western travel, an opinion which would bring him into conflict with others during the course of the journey.

For this venture Udell prepared well. He equipped himself with a good wagon, an excellent team of four yoke of well-broken oxen, two good milch cows, a good riding horse, and everything needed to make this trip as comfortable as possible. He hired (or more likely grubstaked) two young men, Tamerlane Davis and John Anspach, to take care of the team and perform all the necessary labor during the journey. Udell knew what was needed to make the trip a success.

The Udells started their journey to California on April 8, 1858. They traveled at a leisurely pace across northern Missouri, stopping frequently to say goodbye to friends along the way and, wherever possible, having a meal with them. They were usually able to spend each night at a friend's house, sometimes laying over for an extra day. Udell seems to have had a lot of friends in Putnam and neighboring counties.

The first day they traveled ten miles and put up with a neighbor, a Mr. William Graham. The next day, Udell recorded, "We took dinner [lunch] at Mr. John Daily's [John Lucas Daly] in Yreka. We expect Mr. Daily with his large family, will overtake us at the Missouri River, and travel with us to California. We traveled fifteen miles today and camped near Mr. Herriman's." The Dalys were obviously close friends of the Udells, probably members of the same church. The Dalys were not quite ready to begin the trip to California, but knowing the slow pace of the Udells, the Dalys knew they would have no trouble overtaking them.

On April 23, 1858, the Udells arrived at Westport, where, for a two-dollar fee, they crossed the Missouri River by steamboat and arrived in the Kansas Territory. Because it was getting late in the day, they traveled only a short distance before establishing camp. They remained at this location until April 26, on which date Udell recorded, "We moved out four miles, to the encampment of a friend from Keosauqua, Iowa, consisting of fifteen men and a number of women and children. Mr. J. L. [L. J.] Rose was the proprietor, and Alpha Brown superintended it. I made arrangements to travel with this company, as they were bound for California. We all agreed to travel the Santa Fe Route, through New Mexico." This statement indicates Udell may have known Rose previously.

After spending three days in camp with the Rose company getting organized, the emigrants resumed their westward journey on April 30, 1858. "Our course lay through Kansas Territory, over a beautiful rolling prairie, of rich soil; eight miles to Indian Creek; thence ten miles to Cedar Creek—well wooded. Here we camped. To-day Mr. Dailey [Daly] with his large family, and his son-in-law, Isaac Holland and family, overtook us, and will travel with us." The Rose company of the Rose-Baley wagon train was now complete, although this was not the way the two companies would be constituted later in the journey.

The Daly family consisted of John Lucas Daly, a farmer from Putnam County, Missouri, age forty-eight; his wife, Irene Morrow Daly, age forty-three; and six children, ranging in ages from nine to twenty-two. Also traveling with the Dalys were their married daughter, Amanda Melvina Holland, age twenty-seven; her husband, Isaac Taylor Holland, age twenty-six, and their four children, Hiram H., age four; Edward Warren, age two; and one-year-old twin boys, Tom and John. Isaac Taylor Holland was a blacksmith by trade, a most useful person to have along on a wagon train.[8]

John Lucas Daly was born in Bourbon County, Kentucky, November 2, 1809. His wife, Irene Morrow Daly, was born in Kentucky in 1814. They were married in Boone County, Missouri, in 1829. Their eldest daughter, Amanda Melvina, married Isaac Taylor Holland in

Putnam County, Missouri, in 1853. Holland was born in Davidson County, Tennessee, February 21, 1832.

The Dalys and Hollands each had an ox-drawn wagon and a few spare oxen, a couple of riding horses, and perhaps a milch cow or two. They were not burdened by a large number of loose stock like some families in this wagon train. Their destination was Tuolumne County, where Isaac had three brothers living. They had written to Isaac praising the delightful climate of California, and enumerating all the other glories that abounded there. They urged Isaac to bring his family and come out west and join them.

John Lucas Daly had been to California in 1849 during the gold rush and mined on the Feather River. Although he failed to find his fortune, he still believed there were a lot of nuggets in the streams of California just waiting to be picked up. He, too, might have had relatives in Tuolumne County.[9]

During the spring of 1858, four families in northwest Missouri were also making preparations to emigrate to California. These were the two Baley and the two Hedgpeth families. All were farmers in Nodaway County, Missouri. Since Gillum Baley was, by tacit agreement, the acknowledged leader of the group, these families will be referred to as the Baley company.[10]

Gillum Baley, age forty-four, was the older of the two brothers. His wife, Permelia was thirty-eight. They were the parents of nine children ranging from age twenty down to a six-week-old babe. William Right Baley, the younger brother, was thirty-eight; his wife, Nancy, was also thirty-eight. They had eight children whose ages varied from sixteen years to fifteen months. In addition, Nancy was five months pregnant with child number nine.[11]

Gillum Baley was born June 19, 1813, in Gallatin County, Illinois, near the Ohio River. When he was but two years old, the family resettled in Madison County, Missouri, where his father, William Baley, was one of the early farmers and cattle raisers of southeastern Missouri. In 1826 the family moved to Sangamon County, Illinois. After a brief residence there, the family moved again, this time to Pike County, Illinois.[12]

They were living in Pike County in 1832 when trouble broke out between the settlers and the Sauk and Fox Indians in an affair known to history as the Black Hawk War. Gillum and his older brother, Caleb, enlisted in the Illinois Mounted Militia in General Whiteside's brigade. Another volunteer in this brigade, but in a different regiment, was a young man by the name of Abraham Lincoln. Gillum Baley, although only nineteen, was elected second sergeant of his company. The company had a complement of four sergeants. After the expiration of his enlistment, he returned home to Pike County where he married Catherine Decker in 1834. Catherine died of measles after only two years of marriage, leaving Gillum with an infant son, William Moses. Shortly after this tragic event, Gillum left Illinois and resettled in Jackson County, Missouri. Here he married his second wife, Permelia Eleanor Myers, on August 21, 1836.

William Right Baley, called Right (spelled without a W) by his family and friends, was born May 17, 1819, in Madison County, Missouri. He was too young to enlist in the Black Hawk War with his brothers, Caleb and Gillum. In 1836 he joined Gillum and other family members in Jackson County, Missouri. Two years later the families moved to Platte County, Missouri, one of the new counties formed from territory acquired from the Sauk and Fox Indians in 1836 by the Platte Purchase. In 1842 the extended family resettled in Nodaway County, another of the counties created from the Platte Purchase. While living in Platte County, William Right married Nancy Margaret Funderburk. Nancy was born in Davidson County, Tennessee on March 20, 1820, a daughter or George Funderburk Sr. and Sally Scott.

In 1849, the three brothers, Caleb, Gillum, and William Right, got caught up in the excitement of the gold rush. They left their farms in the care of their wives and headed to California by way of the Oregon-California Trail. Caleb died in the gold mines at the Feather River soon after their arrival, but the two remaining brothers continued their mining activities with varying degrees of success until 1852, when they returned to their homes in Missouri by way of the Isthmus of Panama.

After returning home to Nodaway County, the brothers continued farming and improving their herds of thoroughbred Durham cattle, but the pleasant memories of California beckoned them. In 1858, they decided to return, this time with their families. They planned to drive their cattle with them; this would be their grubstake when they arrived at their new homes.

The Hedgpeth families consisted of a father and a married son and their wives and children. In the elder Hedgpeth household were Joel Hedgpeth Sr., age forty-nine; his wife, Jane, fifty; and their four children, varying in ages from twenty to seven years old. The members of the younger Hedgpeth family were Thomas Riley Hedgpeth, eldest son of Joel and Jane, age twenty-eight; his wife, Eliza Jane Elliott Hedgpeth, twenty-four; and their four children ranging in age from seven years to nine months.[13]

Joel Hedgpeth Sr. was born in Kentucky on January 14, 1809. His wife Jane Hudspeth (she may have been a distant cousin) was born in Virginia in 1808. They were married in Green County, Kentucky, in 1829. We know little about their early lives except that, like many other families of that era, they moved to northern Missouri during the 1830s. In 1836, Joel was employed as a teamster in Jackson County, Missouri, by the firm of Russell, Majors, and Waddell, the largest transportation company in the West at that time.[14] During the early 1840s they settled in Nodaway County, Missouri.[15]

The Baleys and Hedgpeths were neighbors and fellow members of the Methodist Episcopal Church, South, in Nodaway County, Missouri. This is likely how they met. Both Gillum Baley and Joel Hedgpeth Sr. had studied law and both had served as justices of the peace in Nodaway County, although neither ever obtained a law degree.[16] Obviously, these four families had a lot in common and were compatible, a positive factor considering the ordeals that they were soon to endure. None of the Hedgpeths had previously been to California, and so far as it is known, they had no close relatives living there. They, too, had heard the tall tales spun by returning miners about the wonders of California, and they believed that a better life awaited them there. They also planned to drive their livestock with them to California.

Another factor that may have encouraged these families to leave Missouri in 1858 was the unsettling times that existed on the Missouri-Kansas border as the result of the passage of the Kansas-Nebraska Act of 1854. This legislation admitted Nebraska into the Union as a free territory, but provided for the people of the Kansas Territory to decide for themselves whether they wanted to be organized as a free or as a slave territory. The result was what might have been expected—open warfare between proslavery and antislavery forces—with each side trying desperately to organize the territory to suit its own political convictions. Ruffians and other undesirable characters moved into the area to take advantage of the strife.

Conditions were exacerbated when John Brown and his abolitionists moved into Kansas. The Territory became known as Bleeding Kansas, so great was the violence. Soon the conflict began to spill over the border into the western counties of Missouri, including Nodaway, creating an atmosphere of fear and uncertainty. To make matters worse, the Panic of 1857 placed financial burdens on farmers everywhere in the country, but it was particularly hard on those in the Midwest. It was a combination of these factors plus the exaggerated glories of California that persuaded these families to pull up stakes and emigrate.

The Baleys and Hedgpeths said goodbye to their friends, relatives, and neighbors in Nodaway County on April 22, 1858, and set their course for St. Joseph, Missouri. After some last-minute shopping in St. Joseph (the elder Hedgpeths had their pictures taken here), they crossed the Missouri River on a steamboat and entered the Kansas Territory.

The Baley outfit consisted of five Murphy wagons, nineteen yoke of oxen (thirty-eight animals), twenty thoroughbred Durham cows and heifers, one thoroughbred Durham bull, and an unrecorded number of riding horses. The Hedgpeth outfit consisted of three Murphy wagons, twelve yoke of oxen (twenty-four animals), fifteen milch cows, forty head of loose cattle, and three riding horses.[17] In addition, each family had "an outfit for crossing the plains," consisting of a supply of food, clothing, and all the paraphernalia needed for such a long journey. Both the Baleys and the Hedgpeths made room in their crowded wagons for small libraries.

To herd the loose stock, and perform the myriad duties connected with a trip of this nature, six to ten young men (the exact number is unknown) were hired or grubstaked jointly by the two families. One of these young men was a German immigrant by the name of August Block who was hired as a wheelwright, an indispensable person for a wagon train.[18] Another German immigrant hired for the trip was a carpenter by the name of William Krug. We will hear more about these two later.

Other young men who accompanied the Baley train, as identified by the affidavits that they signed in support of the Baley and
Hedgpeth Indian depredation suits, were: William Garton, John and
Thomas Billings, and Wesley Gadsbury.[19] There may have been three
or four others whose names are not recorded.

Gillum Baley, having spent his entire life on the western frontier, was well suited for leading a wagon train across the plains. He was
forty-four years of age, old enough to possess mature judgment, yet
young enough to still have the physical stamina necessary for such a
demanding endeavor. Having served as a justice of the peace and as a
lay minister, he had demonstrated his ability to work in harmony with
others. In addition to these virtues, he had also been to California during the gold rush and had experienced firsthand the rigors of crossing
the plains. His brief service in the Black Hawk War gave him at least a
modicum of military discipline and some knowledge of fighting
Indians. He was known to be an expert shot with a rifle, a skill which
would soon come in handy. These qualities, combined with a hardy
constitution and an optimistic outlook on life, proved Gillum Baley to
be a worthy counterpart to the younger but less experienced Rose as
co-leader of the Rose-Baley wagon train.

By 1858, there was nothing new or unusual about emigrating to
California. Americans had been doing this since the early 1840s. What
was different about this emigrant party was the route they chose and
what happened to them while traveling this route.

CHAPTER 2

The Santa Fe Trail

The Santa Fe Trail was pioneered by mountain men and explorers working their way southwestward during the early 1800s. By the 1840s it had become a major trade route between the United States and New Mexico. Although it is called the Santa Fe Trail in literature and folklore, it was really a well-traveled road for heavy-duty freight wagons. The route originally began in Franklin, Missouri, but after that town was nearly destroyed by a disastrous flood on the Missouri River, Independence became the eastern terminus, until it, too, suffered the ravages of the capricious Missouri River and had to yield its place to Westport (Kansas City). The route ran 780 miles in a southwestward direction through Kansas by way of modern-day Olathe, Gardner, Council Grove, Diamond Springs, Durham, and to the Great Bend of the Arkansas River. It followed the Arkansas River to a point near today's Cimarron, Kansas, where it divided into two branches, the Mountain Branch and the Cimarron Cutoff.

The Mountain Branch followed the Arkansas River westward to Bent's Old Fort, near present La Junta, Colorado, and from there it turned southwest and passed through Trinidad, Colorado. It entered New Mexico over 7,834-foot Raton Pass, then continued down through Northern New Mexico by way of Fort Union to another La Junta (now called Watrous) near Las Vegas, New Mexico, where the two branches of the trail joined.[1] The Mountain Branch had the advantage of splendid scenery, and in most places there were plenty of wood, water, and grass. It was safer than the Cimarron Cutoff, although not totally immune from Indian attack. Its chief disadvantages were that it went over high mountains, making travel more difficult, and in winter it was closed to wagon traffic because of heavy snow.

The Cimarron Cutoff, as the name implies, was developed as a shortcut; it saved the traveler about one hundred miles. This route did not cross any high mountain ranges, thus making it easier for wagons. It could also be traveled by wheeled vehicles in winter. However, this branch did have some disadvantages: Between the Arkansas and the Cimarron Rivers lay the Cimarron Desert, a stretch of waterless wasteland more than fifty miles across called the Water Scrape by the Americans and La Jornada del Muerte by the Mexicans. Another disadvantage was that it went through territory inhabited or frequented by the fierce Comanche and Kiowa Indians. It was while traveling this route in 1832 that the famed mountain man and explorer, Jedediah Smith, was ambushed and murdered by Comanche Indians. But in spite of its aridity and the danger from Indians, most travelers preferred this branch of the Santa Fe Trail. This was the route chosen by the Rose-Baley wagon train.

After crossing the Missouri River at Westport, the Rose company came to the trailhead of the Santa Fe Trail and started their journey down this fabled route. The Santa Fe and the Oregon-California Trails ran together for the first thirty or so miles from Westport before separating. As the emigrants advanced westward, civilization fell behind. The countryside gradually began to change. The landscape became more arid and farmland was replaced by open prairie. Kansas was still sparsely settled in 1858, with most of its population living in the eastern part of the state near the Kansas-Missouri border.

Soon the emigrants came to land inhabited by the Osage Indians, but the emigrants felt no fear as this tribe had long been subjugated and posed no threat. The same could not be said of some of the Whites in the area. The border warfare between proslavery and antislavery factions had brought a special breed of ruffians to the territory; murders and robberies were everyday occurrences, and no one's life was safe. Bands of cattle rustlers and horse thieves roamed the countryside looking for victims, and if they happened upon a small, weakly armed outfit, they would not hesitate to kill anyone who offered resistance. On several occasions suspicious-looking characters rode into the Rose camp, but after observing the large group of well-armed young men, they soon rode off in search of easier prey.[2]

Because of the Mormon War, the Baley company also chose to travel to California by way of the Santa Fe Trail and the Southern

Route.[3] They crossed the Missouri River by steamboat at St. Joseph, Missouri, because it was nearer to their homes in Nodaway County than was Westport. After crossing the Missouri River and entering the Kansas Territory, they followed one of several feeder trails that connected with both the Oregon-California Trail and the Santa Fe Trail. This road took them through Topeka, soon to become the capital of Kansas Territory. They struck the Santa Fe Trail at Council Grove, which in 1858 was the last place where goods and services could be procured before reaching Santa Fe, New Mexico. They laid over here a couple of days to replenish their supplies and make final checks to their equipment before plunging forward on the long journey ahead.

The two companies, the Roses and the Baleys, met on the evening of May 12, 1858, at Cottonwood Creek near present-day Durham, Kansas. Udell describes the meeting:

> We came seven miles to Cottonwood Creek, and camped, to dry our provisions and clothing, it being a pleasant day. At night a large train from Nodaway County, Mo., called the Bailey [Baley] train, came near us and camped. Messrs. Bailey and Messrs. Hedgespeth [Hedgpeth] were the owners. They were also bound for California. Grass, wood and water plenty here, and a good road. Travel today, 7 miles, and 178 from Missouri River.[4]

The two groups apparently found each other compatible and agreed to travel together to California. From this point to the Colorado River, they can properly be called the Rose-Baley wagon train. However, the two groups never formally merged, each retaining its separate identity. They kept their livestock (which were unbranded) separate and camped separately but near each other. They realized they would soon be entering country inhabited by unfriendly Indians, and they knew there was strength in traveling in large groups. Indians seldom attacked large well-armed trains, but were quick to pick off stragglers or small groups. Udell reported, "Since Messrs. Bailey [Baley] came up with us, we number forty men and fifty or sixty women and children, and nearly 500 head of cattle, mostly cows and oxen, and twenty wagons."

Each night in his journal Udell recorded the location of the campsite, the weather, road conditions, the availability of wood, grass, and water, the number of miles traveled that day, and the distance of the campsite from the Missouri River. One might wonder if he had an odometer or some other type of measuring device for this purpose, but he tells us that his calculations were made by using a simple procedure utilizing time and gait.[5] He kept track of the time traveled and was able to estimate from the gait of the oxen the distance covered in one hour. Multiplying this by the number of hours traveled gave the distance covered that day; the sum of the miles traveled each day gave the approximate distance from the Missouri River, measured from their crossing at Westport. This method is something like dead reckoning used by sailors at sea in estimating their location. Udell's estimates of distances were surprisingly accurate for such a primitive method of measurement.

Soon the wagon train was in buffalo country; in 1858, buffalo still ranged over the western prairie in great numbers. Most members of the wagon train, having never seen these shaggy beasts before, were thrilled by the prospect of a buffalo hunt and fresh meat cooking on the campfire. Joel Hedgpeth Jr. tells about one such hunt which took place during the journey:

> One hunt I well remember and will not forget. That hunt was on Sunday. We did not usually travel on. Sundays but that day it seemed necessary to travel part of the day at least to find a suitable camping place. Father had somewhat sharply—but wisely—chided the boys for recklessly running the horses. That day he chose to ride horseback and the animal he rode was my saddle horse; we called him Pioneer. During the travel that day someone found a buffalo and started in pursuit. Father joined in the chase and succeeded—on Pioneer—in getting near enough to the buffalo to deliver several telling shots with his pistol. The buffalo was killed and part of it brought into camp. When father rode up I heard Mother say to him very quietly and pleasantly, "Didn't you know this is Sunday?" Father threw up his hands—almost in horror—and explained, "Well, I forgot all about it being Sunday." And I'm sure this he never forgot until he joined the great Sabbath Anthem on High.[6]

It was on this part of the journey that Thomas Hedgpeth caught a buffalo calf. The calf was adopted by a cow that had lost her calf; it remained with the family until it was killed by Indians near the end of the journey. Quantities of buffalo meat were dried and made into jerky or *carne seca* as the Mexicans called it. Unfortunately, much meat was wasted and many animals unnecessarily killed. Udell described one such incident: "We Came twenty-two miles and camped on a small creek, twelve miles from Big Turkey Creek. Plenty of grass and water, but no wood. Immense numbers of buffalo. Our young men shot them down for sport and left them for the buzzards and wolves . . ." Apparently, the young men of this emigrant train, succumbed to the pleasures of the hunt and let excitement and emotion overrule their good judgment.

The road through this part of Kansas, having been traveled for some years, was reasonably good except when there had been heavy rain. Then, the ground would become a quagmire causing the wagon wheels to sink deep into the wet soil, making it difficult for the poor oxen to pull the wagons. Rain also caused rivers and creeks to become swollen and difficult to ford. Few bridges had been built on this part of the road, and since most of the streams were small and shallow, no ferries were in operation. Streams with steep banks were especially difficult to cross in wet weather because the animals could not get traction on the slippery slopes. Udell complained, "We had much wind and rain all the way from home." Rain might have made travel more difficult but it was great for grass and water. As they traveled across the prairie, wood began to become scarce. When they came to a good supply they would gather up as much as they could haul in their wagons, and when wood was not available, they were sometimes able to substitute buffalo chips. Whenever they came to a place where grass, water, and wood were in plentiful supply, they frequently laid by for a day or so to give the women a chance to get caught up on their washing and baking and to give the men a chance to do some hunting or make repairs to their wagons.

Scouts were sent ahead to look for danger and to find suitable campsites. When camp was established, the work teams would be unhitched and turned out to graze with the loose stock, unless there was perceived to be a danger from rustlers or Indians, in which case they would be kept tied to the feed boxes on the wagons. At night, mounted guards were posted along the perimeters to keep the stock from being stolen or wandering off. After the evening meal was eaten and the dishes washed and put away, many emigrant parties would gather around the campfire for some music, singing, or storytelling. Several members of this wagon train had brought along violins, guitars, harmonicas, and jews' harps.[7] Emigrant trains would sometimes hold impromptu dances around the blazing campfire, but given the strict religious background of some of the members of this group, it is doubtful that much dancing took place.

In spite of wet weather the wagon train made good time in traveling across the flat prairie lands of Kansas Territory. One day Udell recorded a distance of thirty miles traveled, and on several other occasions he recorded distances of twenty-two, twenty-four and twenty-six miles.

They arrived at the Great Bend of the Arkansas River on May 17, where they camped for the night. The trail did not cross the river at this point, but veered west from the river and crossed Walnut Creek near a large sandstone pinnacle known as Pawnee Rock. Travelers frequently stopped here and recorded their names on the soft rock. The members of the Rose-Baley wagon train apparently resisted this temptation, for according to Udell, they passed this spot on May 18 but did not stop. Even if they had carved their names on Pawnee Rock, the inscriptions would probably not be there today because in later years it was heavily quarried for its rock and gravel. The day they passed Pawnee Rock was also the day that the wagon train traveled a record distance of thirty miles. Perhaps speed was more important to the travelers than vanity, or at least it was that day.

The wagon train crossed the Arkansas River on May 24, 1858, at Middle Crossing. Udell described the river at this point as a swift-running stream about one-half mile in width, but only three feet deep. Some difficulty was encountered in fording the river due to the swiftness of the current, and quicksand on the bottom, but all crossed safely. Quicksand was a problem not only on the Arkansas River, but on many other Western streams. Experienced travelers developed a strategy for dealing with this menace. First, they would drive the loose stock across the stream, the large number of hoofs striking the bottom in rapid succession would tramp the quicksand under and firm the bottom. Then the wagons could be driven across with relative ease. Alpha Brown, Udell, and others, must have been well aware of this trick.[8]

Near the Arkansas River, the wagon train came upon a small village of about one hundred Indians. At first the emigrants were somewhat alarmed, but when the Indians exhibited no hostility, tensions eased. This is the only Indian encounter on the Santa Fe that Udell mentions in his journal. No doubt Indians kept the wagon train under observation, but seeing that it was large and well-armed, they did not molest it. Indians continued to menace the Santa Fe Trail until long after the Civil War.

On May 26, they traveled eighteen miles and camped at Sand Creek. Udell reported, "No running water, but it remains in holes, as yet. No wood, but good grass and good road. Weather pleasant." And on May 27 he wrote, "We came ten miles to Semanone Creek [probably the Cimarron River], which we reached at 12:00 o'clock noon, and camped to rest until morning. The water brackish, with saltpetre. Grass plenty, but no wood. We have brought enough wood from Pawnee Fork to last us more than one hundred miles; but we have now to burn buffalo-chips."

They frequently met large trains from New Mexico going to Missouri or to other places in the United States. Udell described one such encounter, "Yesterday we met a train of Government officers with their families, going from their stations in New Mexico to visit their connections in the States. They travel in fine style, with their servants to attend them in this wild and savage country." After reaching the Cimarron River, the wagon train was out of the worst part of the Cimarron Desert. This river is dry most of the year, but water can usually be found by digging in the dry stream bed. Since the spring of 1858 was unusually wet, they were able to find water in pools and ponds, although of poor quality, as Udell describes. The road followed the Cimarron River for some distance into what is now Panhandle Oklahoma before reaching the New Mexico border.

In his May 30 journal entry, Udell complains that Tamerlane Davis, one of his hired men, had changed places with Paul Williamson, one of Mr. Brown's hands, "Not with my consent, but I hope it may be for the better." Could it be that the young hired hand was finding the Baptist minister a little difficult to get along with?

The wagon train crossed into the New Mexico Territory on June 1. The scenery began to change as they slowly gained elevation; the ascent was gradual with no steep hills to be climbed. They were now entering the high desert. The higher elevation brought with it a change of both scenery and climate. The hills were wooded with pine, oak, and cedar, and in the canyons flowed rushing streams with water, pure and clear. The days were warm but the nights were cool and refreshing. These changes were most welcome after viewing nothing for weeks but the flat and endless prairie. Even Udell seemed to have switched into a more optimistic mood, for on June 3, he recorded, "Our large company continues harmonious and healthy, for which I am thankful to the Lord. Travel today, 22 miles, and 549 from Missouri River."

They laid over at Rabbit-Ear Creek on June 4 to get caught up on their domestic chores, "A busy day with us," Udell recorded. The next day they came eleven miles to Rabbit Creek where they found abundant grass and water; they traveled another nine miles and camped at the foot of a mountain, but without wood or water. "The country begins to assume a mountainous appearance," Udell reported, "we passed several [mountains] to-day." On June 6, they crossed Rock Creek and camped that night at Whetstone Creek. Udell stated that they traveled twelve miles over a good road between low mountains and came to the "Red River," which they crossed at 10 a.m. on June 8. He apparently confused the Red River with the Canadian River, because the Red River flows many miles to the southeast of this location. Udell may be forgiven for occasional errors in place names because many of the rivers, streams, and other geographic features in the West had not yet been officially named, nor were there road signs or location markers conveniently placed along the route to inform travelers as is the case today.

After crossing the Canadian River on the morning of June 8, the emigrants decided to camp and take it easy for the remainder of the day. Udell took advantage of the layover to do some hunting. "I, with my horse, ran down and caught a young antelope, and we had excellent fresh meat for supper. The Rocky Mountains, snow capped, are in sight. Travel to-day, 12 miles and 621 from Missouri River."

The next day they traveled twenty miles and camped near Wagon Wheel Rock [probably Wagon Mound]. "Here we camped; good road and grass all the way, but no wood; some of us went three miles off and brought wood into camp—some on horses and some carried it on their shoulders; now distant 641 miles [*sic*] from Missouri River." On June 11, they arrived at Water's Ranch, home of the first white settler whom they had encountered since leaving eastern Kansas. "He is quite an intelligent, persevering man, from Vermont," Udell writes. "His ranch is situated on Moho [Moro] Creek, a considerable tributary of Red River [Canadian River]. Fort Union is situated six miles above; it is quite a large military post. We came two miles farther and camped on the creek; 671 miles from Missouri River."

Udell does not mention visiting the fort, but it must have been a comforting feeling to be traveling in the vicinity of a large military installation staffed by fellow Americans. Fort Union was established in 1851 to replace Santa Fe as military department headquarters for the New Mexico Territory, because Santa Fe at that time was regarded as a pit of vice and immorality, and unfit for soldiers.

The emigrants now entered a more attractive countryside that showed definite signs of civilization. Farmers in the area, mostly Mexican, tended small plots irrigated with water that they were able to obtain from canyons and small streams. They grew small patches of corn, grain, vegetables, and a few fruit trees. This might have been the first time that many members of this wagon train had ever seen irrigated fields. The farmhouses were flat-roofed adobe brick structures and usually festooned with garlands of red chile peppers and garlic. There also were some large sheep and cattle ranches in the area.

Soon they arrived at the settlement of Las Vegas, New Mexico, which Udell called "Los Bayas." Las Vegas was a small village at the time, inhabited mostly by Mexicans. Its buildings were all constructed of adobe brick, but to the weary emigrants it must have appeared as a metropolis built of alabaster and marble. In town, Udell wrote, was a large general store, a blacksmith shop, a flour mill, a Catholic Church, several saloons, and other small businesses. Near Las Vegas was the famous Montezuma Hot Springs. Many of the emigrants took advantage of its hot mineral water and had their first tub bath in weeks. If Udell was one of the bathers, he doesn't mention it in his journal, but then, a Baptist minister wouldn't be expected to comment on pleasures of the flesh!

After a short stay in Las Vegas the wagon train continued its westward journey. About three miles south of town the road forked; one fork went to Santa Fe while the other went toward Albuquerque. "From wrong information, we took the Santa Fe road, which we afterwards learned was much further and a worse road," Udell complained. "The numerous herds of sheep, goats, and jackasses have eaten out the grass through here, so that our stock are pinched with hunger." On June 16, they camped in the vicinity of the well-known Pigeon Ranch, near Glorieta Pass, where just four years later a Civil War battle would be fought. His entry for June 17 stated: "At Rock Correll [Corral] we left the Santa Fe Road, twelve miles South of Santa Fe; we took the left-hand road, down through a ravine, past a spring, leading on to Albuquerque; came six miles and camped; no water; plenty of wood; little grass. . ." Udell says nothing about going into Santa Fe. The fame of Santa Fe was known far and wide; it seems incredible that they would come this far and this close to such a celebrated place without paying it a visit. It was by far the largest town that they came to on their journey to California.

L. J. Rose Jr., in his biography of his father, stated that the Rose company did go into Santa Fe and make some purchases of clothing and other articles. He wrote, "One can readily believe that the women fairly reveled in a shopping expedition, the first in three months."[9] Apparently the wagon train made a temporary split at this point, the shoppers going into Santa Fe, while those not interested in shopping continued on toward Albuquerque. As they were now in relatively safe country, there was no compelling reason for them to stay together; they would reunite before continuing to California. Udell mentions a shortage of grass and water near the settlements, and since they were driving a large herd of cattle, this would be another reason to separate. It is unknown whether any members of the Baley company went into Santa Fe. We know that Rose was very favorably impressed by what he observed in Santa Fe because he later returned there and purchased a hotel.

Why wouldn't Udell and possibly some of the others want to go into Santa Fe after such a long and arduous journey? The reasons are probably the personalities of the individuals involved and the conditions that existed in the place at that time. Santa Fe had the reputation of being a wide-open town; saloons, fandango halls (dance halls), prostitutes, and gambling dens were everywhere. Desperados roamed the streets looking for victims, and gun fights and stabbings were daily occurrences. This might have been the reason that Udell and possibly others avoided the town.

CHAPTER 3

A New Road West

The Rose-Baley wagon train reached the Rio Grande on June 19 at a point approximately thirty miles north of Albuquerque. From here to Albuquerque they would follow the river. Water was plentiful, but Udell complained that the grass had been eaten short, making for poor grazing. He also complained that they had to buy wood since there was none along this well-traveled road; civilization has its price! On the evening of June 22, they camped two miles from Albuquerque. Udell noted that "according to my calculations by time and gait," the wagon train had traveled 826 miles since crossing the Missouri River at Westport. June 22 also happened to be Udell's birthday. Being in a pensive mood that evening, he recorded in his journal, "This is my sixty-third birthday. My three-score-and ten years are almost spent; may I so appreciate it that I may be prepared to leave this earthly house even sooner than that, if my Lord should call me?"

In 1858, Albuquerque was a much smaller town than Santa Fe. It was mainly a military outpost and the headquarters for the Ninth Military District. Dr. William P. Floyd, who served as the physician for Beale's second expedition in 1859, had this to say about Albuquerque in his journal:

> Thursday, March 3, 1859. I left camp this morning and have come to the famed town of Albuquerque. It is inferior to Santa Fe and not much in fact for a Mexican adobe town, three fourths apparently taken up by the military. I see no use in their being here. There are no hostile Indians near and it is one of the furthest points of transportation in the Territory for provisions and therefore should not be made the depot for the supply of food to the other posts. I am no military man, however, and cannot know.[1]

The next day, Udell and Emily went into Albuquerque to have some repairs made to their wagon. While waiting for the completion of the repair work, Udell struck up an acquaintance with Judge Samuel Winslow. Udell was able to get himself and Emily invited to the Judge's home where, Udell wrote: "My Wife and I partook of an excellent dinner [lunch] with them. Judge Samuel Winslow is a gentleman of good attainments, much general information, pleasing in his manners, and benevolent and kind to all. And his lady is also possessed of those graces."

Judge Winslow was a very important individual in Albuquerque; not only was he one of the town's leading merchants, but he also was the justice of the peace and postmaster. In addition to these duties, he served as a sutler for the army. Udell's newly acquired friend would prove to be a godsend in the months to come.

That evening the wagon train moved farther down the Rio Grande in order to find grass for their animals. They planned to spend several days here recruiting their stock and making final preparations for the journey to California. During their stay in Albuquerque, L. J. Rose persuaded some of the army officers to inspect his fine herd of thoroughbred cattle. He had the foresight to obtain letters from two of these officers testifying to the high quality and excellent condition of the animals. This would serve a very useful purpose at a later date.[2]

At Albuquerque the emigrants heard about a new route to California that was recently surveyed by Edward F. Beale at the request of the United States government. This route closely followed the thirty-fifth parallel and was said to be a more direct route to California than the Southern Route usually followed by emigrants. According to its proponents, it would save travelers approximately two hundred miles. At an average of fifteen miles traveled per day, this would be a saving of thirteen days. Both the army officers and the citizens of Albuquerque spoke enthusiastically about this new route, saying there was plenty of grass and water the entire way, and that no hostile Indians would be encountered. Beale was in Washington, D.C. preparing reports on his newly surveyed road for the War Department and Congress, and thus, was not available to give the emigrants firsthand information

The proposed new road would run from Fort Smith, Arkansas, to Los Angeles, California. It was intended to be used both as a military and as an emigrant road. It was envisioned that, later, a railroad would be built over this same route. Beale had been given an appropriation of $50,000 and instructed by the War Department to survey that portion of the route from Fort Defiance to the Colorado River. A military road already existed between Fort Defiance and Albuquerque, but it could not be incorporated into the new road because it ran only to the fort and was off the direct route to California. Fort Defiance was located near the present-day New Mexico-Arizona border, and about one hundred and fifty miles northwest of Albuquerque. Beale was chosen to conduct this survey because of his distinguished naval career and his previous explorations and travels in the Southwest.

Some confusion exists as to Beale's actual title at this period. He is sometimes referred to as Lieutenant Beale of the U.S. Army, and sometimes as Lieutenant Beale of the U.S. Navy. To add even more confusion he was also sometimes addressed as General Beale. In actuality, Beale was not a member of any military or naval unit at the time. When he resigned from the navy in 1852, he held the rank of lieutenant. In 1852 he was appointed as the superintendent of Indian affairs for California by President Fillmore. In this position he frequently had to deal with army officers. To give him more clout in dealing with these officials, he was assigned the rank of brigadier general in the California State Militia by Governor Bigler.[3] He apparently liked this title and was never known to scold anyone who addressed him as General, even long after he had left the Department of Indian Affairs.[4] He also served as surveyor general of California, and this title might have helped reinforce the title of general in the public mind.

This was not the first to attempt to open up a route along the thirty-fifth parallel. Lieutenant Lorenzo Sitgreaves, of the U.S. Army Topographical Engineers, led an exploration team across this area in 1851. Lieutenant Ariel Weeks Whipple, also an army topographical engineer, came through this area in 1853–54 while searching for a transcontinental railroad route. Even private individuals got involved. Francois Xavier Aubry, a Santa Fe merchant, made two trips, one in 1852–53, and another in 1853–54, over this proposed route. Each of these expeditions gained valuable knowledge about the area, but none was successful in opening a railroad route or a wagon road.[5]

Beale succeeded where the others failed. His well-equipped expedition, escorted by twenty soldiers from Fort Defiance, had little trouble in getting wagons across Northern Arizona. He started his survey from the Indian pueblo of Zuni on August 31, 1857, and arrived at the Mojave Villages on the Colorado River on October 17, 1857, having completed the trip in a little more than six weeks.[6] For this expedition, Beale was authorized the use of twenty-five camels for the purpose of testing their usefulness and endurance on the Western deserts. This is the famous camel experiment about which much has been written. However, as Dennis G. Casebier carefully points out in his book, *The Mojave Road*, the main purpose of Beale's expedition was to survey a wagon road and not to experiment with camels.[7]

Beale described the Mojave Indians living along the Colorado River as, "fine-looking, comfortable, fat, and merry." Although he didn't feel threatened by them, he did insert this caveat in his report to the secretary of war:

> I regard the establishment of a military post on the Colorado River as an indispensable necessity for the emigrant over this road; for, although the Indians, living in the rich meadow lands, are agricultural, and consequently peaceable, they are very numerous, so much so that we counted 800 men around our camp on the second day after our arrival on the banks of the river. The temptation of scattered emigrant parties with their families, and the confusion of inexperienced teamsters, rafting so wide and rapid a river with their wagons and families, would offer too strong a temptation for the Indians to withstand.[8]

Beale's instructions were to go to Fort Tejon (near present-day Bakersfield) if he were in need of supplies, and then go back over the road which he had just traveled. His supplies being low, he exercised this option and proceeded to Fort Tejon. This was convenient for him since he owned a large cattle ranch nearby.[9] After crossing the Colorado River on inflated India rubber rafts, he proceeded to Fort Tejon. The camels and other livestock swam the river.

He detached two camels and sent them with their handlers to Los Angeles. The people there were disappointed since they had expected him to come to their city with his full camel corps. They accused him of going to Fort Tejon just so he could visit his ranch, but these charges were unfair because he had been instructed to go to Fort Tejon for his supplies and not to Los Angeles.

Beale left Fort Tejon for the return trip on January 10, 1858. He waited until then to go back because he wanted to prove that the thirty-fifth parallel route was an all-season road and could be traveled in the dead of winter as well as any other season. He must have had some second thoughts about the peaceful intentions of the Mojave Indians, however, because for this trip he brought along fifty dragoons from Fort Tejon. Camels were included on the return trip. Although Beale wasn't overly enthusiastic about the camels in the beginning, he had by now formed a very favorable impression of these exotic beasts.[10]

When the expedition reached the Colorado River, the men were pleasantly surprised to find a steamboat, the *General Jesup*, with Captain George Alonzo Johnson in charge, waiting to ferry them across the river. Captain Johnson was on a private exploration trip at his own expense to determine the navigability of the Colorado River. He had stopped to take on wood for the engines of the *General Jesup* when he saw Beale's party coming over the horizon. What a surprise it must have been for Beale to have such an easy crossing of the Colorado River!

The expedition encountered no severe weather on the return trip and arrived safely back in Albuquerque on February 24, 1858. By mid-April Beale was in Washington, D.C., writing his reports for the War Department and Congress. In his report to Secretary of War John Floyd, Beale stated that the thirty-fifth parallel route would inevitably become a great emigrant road to California. To relieve the emigrants of some of the hardships of travel, Beale recommended that the government establish military posts, build bridges, and construct dams to insure a more reliable water supply, and as previously stated, he reported that the establishment of a military post at the Colorado River was an indispensable necessity before the road be opened to emigrant travel. It is quite clear from this report that Beale did not expect emigrants to use this road until all of these things were done.

Given the slow means of transportation available during that period, it is doubtful that a copy of Beale's report had yet reached Albuquerque at the time the Rose-Baley wagon train arrived there on

June 23, 1858. Some of the army officers had talked with Beale and members of his expedition about the proposed new route when Beale returned to Albuquerque in February. Just what claims Beale made for the road in conversations with army officers, or what they understood him to say about it, is unknown. What is known is that the U.S. Army officers stationed in Albuquerque and the citizens of that town had the impression that the road was ready for emigrants.[11]

No name was given to the road by Congress, nor did Beale suggest any. He simply referred to it as the thirty-fifth parallel route in his report to Congress. However, the army and the citizens of Albuquerque began calling the new route Beale's Wagon Road or the Beale Road, which must have made Beale proud. We, too, will call it Beale's Wagon Road. It is only fitting that the road was named for him since he was the one who led the successful survey.

The town of Albuquerque had much to gain from Beale's Wagon Road. All the traffic moving between Fort Smith, Arkansas, and Los Angeles, California, would have to pass through Albuquerque. It was already on the Southern Route and on El Camino Real, the ancient trade route between New Mexico and Mexico City. Had there been a chamber of commerce in Albuquerque at that time, it too, would have been assiduously promoting Beale's Wagon Road.

The army might have had an ulterior motive in advising this new route to the Rose-Baley wagon train. In past years the army had furnished escorts for emigrants taking the Southern Route, since this road traversed territory inhabited by the feared Apaches. But this year (1858), because of possible trouble brewing with the Mormons in Utah, the army might have felt that it was not in a position to fight Mormons and escort emigrants at the same time. Besides, there was no known tribe of Indians on this new route that could match the ferocity of the infamous Apaches. Most of the Indians in this part of the country were thought to be harmless. They might be a nuisance because of their proclivity for thievery but presented no real threat to the lives of the emigrants. Problems with the Navajos would seem to have put this theory to rest, but apparently they hadn't.

For their protection, the emigrants were advised by the army to stay together along the route and not wander off in small groups. The equipment and livestock of the Rose-Baley wagon train appeared to the army to be of very high quality, and the emigrants presented a hardy appearance. Although there were women and young children and some older people in the group, they were outnumbered by the young men. The army did insist, however, that the emigrants procure the services of a guide before they would be given permission to travel this new route.

After hearing the glowing reports about Beale's Wagon Road from the army and the citizens of Albuquerque, all the members of the Rose-Baley wagon train agreed that they would travel together over this new route—all but one, that is. As the reader might have already guessed, the lone dissenter was the old Baptist preacher, John Udell. Udell argued that it was unwise for them to start so long a journey with so many women and children over a new and completely unproven route. He recited an experience of his own when a group that he was crossing the plains with took a cutoff. Indians stole all of their horses leaving the emigrants to suffer many days of hunger before they could return to civilization—and they had no women or children with their party! Udell, having made three previous trips across the plains, clearly considered himself the elder statesman of the group. But when even his own wife and hired hands urged him to accept the group's decision, he had little choice but to agree.[12]

Udell was perfectly correct in his opposition to traveling a new and unproven route for such a long distance accompanied by so many women and children. Although Beale had taken a few wagons over the route, the road was little more than a survey trail marked only by faint wagon tracks, an occasional stone cairn, and perhaps a few axe blazes on trees. For much of the way it followed existing Indian trails, which in turn followed animal trails. Little or no road work had been done and not a single bridge had been built anywhere along the route. Water could be found in most places along the way, but there were long waterless stretches (*jornadas*), and in many of the places where water did exist it could be found only by experienced desert travelers. In the area between the San Francisco Mountains and the Colorado River, wood and grass as well as water were scarce. Another disadvantage of this proposed route was the fact that between Albuquerque, New Mexico, and San Bernardino, California, a distance of nearly six hundred miles, there existed not a single outpost of civilization, except the small pueblos of Laguna and Zuni. Even these were located near Albuquerque, not far into the journey. This meant that there would be no friendly trading post where supplies could be purchased or fresh horses or oxen obtained, and no protective fort where travelers could take refuge in case of an Indian attack.

Being the first emigrant party to use this route, they knew there would be no one in advance whom they might overtake in case of trouble, nor could they be sure there would be others following them. They knew only one thing for certain: They were in for the adventure of their lives! But in spite of all its disadvantages, the new route, with its promise of shorter distances, plenty of wood, grass, water, and friendly Indians all the way, was too much of an inducement for these emigrants to ignore.

About the only thing that Udell and his fellow emigrants could agree upon was the need for hiring a guide. A meeting for this purpose was held in Albuquerque on June 25:

> We all agreed that we could not travel it [Beale's Wagon Road] without a guide, so I, with the other heads of families and owners of property, assembled for the purpose of hiring one. Mr. J. L. [L. J.] Rose and Mr. Gillum Bailey [Baley] were the largest owners in the train. We all expected to participate in the hiring of the guide; but as I commenced talking on the subject, says Mr. Rose: "Mr. Udell, Mr. Bailey and I can attend to this business without your help, and after the guide is hired, you can have the benefit of him with the rest, by paying what we think is right." Such an insulting expression from a German aristocrat caused the blood of a free-born American to rankle in my bosom. But under my circumstances I thought it best to pass it over in quietness.[13]

Udell was even further incensed when he learned how much he was to be assessed for his share of the guide's fees. He believed that it was at least double what it should be, based on the value of his property and the number of persons in his group. He appealed to Gillum Baley, and through the latter's influence, a considerable amount was deducted from his assessment. Udell recorded in his journal, "It appeared that the latter [Rose] wished to make a speculation off us poor people, just in hiring the guide." Udell then says that he resigned from Rose's train and enrolled in Gillum Baley's train. He also persuaded his friends, the Dalys and the Hollands to do likewise.[14] Actually, the change made little difference since they all agreed to travel together.

Not only did the army recommend Beale's Wagon Road as the safest and shortest route for the emigrants to travel to California, but it also recommended a guide. According to L. J. Rose, the emigrants were advised by the commanding officer in Albuquerque, Colonel B. L. E. Bonneville, that:

> The Beale Route or 35th Parallel Route was a much pleas-anter and safer route, and shorter, too, and that there was plenty of grass, wood, and water all the way—and the Indians were friendly. Well, they were so much in earnest in this matter that they recommended a guide who had been over the route before, and paid part of his expenses.[15]

The guide recommended by the army was one Jose Manuel Savedra, a fifty-eight-year-old Mexican.[16] Savedra's credentials as a guide were impeccable. Some years before he had accompanied the Moqui (Hopi) Indians to the Colorado River country in a raid against the Mojave Indians. He had been one of the two guides on the Whipple expedition in 1854, the other guide being the famed mountain man, Antoine Leroux.

More recently Savedra had been the sole guide for Beale's expedition which had just completed the survey for Beale's Wagon Road. With qualifications like this, Savedra must have seemed like a godsend to the eager emigrants. Not only was his résumé impressive, but also his fee was quite reasonable for a guide with this kind of experience. He was willing to serve the emigrants as their guide for only $500, to be paid in advance, of course. This fee also included the services of Savedra's friend, Petro, who would act as interpreter. (What languages Petro spoke have never been revealed.) This was quite a bargain because only the year before Savedra had been paid $1,200 for his services on the Beale expedition. Making the deal even more tempt-ing was the fact that the good citizens of Albuquerque, including some of the army officers, agreed to pay $180 of the guide's fee. How could the members of the wagon train pass up a bargain like this?

What the emigrants didn't know was that both Whipple and Beale had found Savedra's services as a guide to be less than satisfac-tory. Whipple hired Antoine Leroux, a friend and frequent companion of Kit Carson, as his principal guide. Antoine Leroux had served as guide for Lieutenant Colonel Philip St. George Cooke's famed Mormon Battalion in 1846. Neither Whipple nor Leroux had traversed the entire thirty-fifth parallel route before, and having heard that Savedra had accompanied the Moqui Indians in an expedition against the Mojaves, Whipple hired him as extra insurance. "In order to omit nothing that may contribute to success, we have secured the services both of Leroux and Savedra for the journey," Whipple wrote in his journal.[17]

Savedra had difficulty finding water for the Whipple expedition. Once, while they were on a scouting expedition, Whipple stated, "Savedra thought that he recognized a point on the route he pursued with the Moquis twelve years since, and a few of us followed him to the top of a high hill to reconnoiter. He was entirely lost."[18] A guide who gets himself and his companions lost does little to inspire confidence in his leadership or improve the expedition's morale. Had Whipple investigated Savedra's claim more thoroughly, he would have found that Savedra had accompanied the Moqui Indians on a raid for the purpose of stealing children from other Indian tribes and selling them into slavery or keeping them as their own slaves. The slave-procuring expedition was thoroughly routed by the Yampai Indians, and the slave stealers were lucky to have escaped with their scalps intact. Child stealing and slavery hardly speak well of Savedra's moral character. Fortunately for the Whipple expedition, it also had the services of Leroux.

In comparing the value of the two guides, Savedra and Leroux, Lieutenant David Sloane Stanley, a member of Whipple's staff, had this to say about Savedra: "He pretends to know the country we are to explore, but he knew nothing, and Lieutenant Whipple, to utilize him, put him to work with the pack train." But about Leroux, Stanley had this to say: "Leroux was a man of another sort. He pretended to nothing he did not know. His knowledge and experience were wonderful, and yet part of the route he had never seen."[19]

Beale, who had allotted only one guide for his expedition, let himself be talked into hiring Savedra by the citizens of Albuquerque. What qualities Savedra lacked as a guide he made up for as a public relations man. Beale soon realized his error, but unlike Whipple he had no Leroux to fall back upon. As a consequence he was forced to do his own scouting and exploring. He, too, soon relegated Savedra to the pack train as a simple packer. In his report to the Secretary of War, Beale was much more critical of Savedra than Whipple had been. He said this about Savedra:

> We unfortunately have no guide, the wretch I employed at the urgent request and advice of everyone in Albuquerque, at enormous expense, being the most ignorant and irresolute ass extant. This obligates us to do the double duty of road making and exploring which is very arduous, besides adding infinitely to my anxiety and responsibility.[20]

Fortunately for Savedra, but unfortunately for the members of the Rose-Baley wagon train, neither Beale nor Whipple was anywhere near Albuquerque at this time. Beale was in Washington, D.C., writing his reports to the secretary of war, while Whipple was serving at another post far from Albuquerque. Careful inquiry might have turned up deficiencies in Savedra's résumé—but then, the unsuspecting emigrants had no reason to suppose that Savedra wasn't everything that he was represented to be. Even if Savedra's poor performance as a guide on the Whipple and Beale expeditions had been known to the emigrants, it is doubtful that they could have found another guide in Albuquerque or Santa Fe who was familiar with the thirty-fifth parallel route all the way from Albuquerque to the Colorado River and to California. Neither Kit Carson nor Antoine Leroux was available at that time.

The *Santa Fe Gazette,* in its July 10, 1858, edition published the following letter to the editor from a citizen in Albuquerque who claimed to be a member of the Committee of Information, whatever that was.

Albuquerque, N.M., June 28, 1858
　Mr. Editor:
　I am happy to inform you that the Great Central Route to California, is in a fair way of being opened at last. There is here now a large train of emigrants who will start tomorrow by Zuni for the Colorado. They have nearly forty wagons, and over fifty men and a great many loose cattle. Their stock is all in fine order, the wagons new, light and strong, the men, women and

children in the best of health and spirits; and at last, but not least, they have for a guide, Laavedra [Savedra] who took Mr. Beale over so successfully.

Please insert in your valuable Gazette, that persons intending to emigrate, may feel assured of finding hereafter a beaten road over the shortest route.

Respectfully, Sir yours,
W.H.B. for Com. of Information

The *Gazette* also saw fit to publish in the same edition a few comments of its own regarding the arrival of the emigrants in Albuquerque and their intent to travel Beale's Wagon Road to California.

It will be seen by our Albuquerque correspondence, that a large number of California emigrants arrived there during the past week and have determined to take the Beale or 35th Parallel route to accomplish their journey. This circumstance is a flattering indication of the prospects of the route as the great overland highway to the Pacific. The emigrant party seemed to be much pleased with their reception at Albuquerque and the interest manifested in their success by the citizens of that city. They employed the services of an experienced and valuable guide, and doubtlessly will have a prosperous and pleasant journey.

Thus, with the hiring of the guide, the Rose-Baley wagon train made its final preparations for plunging into the unknown and its date with destiny.

COUNTIES IN MISSOURI AND IOWA FROM WHICH THE FAMILIES
OF THE ROSE-BALEY WAGON TRAIN DEPARTED

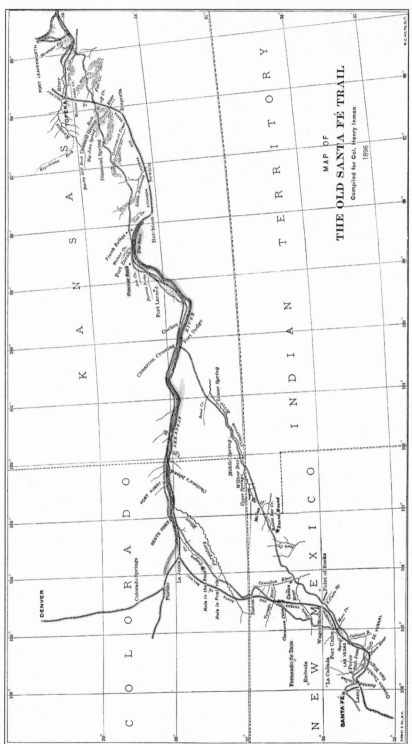

From Henry Inman, *The Old Santa Fé Trail* (New York: McMillan, 1897).

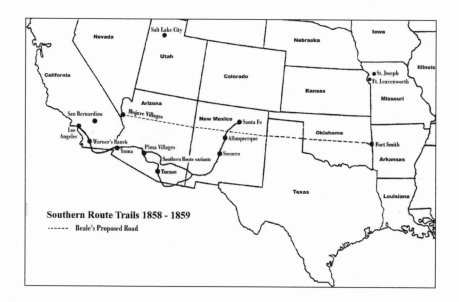

Southern Route Trails 1858 - 1859

----- Beale's Proposed Road

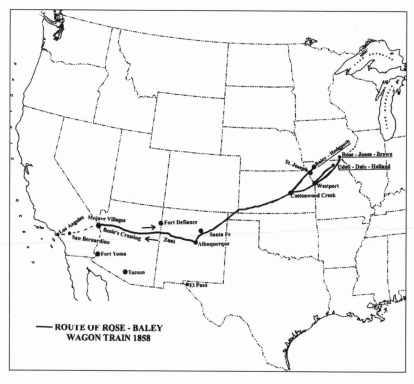

**—— ROUTE OF ROSE - BALEY
WAGON TRAIN 1858**

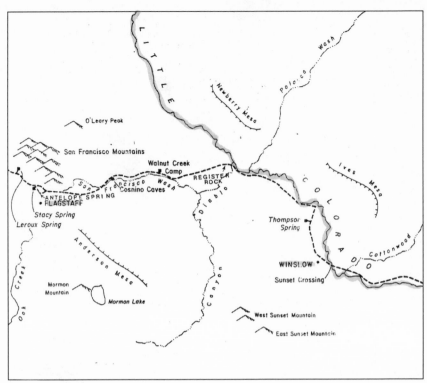

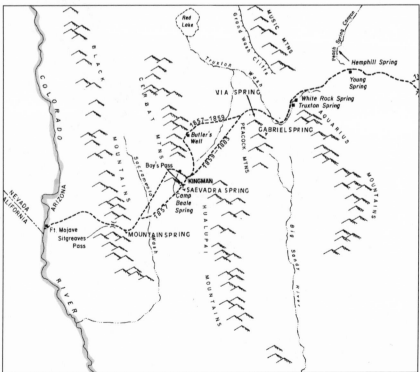

Courtesy of Jack Beale Smith, from John Udell: The Rest of the Story (Flagstaff; Arizona: Tales of the Beale Road Publishing, 1987).

CHAPTER 4

Westward Ho!

Anxious to get on with their journey, the members of the Rose-Baley wagon train did not tarry long in Albuquerque. On June 26, the day after hiring the guide, the Baley contingent, which now included the Udells, the Dalys, and the Hollands, began crossing the Rio Grande by ferryboat. They remained in camp on the west side of the river until Rose got all of his company over.

The first accident of the journey occurred on June 29, when Frank Emerdick, one of Rose's herders, drowned while crossing the river. This was the first death on the trip, and it cast a somber mood over the entire group.

The next day, June 30, 1858, they again resumed their westward march. "We all left the Rio Grande River, with our guide before us, rejoicing in being again on our journey," Udell recorded. The first day's travel took them over some irrigation ditches and through a string of sand hills. The going was rough for their livestock, but because they were fresh and eager for the trail, the travelers were able to make twenty miles that first day in spite of the difficult terrain. That night they camped on a stream which Udell called Rio Pered Creek (probably the Rio Puerco). The stream was dry at the time, but they were able to find water by digging in the streambed.

They were now entering the territory of the Lagunas, a tribe of friendly Pueblo Indians. A Baptist mission had been established among them, and on the evening of July 2, a missionary by the name of Samuel Gorman visited the wagon train and preached a sermon.[1] Udell recorded that the talk was very edifying and gratifying to him. Its impression on the other members of the group is unknown.

Unlike most American westbound emigrants, the members of this wagon train did not stop to celebrate the Fourth of July in camp, but spent the day traveling instead. They were not near any well-known camping spots, and being only five days out from Albuquerque, they were eager to get on with their journey. About fifty miles west of Albuquerque they came to a fork in the road; the right-hand fork led to Fort Defiance, while the left-hand fork led to the Indian pueblo of Zuni.[2] Fort Defiance, fifty-five miles northwest of Zuni, was built in 1851 by the United States government in an attempt to establish control over the Navajo Indians. The road went only as far as the fort, and since the emigrants had no need to go there, they took the road toward Zuni, where they would start Beale's Wagon Road.

Soon they were out of the sand hills and began ascending the Zuni Mountains, a branch of the Rockies. On July 5, they came to a large spring called Cold Spring (Agua Fria in Spanish), so named because of the large volume of pure, cold water that issued from the rocks. Here, they found plenty of grass and wood. It was such a pleasant place to camp they decided to lay by for a day and let the women do some washing and baking, while the men set wagon wheels and shoed horses and oxen.

On July 7, they crossed the Continental Divide which separates the waters that drain into the Atlantic Ocean from those that flow into the Pacific Ocean. The elevation of the Continental Divide in this area varies between 8,000 and 9,000 feet. Formerly, this was a very difficult ascent, but Udell credits Beale with having made some improvements to the road over the summit of the Zuni Mountains that made the passage much easier.[3]

The distance between Cold Spring and the next water at Inscription Rock was twenty-one miles, but because the road was good and they were still fresh, they were able to travel it in one day. That night they camped beside a large pool of excellent water at the base of Inscription Rock. Udell calculated that they were now 116 miles west of Albuquerque and 954 miles from the Missouri River at Westport, Missouri.

Inscription Rock is a high sandstone mesa which, over the eons, has eroded so that from a distance it resembles a castle. The early Spaniards called it El Morro because it reminded them of Moorish castles they had seen back home in Spain. Today it is known as El Morro National Monument, but is still sometimes called Inscription Rock because Spanish soldiers, priests, and government officials traveling between Santa Fe and Zuni stopped here and carved their names in the soft sandstone. The oldest inscription is that of Don Juan de Oñate, the first governor of New Mexico, inscribed on April 16, 1605, fifteen years before the *Mayflower* landed at Plymouth Rock! Early American explorers and army personnel, and later emigrants, also stopped here and added their names to the rock. On top of El Morro are the ruins of two fortified Indian villages.[4]

Although they camped here for only one night, several members from this wagon train carved their names on Inscription Rock. Among them was John Udell, who inscribed his name and the date partially in capital letters, "John Udell AGE 63 JULY 8 1858 FIRST EMIGRANT." Another who added his name was Isaac Taylor Holland, whose inscription in all capital letters reads, "ISAAC T. HOLLAND JULY 8 1858 FROM MO. FIRST EMG. TRAIN." The statements "First Emigrant," and "First Emigrant Train from Mo.," clearly show that these travelers were keenly aware of the fact that they were members of the first emigrant train to attempt Beale's Wagon Road. Also leaving their names engraved on the rock were L. J. Rose, R. T. Barnes, Paul Williamson, W. C. Stidger, W. C. Harper, and one Hedgpeth. At least three female members of this wagon train carved their names here. They were Miss A. C. Baley (Amelia Catherine), Miss A. F. Baley (America Frances), and Sarah (Sallie) Fox. Miss A. C. Baley and Miss A. F. Baley were the daughters of Gillum and Permelia Baley. Sarah (Sallie) Fox was the daughter of Mary Brown, and stepdaughter of Alpha Brown. These girls may very well have been the first females to inscribe their names on Inscription Rock. Others from this emigrant party also might have carved their names here, but if so, time, erosion, vandals, or "internal improvements" by the Park Service have eliminated them.[5]

As pleasant as this campsite was, they camped here for only one night, July 7, 1858. Having just laid by at Cold Spring the day before, they felt they could not justify another layover no matter how enticing the scenery. They were eager to get to Zuni and begin their journey on Beale's Wagon Road.

The names on Inscription Rock were apparently engraved the next morning while waiting to get underway. Since it was late in the evening when they arrived, lack of daylight probably prevented any name-carving that day. This would explain why more of them did not leave their names on Inscription Rock—they simply didn't have time since most of them were too busy with the chores of camp life during the short time they were here.

After leaving El Morro, the wagon train traveled fifteen miles and camped early that day at Fish Spring. Udell describes Fish Spring as a large spring of excellent water with plenty of wood nearby for camp-fires, and plenty of good grass for grazing the animals. The travelers amused themselves by picking up shards of prehistoric pottery which they found in abundance around the campsite. An ancient Indian village had occupied this spot; some of its walls were still standing. After carefully studying the artifacts found at the site, Udell came to a conclusion, "The ruins show the work of a more intelligent race than the present inhabitants of the country."

The following day, Udell recorded, "We came seven miles to a creek, where there is water, wood and grass, and we concluded to lay by until to-morrow, as we were informed there was no grass ahead for a long distance; road good yet. Travel to-day, seven miles, and 997 from Missouri River."

The next day they traveled eight miles and arrived at the Indian pueblo of Zuni. Because they were driving a large herd of livestock, it was necessary to camp some distance from the village.

Zuni was one of the fabled Seven Cities of Cibola, whose houses, the Spanish had heard, were built of marble, and whose streets were paved with silver and gold. What the Spanish found was a typical Indian pueblo with houses built of adobe, and streets paved with mud and dust.

In 1858, Zuni was occupied by some fifteen hundred to two thousand industrious Pueblo Indians.[6] They were agricultural people who grew corn and vegetables by the use of limited irrigation in the fields adjacent to their pueblo. They not only grew enough food for their own use, but they also produced a small surplus for sale or barter. In addition, they made excellent pottery and jewelry. In the past the Zunis had suffered severely from raids on their villages by the Navajos and the Apaches. For protection against these enemies they built their homes with two or more stories. Instead of entering their homes from the ground floor, they entered by climbing a ladder to the flat-topped roof, pulling up the ladder behind them, then climbing down another ladder to the ground floor.

Fort Defiance was established in 1851 by the army for the purpose of controlling the Navajos and protecting the Zunis from these and other marauders. This helped, but the problem wasn't completely solved until 1863, when most of the Navajos were rounded up by General Carleton and Kit Carson and moved to Fort Sumner (the Long Walk). The army contracted with the Zunis for corn and vegetables to feed the soldiers at Fort Defiance; this helped the Zuni economy.

Spanish Padres established a small mission in the pueblo of Zuni in the early 1600s and were successful in converting some of the population to the Catholic faith (at least outwardly), but despite alien influences, the Zunis were able to keep their unique culture and religion in tact.

The emigrants spent a few hours in the pueblo visiting and sightseeing. They found the Zunis friendly and helpful, and they were able to obtain some cornmeal and vegetables, since this was the last opportunity for such purchases before reaching San Bernardino, California, more than five hundred miles away. This might have been the first Indian pueblo that many of the travelers had ever visited; although they had passed the pueblo of Laguna on July 2, they had not stopped. This might also have been the first Zuni encounter with American women and children, for this was the first documented American emigrant train to travel the thirty-fifth parallel route; thus, it was a new experience for both groups.

The Americans found the pueblo both strange and interesting. The Zuni impression of the Americans is not recorded, but it must have been favorable for the Zunis were always kind to the Americans. Among the many strange sights the emigrants observed in Zuni, the one that seems to have impressed them the most, according to Joel Hedgpeth, Jr., was albino Indians. These were the first albinos that many of the Americans had ever seen. Their white skins and pink eyes contrasted sharply with the dark skin and dark eyes of the other Indians. Fellow Indians viewed them as unfortunate.[7]

The wagon train left Zuni in the late afternoon of July 10. They had to traveled four miles west before finding a campsite with sufficient water and grass for the stock. While going for water at the creek after dark, Udell fell from an eight-foot embankment and wrenched his back. The injury was serious enough to keep him confined to his wagon for several days, but fortunately for posterity, not serious enough to curtail his nightly journal entries.

From Zuni westward the emigrants' journey into the unknown really began. Up to this time they had crossed primitive but well-traveled roads; now they were about to plunge into a land previously traversed only by wild Indians and a handful of intrepid explorers, padres, and mountain men. They would be the first emigrant party to attempt Beale's Wagon Road. Terra Incognita, here we come!

The road from Zuni to the Colorado River was mostly over a high rock desert and locating water would be critical. The next adequate water west of Zuni was at Jacob's Well, a distance of thirty-six miles. Since they had already traveled four miles west of Zuni before establishing camp, they had thirty-two miles to go before reaching water. Instead of a well-traveled road to follow, they now had only the faint tracks of Beale's wagons and a few rock cairns for guidance. They had to be careful not to get lost between water holes. They traveled all day and all night on the 11th, but didn't reach Jacob's Well until about 8:30 the next morning. That night Udell made the following entry in his journal: "Wood and grass plenty half a mile off; warm in daytime but cool at night. I suffer much pain from my hurt. [His wrenched back]."

At that time Jacob's Well was a deep well encircled by a high sand bank. Today, the deep well of the trail period is filled in; deep holes appear from time to time in this area and then gradually fill in, probably with wind-blown sand. Early emigrants thought the well looked like a huge round pot set into the earth. It was a long way down to the water and the sides were so steep that it was extremely difficult for the stock to reach the water, and even more difficult for them to get back out. The water was brackish, but the cattle seemed to like it. After traveling all day and all night, the wagon train spent the remainder of the day at the well, resting and watering their stock.

That evening they hit the road again and traveled eight miles to the next water at Navajo Springs, arriving about 1:00 a.m. They camped here for the remainder of the night, and laid over the next day. Having traveled forty-one miles in two days over an almost trackless desert, they were exhausted and sorely in need of rest. Udell had a word of warning about Navajo Springs:

> The water of these springs is tinctured with sulphur, and there are concealed mire holes around them. The ground will appear perfectly hard where a person or animal is walking, and in an instant they will drop through, and it takes hard labor to get either out.[8]

As the name Navajo Springs implies, the emigrants were now entering country inhabited by the Navajo Indians. The Navajos did not take kindly to outsiders entering their territory, be they Whites or other Indians. Neither Udell's, nor any of the other accounts from this wagon train, speak of any problems with the Navajos, or even the sighting of Indians of any tribe while passing through the country between Zuni and the San Francisco Mountains. Since it was summer, the Navajos might have been in the high country where there was better grass and more water for their flocks.

Past Navajo Springs, the next reliable source of water was the Little Colorado River, a distance of approximately forty miles. However, in between there were several small streams which were dry in summer, but sufficient water could be found by digging into the sand of the dry stream beds. The wagon train laid by at one of these locations on the 13th.

They were entering the area of what is now the Petrified Forest National Park. Apparently Udell was not impressed by the sights found in this unique place, for he makes no mention of it in his journal. Some of the other members of the party, apparently more attuned to the wonders of nature, did gather specimens of the petrified wood as souvenirs.[9]

The emigrants arrived at the Little Colorado River near modern Holbrook, Arizona, on July 16. They would follow this river all the way to Canyon Diablo, approximately eighty-five miles. On this segment of the road the Little Colorado River assured them of a reliable source of water. The river was muddy and shallow, but they were able to get clear water by digging holes beside the river bed and letting the water settle until it cleared. The water was brackish but drinkable. The river was also full of quicksand.

Progress down the river was slowed by the stock getting mired in the soft soil near the river. Recent showers made the ground soggy and the road slippery. They were able to avoid the worst of this by moving back from the river. In general, everything seemed to be going well for the wagon train at this point of the journey. Udell's journal entry for July 18 projected an optimistic mood:

> Our large company continue to be harmonious, friendly and kind to each other. My wife was quite ill yesterday and last night, but is much better this evening. I am recovering from my fall. General good health prevails among the company. For all these favors I feel thankful to that Being from whom we derive all our blessings, both temporal and spiritual. Travel to-day, 10 miles, and 1,112 from Missouri River.[10]

By July 22, Udell's mood shifted from optimism to deep pessimism. He had recovered from his back injury, but now it was his eyes that were troubling him. He writes that his eyes have been bothering him for three or four weeks, but now they were so painful that he could scarcely see to write in his journal. He also complained of an old rupture and writes that he was really unfit to travel, but of necessity he must travel with the company or stay alone and perish among the savages. Although his infirmities were not serious, they were painful.

The wagon train left the Little Colorado River on July 23 at its juncture with Canyon Diablo near present-day Winslow, Arizona. Canyon Diablo (The Devil's Canyon) was so-named by Lieutenant Whipple because he found it a great natural obstacle to his thirty-fifth parallel survey. In places the canyon is two hundred and fifty feet deep. He was forced to veer north about twenty-five miles to a point near the canyon's junction with the Little Colorado River before he could cross with his wagons and mules. Beale, likewise, had to extend his survey road farther north than he wanted in order to find a suitable crossing. Neither Udell nor any of the other members of the wagon train wrote of any difficulties encountered in getting across Canyon Diablo. Apparently they crossed at the same point as Whipple and Beale. Udell does mention that they had some difficulty in locating the road at this point, but they finally found it.

Savedra was uncertain where they would find the next water, so they decided to camp here at Canyon Diablo and let the guide, along with two or three members of the wagon train, go on ahead and search for water. While waiting here for a favorable report from the guide, some of the men took advantage of the delay and went hunting. John Daly was able to kill a fine deer, providing the company with a dinner of fresh venison that night.

While camped at this site, several of the emigrants carved their names on a large rock nearby, known today as Register Rock No. 4.[11] When the Santa Fe Railroad came through this section of the country in the 1880s, many of its workers also carved their names on this rock. Time and erosion have erased most of the names, but on the leeward side where it is better protected from the wind, the name Gillum Baley, with the date, July 24, 1858, is clearly visible. The date corresponds exactly with the date Udell says that they camped at this spot, thus giving credibility to his journal, or at least to his chronology of events. Also from this wagon train, the name of R. T. Barnes, one of Rose's men, and the name, M. Rose, are still readable. M. Rose, Amanda Rose, was L. J. Rose's wife; her family and close friends called her "Mande."

At 4:00 p.m. on July 24, Savedra and the other men who had gone out to look for water returned to camp with good news—water had been found! They immediately yoked their oxen and got underway that evening. Due to the heat, they had been traveling a lot at night and were becoming accustomed to night travel. They journeyed seventeen miles and arrived at Walnut Creek about 2:00 a.m. on July 25. The creek flowed through a canyon with sides so steep it was impossible for the animals to climb down to the water. The only way that the stock could be watered was for the men to climb down sixty or seventy feet and bring the water up in buckets. Udell claims he brought up twenty buckets of water from the canyon, not bad for a sixty-three-year-old invalid!

After watering the stock and resting for a while, the wagon train moved down the creek twelve miles to Cosnino Caves where they found three large water holes, all containing excellent water. They camped here for the night. That evening several members of the wagon train became ill with a stomach ailment that they blamed on the water, but Udell thought a more likely cause was the half-green fruit that some of them had eaten that day. He wrote that he and his wife had drunk the same water as the others, but they didn't become ill. Neither had they eaten any of the fruit. The illness was not of long duration, however, since they were able to travel twenty miles the next day.

The wagon train now left the desert temporarily and entered an area of cool forest and stately pines on the lower reaches of the San

Francisco Mountains. These mountains, with a summit of more than 12,000 feet in elevation, are the highest range in Arizona and can be seen in most directions for a distance of nearly one hundred miles. On the night of July 26, they camped at San Francisco Spring where there was an abundance of good water, grass, and wood.

The next day they traveled another seven miles and camped at Leroux Springs on the west side of the San Francisco Mountains. These springs were named after Antoine Leroux, the famed mountain man and guide for the Whipple expedition of 1853–54. The place was so beautiful they decided to lay by for a few days while the guide went ahead to locate water. Udell was greatly impressed by the area, calling it the richest soil he had seen in New Mexico (Arizona was then still part of the New Mexico Territory). He stated, "All it lacks of making it as delightful, and, I think, as healthy, a place as can be found is a settlement of good, civilized, intelligent Christians, and a railroad through it." Today, the thriving city of Flagstaff, Arizona, is nearby.

While camped at Leroux Springs, several of the younger and more ambitious members of the group climbed to the 12,633-foot summit of the San Francisco Mountains (Humphreys Peak, the highest point in Arizona). From its lofty perch they could see almost one-hundred miles in all directions. In the far distance they were able to make out the Little Colorado River, appearing like a green ribbon as it wound its way through the brown desert. High up on the mountain where it was sheltered from the sweltering sun, the intrepid climbers came upon a large snowfield. They were amazed to see snow in July. Someone in the group suggested that it might be great fun to roll a large rock down the side of the mountain. A splendid idea, they all thought! They laboriously pried a huge boulder from its mountain fastness and sent it on its way. They watched with glee as it leaped and thundered down the mountainside.[12] Look out below!

The layover at Leroux Springs gave the men a chance to do some hunting. They were able to bring into camp a good supply of deer, antelope, and wild turkey. So far, the journey to California had been one grand outing: plenty of good campsites; a fairly good road; enough water to get them through; a sufficient, if not plentiful, supply of wood and grass; friendly Indians or no Indians at all; and scenery that was both beautiful and interesting. However, this was soon to change!

CHAPTER 5

Little Water—Many Indians

While the wagon train camped at Leroux Springs, Savedra went ahead to search for water. On the evening of July 29, he returned to camp with a gloomy assessment. He reported that there was not a sufficient supply of water for the stock for seventy or eighty miles ahead, and there would not be until the start of the rainy season in October or November. Many in the wagon train thought that their stock could not travel that distance without water, and that perhaps they should remain where they were at Leroux Springs until the start of the rainy season. At least the springs provided plenty of water and grass. Most were reluctant to risk their animals on such a long, waterless stretch, for they were all well aware of the high prices that cattle were selling for on the California market; their stock was to be their grubstake when they arrived at their new homes. They had brought their cattle this far, and by God, they were not going to lose them now! Udell strongly opposed staying put:

> I contended that we had better travel on, for, with careful and proper treatment, we could get the stock through to water, and if we remain here until the rainy season, in all human probability our provisions would be exhausted, and we should perish with starvation—and to me death by starvation is the most horrible thing I can imagine. But all my entreaties were in vain—none would agree to go on.[1]

After a thorough discussion of their situation, the emigrants decided that maybe Savedra could be mistaken, and perhaps they should send some of their own members ahead to see if they could find water. The next day, July 30, six men volunteered to go and search for water. They took enough provisions to last four or five days. On the evening of the following day, one of these men returned to camp and reported that a weak spring had been discovered fifteen miles ahead, but its capacity was insufficient to accommodate the whole wagon train at one time. There was some discussion of dividing the wagon train into two sections, with one section traveling a day ahead of the other, at least while journeying through this arid section of the country. This would reduce the pressure on the limited supply of water and grass. Remembering what they had been told by the army back in Albuquerque about staying together while traveling through Indian territory, most of the group were fearful of dividing the wagon train. Udell argued that they should move forward in smaller companies, rather than risking starvation or thirst by traveling in one large group. But others argued that it was too risky to separate for fear of Indians. In later years while preparing his journal for publication, Udell could not resist the temptation to insert these words of retrospective wisdom:

> If our company had been as fearful of separating when among the Mojave Indians as they were here, where no Indians lived near, we might probably have saved a number of lives of the company, and all our property and much suffering.[2]

After much discussion on the subject, they came to the conclusion that their best chance for survival was to divide the train into two sections, at least temporarily. So far, they had not been bothered by Indians, and maybe this threat had been exaggerated by the folks in Albuquerque. They agreed that the Rose company would start forward the next day, while the Baley company would wait until the following day.

On the evening of August 1, after the Rose company had moved ahead, the five men who were out searching for water returned to camp and reported that they had found plenty of water in different places for the next fifty miles. One of these scouts, Thomas Hedgpeth, succeeded in killing a bear and brought part of the meat back to camp with him. The fresh bear meat and the news that water was discovered ahead improved everyone's mood.

The Baley company departed Leroux Springs the following morning. The first day out they traveled twenty miles and camped that night at the springs where Thomas Hedgpeth killed the bear the day before. Some of the emigrants called these springs Hedgpeth Springs, while others referred to them as Bear Springs.[3]

The next morning they caught up with the Rose train camped at Spring Valley. Udell doesn't say why the Rose train stopped here, but it was probably to let their stock do some grazing while waiting for the scouts to return with reports of water and feed conditions ahead. The united wagon train then traveled another twenty miles that day. That evening they were forced to make a dry camp, but fortunately they had brought enough water with them for domestic purposes; the stock, however, had to go without. The next day, after traveling five miles, they came to a deep canyon which they called Alexander Canyon (probably Cataract Creek). At the bottom of the canyon they found some pools with enough water in them for all the stock. They laid by the remainder of the day to let their cattle graze and drink their fill of water. Meanwhile, Savedra went ahead to search for the next water hole.

The following day they traveled four or five miles down the canyon, but were unable to locate the road. Realizing that they were heading in the wrong direction, they turned around and began searching for a way out of the canyon. They finally found the road and started in the right direction, but the effort consumed most of the day. That night they camped at the top of the canyon.

While making preparations to get underway the next morning, Udell discovered that his horse was missing. He walked back ten or twelve miles to search for it, but he was unable to find the lost animal. Just as he was about to give up the search, he met Thomas Hedgpeth leading the stray horse back to camp. Udell was overjoyed. He stated in his journal that evening, "My tongue failed to express in full my joy and gratitude to him." The wagon train traveled twenty miles that day, but Udell probably walked and rode more than forty miles, not bad for a sixty-three-year-old man who claimed to be in ill health! That night they again had to make a dry camp.

They expected to find water within six or eight miles the next day, but were unsuccessful. After traveling another six miles, they met Savedra returning from his scouting trip. He stated that the water he expected to find had dried up, and there was no certainty of finding more short of sixty miles. This was indeed bad news! Under normal conditions of travel, sixty miles would take at least three days. Already the poor animals had gone without water the night before; three more days without they could never do! Another council was held. All but Udell agreed that their only choice was to turn back to the last water holes in Alexander Canyon. Udell logically argued that they might find these water holes dried up when they returned, as the holes contained mostly rain water, and then it would be even farther to the next water. Even if they found water in the canyon, he reasoned, they still faced the danger of starvation since their provisions were almost gone. Again, Udell's arguments were brushed aside, and all turned back. Udell, disgusted with the decision to turn back, wrote in his journal that night, "Had there been a road that I could have traveled without a guide, I should have gone on and risked the consequences." This was the first backward march for the wagon train, an ill omen for the future.

The return trip to Alexander Canyon took all the next day and most of the night. Since it was still dark when they arrived, they were unable to see well enough to get their wagons down the steep-walled canyon to the bottom. They unhitched their thirsty oxen which eagerly found their way to the water, having traveled fifty-two miles without. Luckily, some water still remained in the deep holes, but it had become stagnant and was full of wigglers. The thirsty cattle drank it anyway. So did the thirsty people.

The emigrants were beginning to lose confidence in Savedra, and like Beale on his expedition the year before, they also were forced to do much of their own scouting and exploring. On August 9, several men on horses carrying provisions enough to last several days set out in all directions to scout the countryside for water. Meanwhile, those who remained in camp busied themselves manufacturing casks from the pines and junipers that grew in the canyon floor. With these homemade containers, they hoped to be able to carry enough additional water for the cattle to last for at least one night. "Our water still holds out," Udell recorded, "like the widow's cruse of oil, and tastes more pleasant, having been stirred up so often for us."

On the afternoon of August 13, a hard rain shower partly replenished the rapidly drying water holes. That evening the men who were out searching for water the past five days returned to camp with more good news. They found a large spring eighty miles ahead and only five miles off their course. There was a strong probability that the rain they received that afternoon left water in some canyons that they located forty miles ahead. This, and the water that they could carry in their wagons, should be enough to enable them to reach the newly discovered spring. This favorable turn of events raised everyone's spirits. Udell records that they had hymn singing by some excellent female voices until late that night.

They spent the following day filling their casks with water and making preparations for the next phase of the journey. At 5:30 p.m., the signal was given to start the wagons forward. After traveling all night and most of the next day, they arrived at Partridge Creek late in the afternoon. Partridge Creek was normally dry at this time of the year, but fortunately, the recent thunderstorms deposited enough water in large holes in the rocks for both man and beast. Here, they camped for the night after traveling almost continuously since leaving Alexander Canyon the night before. That evening they were blessed with another heavy thundershower which filled Partridge Creek with water. It was now well into the Arizona monsoon season.[4] Udell noted, "A kind providence has visited us in our needy circumstances for which we should ever praise and honor Him."

The next day's travel brought the wagon train to the vicinity of Mount Floyd, which Udell called Apache Peak. (Mount Floyd was named by Beale during his 1857 expedition; being a prudent man, he named the peak after his boss, Secretary of War John B. Floyd.) Beale had not yet published his map at the time the Rose-Baley wagon train arrived in Albuquerque in June of 1858, so Udell had no way of knowing that the peak was already named. Nine miles farther up the road they came to another deep canyon where they had expected to find water, but there was none. The recent showers did not reach this far. Disappointed, they traveled another twelve miles without finding water, and were forced to make another dry camp.

On August 17, they again traveled all day and well into the night without finding any water except a small quantity discovered by Udell at the bottoms of two different canyons that Udell named Udell's Canyons, (the name didn't stick). At midnight they halted and made camp, having traveled thirty miles that day, tying their record set on May 18. Scouts discovered a large spring that day, but it was some distance from the road and in country too precipitous and too difficult to locate in the dark; they would have to wait for daylight.

Early the next morning they drove their thirsty herds over terrain too steep and too rugged to take wagons. They were rewarded by finding a large spring with plenty of good water. Water from the spring flowed through a small valley of fine grass. This was just what the cattle needed, as they had been traveling almost day and night for eighty-five miles without adequate food, water, or rest. They left the cattle at the spring overnight, to give the poor beasts a chance to recruit. Guards were placed during the night to keep the Indians from stealing any of the stock. Udell took two five-gallon kegs of water back to camp with him that evening. "The mountain was so steep," he wrote, "that I could not carry them on my horse, but had to roll them up half a mile, one at a time."

In spite of careful vigilance during the night, it was discovered the next morning that a mare belonging to Rose and a mule belonging to Savedra were missing. Three of the herders were sent out to search for the missing animals. They soon found the animals' tracks and followed in hot pursuit. They tracked the missing animals all day, but were unable to overtake them. Late in the afternoon, while going through a deep canyon, arrows were shot at the men. Indians were seen darting between rocks, and now and then, an Indian would stick his head up for a quick shot. Fortunately, none of the men was hit. With night coming on and with their horses tiring, the three searchers decided that a more prudent course of action would be to abandon the chase and return to the wagon train.

The next day, while the wagon train was traveling, Savedra spied some Indians on the side of a mountain. With much patience and the use of sign language, he was able to coax them down. Seeing that no harm was meant, they followed the wagon train until camp was made, all the while keeping up a constant jabber. When near the emigrants, they would pat themselves on the chest and repeat over and over the words, "Hanna, Hanna, Hanna" (good Indians). Udell, and others, called these Indians Cosninos or Cosniños, but most likely they were members of the Hualapai tribe as the wagon train was now entering Hualapai country.[5]

The Indians knew a few words of Spanish and English, and Savedra understood some of their dialect. Through this medley of languages combined with the use of sign language, Savedra was able to get this story from them: Yes, they had the emigrants' horses, but they had taken them from the Mojaves, who had stolen them from the emigrants, and they would bring them in the following day. They said that they were good, or "Hanna, Hanna" Indians, and that the Mojaves were bad Indians. Not wishing any trouble, the emigrants treated them kindly and fed them all the food they wanted. They were inclined to believe that these were the same Indians who had stolen the horses, and they held little hope that they would ever see the missing animals again. Savedra said that the Mojave Indians never came this far from their own country.

Resigned to the loss of the livestock, the wagon train continued onward, arriving at Peach Springs (Beale's Hemphill Springs) on the evening of August 19. The next morning, to the surprise and delight of the emigrants, about twenty-five Indians came into camp leading the stolen animals. It quickly became apparent that they expected to be well rewarded for their trouble. L. J. Rose had this to say about them:

> It was soon evident that they anticipated very extravagant rewards, all expecting shoes, clothing and trinkets, besides some cattle. I gave each of the two [the two who claimed to have actually recovered the horses] a blanket, shirt, pants, knife, tobacco and some Indian trinkets, and the balance tobacco and some trinkets, also preparing an ample dinner for them, and again a supper. I also gave the two who returned the horses a certificate that they had voluntarily returned them, and that I believe they had also stolen them. Many remained in camp with us that night, doubtless for the purpose of stealing, but the guard kept so sharp a lookout that they found no opportunity.[6]

The next morning, to the great annoyance of everyone, about fifty more Indians came into camp also expecting to be rewarded. They asked for shoes, claiming that they had worn out their moccasins in retaking the horses from the Mojave. They also wanted cattle. After being fed and given some tobacco and trinkets, they left at about 11:00 a.m., to the great relief of all members of the wagon train.

After dinner, while making preparations to get underway, it was discovered that six oxen were missing. Several men were sent back to look for them. After tracking the missing animals for some distance, the searchers came upon four carcasses. Two of the carcasses had all the meat cut away while the other two were partially butchered. A short distance farther, the other two oxen were found. They were freshly killed and still warm, the Indians apparently scared off by their pursuers before they could strip the meat from the animals. Due to approaching darkness and the possibility of an ambush, the pursuit was called off.

During this phase of the journey the wagon train was doing much of its traveling at night, owing to the great daytime heat of the desert and the long distances between water holes. At regular intervals during the night they would stop for a short rest. At one of these rest stops, eleven-year-old Ellen Baley, a daughter of Gillum and Permelia Baley, fell asleep and failed to awaken when the wagon train moved on. Somehow, she was not missed until the train traveled some distance. The poor girl awoke to find herself alone in the middle of a vast hostile desert. Filled with fright, she began running to catch up with the wagon train, but in her confusion she took off in the opposite direction. When she was discovered missing, her father and older brother, George, immediately rode back to where they had stopped. To their horror, she was not there! Captured by the Indians must have been their conclusion! Nevertheless, they continued their search by calling out the little girl's name at the top of their voices as they rode back. Their efforts were soon rewarded when, far off in the distance, came a faint cry, "Papa, Papa." Her father immediately answered and kept calling her name until he caught up with her. When reunited with her family and the other members of the wagon train, Ellen had a tale which would be told and retold by family members until the present day.[7]

From Peach Springs to the Colorado River, a distance of approximately one hundred and ten miles, the wagon train was harassed almost constantly by Indians. During the day, from their places of concealment, the Indians would take potshots at the emigrants or at their cattle; at night they would swarm into camp in great numbers and attempt to steal anything they could get their hands on. The Indians became so bothersome they had to be roped out of camp. The constant vigilance was beginning to wear the travelers down. Still, they considered the Indians only a big nuisance and not a serious threat to the wagon train.

On the evening of August 20, they arrived at White Rock Spring (also called Indian Springs) located in Truxton Canyon. This was a large spring with plenty of good water. Because scouts had reported another long stretch without adequate water or grass, the emigrants decided to again divide the wagon train. The loss of livestock from starvation and thirst was considered a more immediate threat to the group than any threat from Indians.

The next day, the Rose train moved ahead. Because of the uncertainty of finding water and grass, Rose left a large portion of his herd behind at White Rock Spring to recruit, under the supervision of his foreman, Alpha Brown. His intent was to move forward as rapidly as possible to the next known watering place, Savedra Spring, thirty-three miles ahead, where their guide assured them they would find an abundance of good water and grass. He would wait at Savedra spring for the Baley company to join him, then send word back to Brown to bring up the remainder of the herd. He wanted the wagon train to be united before moving ahead, as the Indians were becoming more numerous and more threatening.

Savedra discovered this spring the year before while serving as Beale's guide. Pleased with his discovery, he named the spring after himself. Since this was one of the few things that Savedra had done to please Beale, Beale let the name stand.

On the morning of August 22, the Baley train left White Rock Spring to rendezvous with the Rose company at Savedra Spring. That afternoon, some members of this company received quite a scare. Three of the men rode ahead to check on a recently discovered spring. Another small detachment climbed to the top of a nearby hill to scout any possible danger from Indians. Suddenly, the men at the top of the hill heard a volley of shots emanating from the vicinity of the spring. Believing that their comrades at the spring had been attacked by Indians, they let their imaginations get the better of them. They ran back to the wagons shouting, "The Indians have attacked our men who have gone ahead and have killed them all." Some were so excited that they were sure that they had seen the men fall. Several of the women fainted on hearing this tragic news. Cautiously, and with guns drawn, the men slowly advanced toward the spring. Arriving there they found, to their surprise and great delight, that their comrades at the spring had not been attacked by Indians; they had simply been shooting at a large snake, which they succeeded in killing. With sheepish grins the young men who had given the false alarm hurried back to deliver the good news to those waiting anxiously at the wagons.[8]

When the excitement died down, the Baley company again moved forward, traveling another eleven miles before making camp in the Hualapai Valley. This was another dry camp, but they were successful in finding a spring some five miles off to the left of the road. After the evening meal they drove their stock to this newly found spring, but to their disappointment the water issued from the spring so slowly it was impossible for the thirsty animals to get their fill. Nevertheless, they decided to return them to the wagons and move on, as they were anxious to get to Savedra Spring where they hoped to find the Rose company and plenty of water. They traveled another five miles and camped for the remainder of the night without water.

The next day, the Baley train crossed the Cerbat Mountains through Boys' Pass and arrived at Savedra Spring near present Kingman, Arizona.[9] In spite of what Savedra had promised, the spring bearing his name proved to be a great disappointment. It might have yielded a plentiful supply of water the year before when Savedra discovered it, but this year it produced barely enough water for domestic use.

At Savedra Spring they found Rose and most of his company. Rose, too, was unhappy about the inadequate water supply at the spring, but he also realized that it was not wise to let his herd get too far behind the main body. He decided to wait at Savedra Spring until Alpha Brown could bring up the remainder of the stock from White Rock Spring. To deliver the message to Brown to move forward, Rose sent his young brother-in-law, eighteen-year-old Ed Jones, mounted on Picayune, Rose's fastest horse.

On his way back to camp after delivering the message, it being an exceedingly hot day, young Jones decided to stop and rest under the shade of a large tree. While resting, he fell asleep and was spied by a group of Hualapai warriors mounted on ponies. They stalked him until they were close enough to make a charge. To be caught out in the open, unmounted, would mean certain death.

Fortunately for Jones, he was awakened by the hoof beats of the Indians' ponies in time to leap on the back of Picayune. Putting the spurs to the animal, he literally rode for his life. Thanks to a fast horse, the young man gradually pulled away from his pursuers, but not before they released a volley of arrows in his direction. Several of the prickly barbs struck Jones in the back and one penetrated deep into his body, causing a serious wound. By hanging onto the pommel of his saddle for dear life, he retained consciousness and rode safely into camp. When he was removed from his horse, he lost consciousness from loss of blood, and for several days his life hung in the balance. He slowly recovered but it was over a year before he was able to ride a horse again. One of the arrow points remained in his side, making it impossible for him to ever again do any heavy lifting.[10]

By driving hard all day and all night, Alpha Brown reached Savedra Spring with the remainder of Rose's herd on the evening of August 23. He was harassed continuously by Indians on the way and lost seven head of cattle. The scouts reported that the next reliable water supply was thirty miles ahead at a place called Mountain Spring, located at the eastern base of the Colorado (Black) Mountains. In between lay a rocky, scorching valley (the Sacramento). Because of almost constant traveling both day and night during the last few days, combined with a shortage of both feed and water, many of the emigrants feared that their cattle would never make it that far. But they also realized that because of the Indian menace, low provisions, and a scarcity of both feed and water, they could not remain where they were. Udell described their plight in these words, "We concluded to go on as far as we could; perhaps some of the stock might get through, which was our last forlorn hope."

As soon as Alpha Brown arrived at Savedra Spring with the remainder of the Rose company's stock, the wagon train began making preparations to move ahead. After the evening meal was finished, they hitched their oxen to the wagons and got under way. Because the weather was still very hot, they believed that their famished stock would have a better chance of survival if they again traveled at night. To better protect their cattle against night forays by the Indians, the two companies combined their stock, which had heretofore been kept separate, into one united herd (they were unbranded). In this manner they could double the number of herders and keep a better vigil.

At about 11:00 a.m. on August 24, the wagon train arrived at Mountain Spring, having traveled thirty miles during the night and morning. The cattle stood the trip better than expected considering their poor condition, but three or four head were missing, either stolen by Indians or dead of exhaustion during this leg of the journey. At Mountain Spring they found plenty of water but no grass. They were now within twenty-five miles of the California border, but in between stood some very formidable obstacles: The Colorado (Black) Mountains, the Colorado River, and the Mojave Indians.

The Black Mountains, which both Whipple and Beale called the Colorado Mountains, are not high, most peaks being less than 6,000 feet in elevation. Nevertheless, they are extremely steep and rugged, as well as arid and barren. They extend along the east side of modern-day Lake Mead and the Colorado River in Arizona to a point near Needles. Beale's Wagon Road crossed this range at Sitgreaves Pass at an elevation of 3,652 feet. Sitgreaves Pass is named after Lieutenant Lorenzo Sitgreaves of the U.S. Army Topographical Engineers who led an expedition through this region in 1851, although he actually crossed these mountains through Union Pass ten miles to the north. Lieutenant Joseph C. Ives, also of the topographical engineers, named this pass after Sitgreaves in 1858 because Ives mistakenly thought this was where Sitgreaves had crossed the range. Beale called this pass John Howell's Pass after one of his men.

Union Pass is a much easier pass than Sitgreaves, but the emigrants had no way of knowing this. They were only following the trail that Beale had marked. In some places on the west side of Sitgreaves Pass the terrain was so steep that Beale had to let his wagons down by ropes. One of his wagons was smashed to pieces while being lowered.

The Rose-Baley wagon train spent all day of August 25 at Mountain Spring watering their stock and resting for the difficult climb over this rugged range of mountains. All the next day was devoted to clearing rocks and improving the road in preparation for the journey ahead. In many places the road was all but impassable because of its precipitousness. That night, by the light of a full moon, the emigrants began their toilsome climb to the top of Sitgreaves Pass. The going was tedious and slow; double-teaming was necessary in many places, but finally in the late afternoon of August 27, the wagon train reached the crest of the highest ridge of this desert mountain range. From its lofty summit they could plainly see the Colorado River flowing in the distance, its silvery surface shimmering in the late afternoon sun. Shortly, they would be pitching their camps under the shady cottonwood trees that lined its banks, and watering their thirsty animals in its cool, life-giving waters. Fresh fruits and vegetables for the weary travelers and feed for their starving animals could surely be purchased from the Mojaves—for didn't Beale say they were agricultural Indians? They had brought along an ample supply of tobacco, calico, trinkets, beads, and other trade items for bartering with the natives. Soon they would be in California, the land of milk and honey, and all their troubles would be behind them. But, alas, fate had decreed a different scenario.

CHAPTER 6

Battle at the Colorado

The Rose-Baley wagon train was now entering the domain of the Mojave Indians. The Mojaves are members of the Yuman language group. They inhabited an area along the Colorado River stretching from about fifteen miles north of the present Davis Dam southward to a group of three sharp mountain peaks known as the Needles (from which the modern city of Needles takes its name), and eastward from the Colorado River to the crest of the Black Mountains. Their territory lay in three different states: Arizona, Nevada, and California, but the vast majority was in Arizona. These Indians occupied approximately the same area in 1858 that they occupied when first encountered by the Spaniards in 1604. They still occupy this same area today. The Spaniards never established missions or colonies among them. The first European to visit the Mojaves was Father Francisco Garcés in 1776. He estimated their population at approximately three thousand.[1]

The Mojaves practiced a form of agriculture by planting their crops in the rich silt deposited by the annual flooding of the Colorado River, much like the ancient Egyptians did on the Nile River. Their principal crops were corn, beans, pumpkins, squash, and various types of melons, which they supplemented by hunting, fishing, and gathering different types of wild seeds. A reliable and varied food supply helped to promote good health and proper physical development. Whipple described the men as tall, erect, and finely proportioned.[2] They made some pottery and baskets, but their workmanship in these crafts was mainly utilitarian.

Although divided into several bands and family groups, the Mojaves thought of themselves as a national entity, enabling them to present a united front against any potential enemy. They prized courage above all other virtues.[3] These qualities made them splendid warriors. Raiding parties of young Mojave warriors would travel great distances to raid other tribes, but these expeditions were more for curiosity and gaining knowledge about new lands than they were for acquiring booty or new territory. However, they did sometimes capture young women and girls for slaves. They took enemy scalps and held scalp dances. The scalps would be placed on poles and set up in an open field or playground; the young men and girls would paint their hair white and dance around the scalps for four days and nights.[4]

The Mojaves had hereditary chiefs, in the male line, but it is uncertain how much power they possessed. They might have had more moral influence than actual authority. War leaders and shamans (spiritual leaders or doctors) also played important roles in Mojave society. These leaders were believed to have received great power from dreams.[5]

After crossing the summit of the Colorado (Black) Mountains at Sitgreaves Pass on the late afternoon of August 27, 1858, the Rose-Baley wagon train halted while its members prepared a meal, their first of the day. They labored so hard in getting over the pass they had not taken time to eat. While they were preparing their supper, a small group of Mojaves approached. They acted quite friendly. They had with them a small quantity of green corn and some melons, which the vegetable-hungry travelers eagerly purchased. Speaking a mixture of poor English and poor Spanish, the Mojaves asked how many individuals were in the wagon train and whether or not they intended to settle on the Colorado River. Very unusual questions, the emigrants thought! On being assured by the emigrants that they were en route to California and had no intention of settling anywhere near the Colorado River, the Mojaves seemed satisfied and asked no further questions. Some of them traveled with the wagon train and made themselves useful by pointing out the road and volunteering other help during the night travel.

By traveling all night the wagon train hoped to reach the Colorado River by early morning. From the summit of Sitgreaves Pass, the river appeared tantalizingly close, but the descent proved to be nearly as difficult as the ascent. The road descended into a very deep canyon (Silver Creek Wash), which it followed for some distance before climbing out of the ravine and taking off over some rugged hills. The climb out was so steep the wagons had to be partially disassembled and pulled up by means of block and tackle. The Rose company wrecked one of its wagons when it accidentally bashed against the rocks while being brought up out of the canyon. Beale lost one of his wagons at this same spot the previous year.

During the night the Baley company, traveling in the rear, began falling farther and farther behind. Their animals had become so weak and worn down from lack of food and water and continuous travel that it was feared they might not be able to pull the wagons out of the mountains. Shortly before midnight the company decided to stop and pitch camp. They would unhitch the oxen from the wagons, and drive them and the loose stock to the Colorado River along with the livestock of the Rose company. After the work stock was sufficiently recruited, they would be brought back to camp to pull the wagons out of the mountains and down to the river to join the Rose company so that the wagon train would be united before crossing the Colorado River. The women and children remained with the wagons along with some of the men to protect the camp from Indians. The others, mostly the younger men, went with William Right Baley to help drive the stock to the river. Bentner, from the Rose company, also left his family and light wagon at the mountain camp while he drove his two mules to the river with the other stock. They expected it would take two or three days to recruit the animals sufficiently for them to be returned to the wagons. Those men not engaged in herding the stock would assist Rose's men in cutting trees for the construction of a raft for crossing the Colorado River.

The next morning, August 28, Udell and others who remained with the wagons at the mountain camp began a search for water for domestic needs. They had brought only a small quantity of water with them since they expected to arrive at the Colorado River the next morning. Neither Udell nor the others were successful in locating water, although they searched long and hard. To get more water they had to go back three miles to a small spring they passed the previous day on the east side of Sitgreaves Pass.

Although they were unsuccessful in finding water in the canyon, Udell made an important observation.

I spent the day in examining the road on ahead and looking for water, for we had to bring it three miles over the mountain, from the last spring we passed. I did not succeed in finding
water, but I concluded we could improve the road ahead; here
it leaves the canon, [*sic*] where Mr. Rose broke a wagon. I
thought we could, with some labor, keep down the canon we
were in, and shun those bad hills and shorten the distance half
a mile.[6]

The following day, Gillum Baley and Joel Hedgpeth went with
Udell to examine the route he had suggested. They all agreed it would
be better to construct a road down the canyon than to attempt to take
the wagons out of the canyon at the place where Beale and Rose had
left it. The shattered remains of one of Rose's wagons were clear evidence of the difficulties they would encounter if they tried to leave the
canyon at that point. The main obstacle to continuing down the canyon
was the large boulders that blocked the way, but with some effort these
could be removed. They started work on the project immediately.[7]

Meanwhile, The Rose company, along with the livestock and
some of the men of the Baley company, continued traveling during the
night. After climbing out of the canyon they found the going much easier. By noon they had cleared the last hill and arrived at a grove of cottonwood trees about a mile from the river. From this distance the thirsty
animals smelled the water and made a mad dash for it. The work oxen
were unhitched from the wagons and allowed to join the loose stock,
lest they stampede and overturn the wagons in their rush to water.

As the emigrants neared the river, they encountered many
Mojave Indians, but unlike the friendly Mojaves back at the pass, these
Indians acted in a rude and impudent manner. They asked the same
questions as those back in the mountains: Did the emigrants intend to
settle on the Colorado River? How long did they intend to remain in
Mojave territory? They were assured that the wagon train was en route
to California and would be leaving Mojave territory as soon as the
train got across the river. Their furtive glances and constant jabbering
made it apparent that these Indians viewed the emigrants' answers with
some suspicion.

As quickly as the work oxen were watered, they were returned
to the wagons. When the watering was completed, the Rose company

started for the river to locate a suitable campsite. L. J. and Amanda Rose decided to lighten the load by getting out of their wagon and walking the remaining distance to the river. As they were walking along, one of the more bumptious Indians stepped between them and placed his hands on Mrs. Rose's shoulder and bosom. This frightened the poor woman so that she ran screaming back to the nearest wagon, climbed upon the wagon tongue between the oxen, and remained there until the wagon reached the river. Leonard Rose was naturally incensed by this outrageous conduct, but not wishing to start an incident while surrounded by hostile Indians, he wisely held his anger in check.

A second group of Indians approached the Alpha Brown wagon, which had been unhitched a short distance from the others. Brown was away herding the loose stock to water at the river. As it was very hot day, Mrs. Brown asked the Indians if they would bring some water to her and her children. They said that they would if she would pull off her dress and give it to them. She offered them other articles of much greater value, but nothing else would do. They then took hold of her little boy, saying that they were going to take him. L. J. Rose, seeing what was happening, had the Brown's wagon pulled closer to the others where he could keep an eye on it. This discouraged the Indians and they left. Shortly afterwards Alpha Brown returned to the wagon with water for his family, thus ending any immediate danger.

They made camp that evening, August 28, in the shade of some large cottonwood trees about two hundred yards from the river. The exhausted men, except for those still herding cattle, lay down in the cool shade of the trees and were soon fast asleep. Had the Mojaves chosen this moment to launch an attack, they probably could have wiped out the whole camp. The sharp-eyed Indians, however, did not fail to take notice of the general state of unpreparedness. They took advantage of the situation by driving off cattle in plain sight of the herders, who were too few in number to prevent the depredations. To add insult to injury, some of the cattle were butchered and the meat cooked and eaten in full view of the whites. Whenever the Mojaves were caught in the act of stealing, they would treat the incident as a big joke. There was little the emigrants could do about it without risking a major battle for which they were ill-prepared since a large part of the wagon train was still at the mountain camp ten miles back. They believed their best chance in getting away safely and without further incidents was to get across the Colorado River as quickly as possible and out of Mojave territory. Finally, at nightfall, the Indians departed, leaving the wagon train to enjoy a peaceful night of much needed rest.

The next morning the emigrants awoke feeling rested and refreshed. After a hearty breakfast, camp was moved to the river bank in order to be nearer to water. Some of the men began searching for the best place to cross the river, while others began looking for better grass for the stock. They were successful on both accounts. To their great relief, no Indians had yet shown up in camp.

Bentner, who had left his family and light wagon back at the mountain camp with the Baley company, now decided that his two mules were sufficiently recruited for him to go back to the mountain camp and bring his family and wagon to the river camp. As his mules were well shod, their only suffering had been from thirst and lack of feed. After an abundance of grass and water and a day's rest, his animals were now in good working condition, Bentner believed. Being a member of the Rose company, he was anxious to get his family back with the rest of that group. As soon as he finished breakfast, he set off for the mountain camp astride one of his mules while leading the other. He expected to travel all day and all night and be back at Rose's camp the next morning.

About noon on August 29, the river camp received a visit from a Mojave chief accompanied by about twenty-five of his warriors. When the emigrants complained to him about the theft of their cattle by some of the chief's men, he took his warriors aside and talked with them. Just what he said is unknown as the emigrants did not understand the Mojave dialect, but when he returned he assured them that his men would steal no more. He, too, wanted to know where the emigrants were planning to settle. Again they explained that they were on their way to California and were only passing through. The chief seemed satisfied with these answers and asked no further questions. Presents, consisting of blankets, shirts, pants, knives, tobacco, beads, mirrors, and rings, were then given to the chief, who in turn distributed these gifts among his men. The chief appeared well pleased by this gesture. He told the emigrants they could cross the river whenever and wherever they wished without being molested by any of his warriors.

About an hour after this group of Mojaves departed, another chief, with his entourage of warriors, arrived at the river camp. This chief was a tall, stout individual, his skin decorated with war paint. He spoke with a bombastic style. On his head he wore a gorgeous feather headdress, and on his body he wore many bells and gewgaws. With his tall stature and splendid costume, he presented a very imposing figure. He asked the same questions as the previous chief and received the same answers. He also was given presents and he likewise assured the emigrants that they would encounter no further problems from him or his men. He and most of his warriors then left.

The emigrants noticed that most of the Indians who visited their camp came from across the river. This contradicted information they had received in Albuquerque that when they crossed the Colorado River they would be out of Mojave territory and safe in California.[8] Actually, the Mojaves inhabited both sides of the Colorado River between modern Needles, California, and Laughlin, Nevada, moving their villages and cultivated fields to conform with the annual spring floods of the Colorado. In 1858 all of their villages and cultivated fields were on the west, or California, side of the river.

Late in the afternoon of August 29, the emigrants again moved camp, this time about a mile down the river to a spot near where they expected to cross. This location was selected because it was near a large grove of cottonwoods they intended to use in constructing a raft for crossing the river. There was a good supply of grass here also, and with the river nearby, the cattle could be watered and grazed near camp where a close watch could be kept on them. The men cutting the trees and constructing the raft would be within hailing distance of the camp in case of any trouble with the Indians.

That evening, William Right Baley returned to the mountain camp from the river and reported that the Indians were stealing cattle and driving them across the river before the very eyes of the herders, they being too few in number to stop the depredations. This news alarmed those at the mountain camp. That same evening Baley, his brother, Gillum, and several more men left for the river camp to reenforce those already there, and to expedite driving the work stock back to retrieve the remaining wagons. The men remaining at the mountain camp continued working on the road all the next day so everything would be ready as soon as the work stock were brought back to the wagons.

The work of constructing the raft was not expected to take more than two or three days. By then the Baley company should have all of its wagons and people down from the mountains and the wagon train once more would be united and ready to continue its journey. As they had done in crossing the Rio Grande in New Mexico, each company would take one entire day in crossing the Colorado River. The Rose company expected to cross first since their stock had been resting and grazing for the last few days. Some of the work stock of the Baley company would have to go back to the mountain camp to bring in the remaining wagons and the women and children, and would probably need a day's rest before crossing the river. If all went according to schedule, they should be across the Colorado River and in the Promised Land of California in three or four days.[9]

Crossing a major river such as the Colorado was always a difficult and time-consuming process for a wagon train, especially when there was no established ferry service. The lower Colorado was vastly different in those days than it is today. There were no dams or other diversions on the river; it ran free and wild all the way from its source in the Rocky Mountains to the end of its journey at the Gulf of California. This is how L. J. Rose Jr., described the crossing site:

> The river at this point was about five hundred yards in width, composed of alternate expanses of shallow water and swift running, deep currents in the more confined areas. The bottom throughout, shifting in nature, was composed of atomic particles of silt and sand, which caused the formation of more or less quicksand in the shallow places. Although it would be possible to cope successfully with these conditions with the loose stock and mounted horsemen, to undertake to haul the heavy wagons across would be but to court certain disaster.
>
> It therefore became necessary to construct a log raft and rig a ferry crossing with which to transport the women and children and the wagons.[10]

The new river camp was pleasant and well situated for making the necessary preparations for crossing the river. Although the weather was hot, its effects were somewhat mitigated by a cool breeze blowing off the river. The camp was located in a clearing about one-half acre in size with a huge cottonwood tree providing ample shade in the center of camp. On both sides of camp were trees with a considerable amount of brush growing under them. In front of camp was a large area covered with mesquite and creosote bushes. The river enclosed one end of camp while the other end was open for coming and going. The wagons were drawn up in two parallel rows with considerable space left between wagons, giving the camp a strong defensive position.

No Indians visited camp that night and no cattle were stolen. The next morning found everyone refreshed after a good night's sleep and eager to get started on the day's work. The herders were sent out to graze the cattle, while other men began cutting trees for construction of the raft. The women took advantage of this opportunity to get caught up on baking and washing so that everything would be ready for crossing the river. Only two Indians visited camp that morning, but neither demanded anything nor stayed long.

About 10:00 a.m., a large number of Indians were observed crossing the river at some distance above camp. More than two hundred and fifty were counted and all were carrying bows and arrows and dressed in war paint. The appearance of such a large number of Indians aroused Savedra's suspicion. He turned around and said to Rose, "I don't like the way them Injuns is actin'. We are going to have trouble with them, and I bet before night."[11] Rose took Savedra's concern seriously and sent word to his foreman, Alpha Brown, to have the cattle brought closer to camp. Yet, there was little fear of an attack on the camp; the main concern was for the safety of the stock.

Rose began to feel some uneasiness about the Bentner family. Bentner had gone back to the mountain camp the previous morning to bring in his family and wagon. He expected to be back at the river camp early the next morning. It was nearly noon and they should have returned by now. Rose decided to send someone back to the previous campsite to see if the family might be there, since the camp had been moved again after Bentner left. Since it was now almost dinner time, Rose decided to wait until after the noon meal. Immediately after dinner he sent two young men on horseback, Edward A. Young and Billy Stidger, to see if they could find the Bentner family. During dinner, a lone Indian came into camp. He looked around for a short time and then left.

Shortly after dinner one of the herders came into camp and reported that he saw a good many Indians in the vicinity. They told him that a steamboat was coming up the river and pointed where the sun would be when the boat would arrive. This created some excitement in camp, but the emigrants soon realized that this was just too good to be true. And it was. No regular steamboat service had yet been established this far up the Colorado River; only a couple of experimental runs had been made past this point earlier that year. The steamboat story was apparently a ruse to divert the emigrants' attention while the Mojave warriors made last minute adjustments for a surprise attack on the unsuspecting wagon train.

At approximately 2:00 p.m. on August 30, 1858, the emigrants were enjoying a well-earned siesta after the noon meal, that is, all except the Brown children, who were playing in their parents' wagon. Sallie Fox, the thirteen-year-old stepdaughter of Alpha Brown, was climbing upon one of the wheels of the family wagon, where, from her elevated position, she spied Indians sneaking up through the underbrush on their hands and knees. Terrified, she cried out, "The Indians are coming and they will kill us all!"[12] At almost the same instant the Indians let out a series of bloodcurdling war whoops followed by a hail of arrows. The men in camp, aroused from their slumber by the little girl's cries, quickly grabbed their pistols and rifles and met the charge head-on. Robbed of the element of surprise by the little girl's screams, the Mojave warriors beat a hasty retreat, taking cover in the chaparral in front of the camp just beyond effective gunshot range.

Meanwhile, Young and Stidger arrived at the previous camp and made a gruesome discovery. There stood the Bentner wagon but without the mules or the Bentners. A closer inspection revealed the battered body of the older Bentner girl lying on the ground near the wagon. The body was stripped of all its clothing and the face was horribly mutilated. No trace of the other members of the family was ever found, but during the battle an Indian across the river waved a pole with a number of scalps dangling from it. It was assumed that these trophies came from the Bentner family.

At the mountain camp the night before, members of the Baley company tried in vain to persuade the Bentners not to travel by themselves. William Krug, one of the young men of the company and a fellow German immigrant, remonstrated with Bentner that the Indians might prove hostile, but he would not listen.[13]

Young and Stidger no sooner made their macabre discovery when they heard gun shots from the direction of the river. Realizing that a battle was in progress, they mounted their horses and made a dash for camp, arriving just in time to participate in the beginning of the battle. The young men herding cattle also heard the firing, and they, too, reached camp safely.

The men at the site where the raft was being built, Alpha Brown, Ed Akey, and Lee Griffin, were not so fortunate. Hearing gun shots, Lee Griffin shouted, "What does that mean?" "Great God, it's the Indians!" Brown exclaimed, as he mounted his horse and galloped for camp. He had ridden only a short distance before he was struck by a volley of arrows. One penetrated his back and lodged near his heart, but he was able to keep riding and reached the safety of camp. He rode up to his wife and reportedly said, "Where's my gun, Mother?" He then toppled from his horse and was dead by the time he hit the ground.[14]

Akey and Griffin, who were not mounted, made a run for camp on foot as fast as their legs could carry them. Fortunately they were both armed with Colt revolvers. As they ran, they carried their weapons fully loaded and cocked, with their fingers on the triggers ready for instant action. As Akey rounded a clump of brush near the camp, he found himself face to face with an Indian who had an arrow on his bow string and was about to let it fly. Akey quickly fired a bullet into the Indian's chest, bringing him to the ground and sending his arrow flying feebly up in the air. A moment later he came upon another Mojave and he promptly dispatched him before the Indian could get his arrow away.

As Akey neared camp, he saw Griffin standing in the open space near the wagons in a dazed condition. "What are you standing there for?" Akey asked. Griffin partly extended his right arm, which had two arrows dangling from it, and responded, "That's what for." One arrow had gone almost through his arm just above the wrist, and the other had struck near the same place. Both wounds were bleeding profusely. Akey gave Griffin a vigorous shove in the direction of camp and said, "Run for it." As they both ran across the open space toward the wagons, they received a shower of arrows; one struck Akey just below the left collarbone inflicting a nasty wound.[15]

The death of Alpha Brown and the wounding of Akey and Griffin further reduced the already thin ranks of those fit to do battle. Young Ed Jones was still recovering from his wounds after his narrow escape from the Hualapais; thus, he too, was effectively out of the fight. This left only twenty-five to thirty able-bodied men trying to hold off an estimated three hundred attacking Mojave warriors. Fortunately for this wagon train, the Indians were armed only with bows and arrows.

The battle plan of the Mojaves apparently had been to take the emigrants by surprise, attacking camp before the men could get to their guns. Those not killed by the initial flurry of arrows could then be finished off with knives and war clubs. But the element of surprise was lost thanks to the screams of Sallie Fox, forcing the Indians to change their plans. Their strategy now was to keep the emigrants pinned against the river with no way to escape, gradually wear them down and let them exhaust their ammunition, then make the final charge. The Mojave warriors seemed confident that they would soon have many new scalps to add to their trophy poles and a vast supply of loot to divide. From their concealed positions in the chaparral, and well out of range of the white men's guns, they fired intermittent barrages of arrows at their intended victims. Some arrows they aimed in a high arc so that they came down in the camp and inflicted casualties. Several of the emigrants, including Elizabeth Jones, Rose's mother-in-law, were wounded by this tactic. Now and then an overanxious warrior would advance too close and be picked off by one of the white men.

Ironically, one of the first to be wounded was Sallie Fox. As soon as the battle started, Mrs. Brown herded her children inside the wagon where she placed featherbeds, blankets, and comforters around them for protection. Nevertheless, an arrow pierced this makeshift barricade and struck Sallie in the abdomen causing a serious wound.

One of the most effective fighters was Tom Billings, a young herder with the Baley company. When the fighting began, Tom took a position near a wagon wheel where he could rest his pistol on one of the spokes. Every time an Indian advanced within range, Tom's pistol barked and the warrior would kiss the earth.[16]

While the battle continued, those Mojaves who were not actively engaged in the fighting busied themselves by rounding up all of the emigrants' livestock they could, and swimming them across the river where they were safely corralled near the Mojave Villages. The Mojaves knew that the wagon train would be doomed without animals to pull the wagons and soon the Mojave nation would harvest an even richer bounty.

With neither side able to gain a decisive victory, the battle settled down to a stalemate. The fighting continued in this manner for more than two hours, during which time the emigrants began to run low on ammunition. The women gathered up all their kitchen knives from the wagon beds and put them in a bucket which was placed near the men in case the battle came down to hand-to-hand fighting. But just when things seemed darkest for the emigrants, an event occurred that turned the tide of battle in their favor. One of the Mojave chiefs, who appeared to be directing the battle, stepped out in the open as if to say, "Try and hit me if you can." He was a tall individual, all decked out in a gorgeous array of feathers and gewgaws.[17] He was a very conspicuous figure as he stood out in front of his men. Thinking that he was out of range of the emigrants' guns, he began making defiant gestures and beating himself on the chest as if attempting to rally his warriors for the final victory charge.

To members of the wagon train, Gillum Baley was known as the "Missouri Preacher" because he was from Missouri and a lay minister in the Methodist Episcopal Church, South. He also had the reputation of being an excellent marksman and was probably the only member of this group who had ever had any military experience, having served in the Illinois Mounted Militia during the Black Hawk War in 1832. Knowing this, one of the emigrants pointed out the gaudily dressed chief to Baley, saying, "Why don't you shoot that Indian?" Baley replied that he didn't think his gun would carry true that far. A man wounded by an arrow in the forehead who could not aim his gun because of the blood running down into his right eye overheard the conversation and said to the Missouri Preacher, "Here, take my gun. You can hit him with it." Baley took the proffered weapon but had difficulty holding it steady because it was heavier than his own gun. He then knelt down and rested the rifle on a spoke of a wagon wheel, murmured a quick prayer, took slow, deliberate aim, and gently squeezed the trigger. At the crack of the rifle the haughty chief fell face-down to the ground. His comrades quickly rushed out and dragged away their fallen leader's limp body.[18]

With the death of their chief, the Mojave warriors lost stomach for further battle. They began to disengage and slowly withdrew from the battlefield, taking their dead and wounded with them except for the bodies of those slain at the beginning of the battle near the wagons. Thirty minutes later there wasn't a live Indian to be seen anywhere.

Safe for the time being, the emigrants counted noses. They discovered that, other than the Bentner family of seven who were all exterminated when caught between camps, and Alpha Brown, who had been mortally wounded while riding back to the encampment, there were no other fatalities. However, eleven or twelve were wounded during the battle, some of them seriously. A partial list of the wounded included Sallie Fox, Elizabeth Jones, William Right Baley, Tom Hedgpeth, L. J. Rose, Ed Akey, and Lee Griffin. Of these, the wounds of Sallie Fox, Ed Akey, and Lee Griffin were the most serious. The number of Indian casualties was never determined with certainty, but according to statements they made later to army officers, the Indians admitted losing "heap" warriors in the battle. Seventeen bodies were counted by the emigrants near the wagons.[19]

Some good news for the emigrants was the fact that they were able to save a small number of their livestock. A few animals who happened to be grazing nearby when the fighting started became frightened by the sound of battle, ran into camp, and thus were spared. Some of these were the animals that the men were using to pull the logs from the grove to the river to construct a raft. Rose stated that they numbered seventeen cattle and ten mules and horses. Among these were six oxen, just enough to pull one large wagon, and two mules to pull the light ambulance. There were also two or three riding horses in this group including Old Bob, one of Rose's favorites. Most of the rest were cows, calves, and colts. There were also two or three oxen belonging to members of the Baley company. Except for a small number of riding horses that might still be alive at the mountain camp, these were all that remained of a combined herd of cattle and horses that numbered more than four hundred at the beginning of the journey.

Thomas Hedgpeth was able to save his horse, but he took a serious risk to his life in so doing. At the beginning of the battle Tom had his riding mare tied to a tree about a hundred yards from camp. When he heard the Indians yelling, he made a dash for the animal and was able to untie her and bring her safely back to the wagons, although the Mojaves were chasing and shooting arrows at him all the way. He was criticized by some of his companions for risking his life to save an animal, but he responded by saying, "A man had about as well be killed as be left in this wild savage country without a horse."[20]

Rose had not been so fortunate with his horse. He had a prized stallion, Black Morrill, that he intended to use to start a trotting horse stable when he arrived in California. He always kept this animal near camp and secured by a strong chain so that he could not wander off or be stolen. The Indians attempted to take this horse during the battle, but finding that they could not cut the chain, they satisfied themselves by slitting the horse's throat, leaving his carcass hanging in the halter.[21]

After the Indians departed the battlefield, and the emigrants were certain that the battle was over, they held a council to decide what to do next. It was their unanimous opinion that the only course open to them was to retrace their steps all the way back to Albuquerque, a distance of nearly five hundred miles over a burning desert with little food and an uncertain water supply.[22] Although they were only about one hundred and seventy miles from San Bernardino, the nearest settlement, they felt that their numbers were too small to hold off such a vast horde of Mojave warriors a second time. They knew, too, that they would be especially vulnerable while crossing the Colorado River since they would have to divide their pitifully small force and defend both banks of the river while crossing.[23]

Another factor in their decision was that they were low on ammunition. In addition, their psychological condition was probably not too good either. The sudden, fierce, and unexpected attack from a group of supposedly friendly Indians left them in a state of shock both physically and mentally. The men of the Baley company had an especially good reason for being concerned; their wives, children, and other loved ones were all back at the mountain camp, and for all they knew the Mojaves might have attacked the camp and slaughtered them all.

Given their very limited resources, the emigrants realized that the odds for a safe return to Albuquerque were not good. There was one small ray of hope: They just might meet another westward-bound emigrant party that could render them enough assistance to return safely to Albuquerque where they might be able to refit and attempt the trip again next year. This faint hope was enough to start them on their long retrograde march.

Before they could leave, however, there was one sad and final duty to perform—the burial of Alpha Brown. His arrow-filled body still lay under the shade of a large cottonwood tree where it had been tenderly placed after he toppled from his saddle. The body was carefully wrapped in blankets, and then, after a few short prayers, it was gently committed to the turbid waters of the Colorado River. Logging chains were added as weight so that the body would sink to the bottom of the river where it would not be found and mutilated by the Indians.

This sad duty performed, they now began the unenviable task of selecting the few articles they could take with them. Only the most essential items could be taken; everything else had to be abandoned. Just enough work animals had been saved to pull one wagon and the ambulance. Most of the hauling space of these vehicles was reserved for those too young, too infirm, or too badly wounded to walk. The emigrants had neither the time nor the inclination to cache their property for future recovery. They might have burned their possessions to keep them from falling into the hands of the Mojaves, but this, they feared, would invite a night attack. Besides, perhaps discovering, examining, and dividing all that plunder just might occupy the Indians long enough for the emigrants to slip away undetected.

In the only remaining wagon rode Grandma Jones (Elizabeth Burgett Jones) because of her infirmities and wounds; the Rose children, Nina and Annie, ages four and one respectively; the small children of Mary Brown, Orrin and Julia; and the badly wounded Sallie Fox. Also riding in the wagon was eighteen-year-old Ed Jones who was still suffering from the wounds he received a few days previously from his encounter with the Hualapai Indians. He was still unable to walk. In the ambulance, on an improvised stretcher, rode the seriously wounded Lee Griffin. As many provisions as possible were crammed into the wagon and the ambulance.

Those who had horses, and were physically able to ride them included Amanda Rose, who was mounted on Old Bob, one of the riding horses that had been saved. The newly widowed Mary Brown rode the horse that had carried her husband into camp after he was mortally wounded. Tom Hedgpeth, also wounded, was mounted on the mare he

had risked his life to save. Because he was lame, Grandpa Ezra M. Jones
was assigned the task of driving the ambulance, pulled by two mules
and carrying the wounded Lee Griffin. Everyone else walked.

It was after 6:00 p.m. before the bewildered emigrants got well
enough organized to slip away from the river camp. They traveled only
a mile or two before darkness overtook them. Since the moon hadn't
yet risen, the night was pitch dark; they could not see where they were
going and they kept losing their way. When they came to an elevated
spot, they decided to call a halt and wait for better conditions. They
chose this location because it was free of chaparral and no Indian could
sneak up on them. Fearful of giving away their position, they dared not
show any kind of light, and when they spoke to each other it was in
whispers; even the Brown's little dog Pedro sensed the necessity for
silence and uttered not a sound. The emigrants constantly strained their
ears for any sign of danger; the slightest sound, even the hooting of an
owl or the creaking of the harness of the oxen caused the men to stiffen
the grip on their guns and edge their fingers ever closer to the trigger.

About ten o'clock that night, the evening stillness was shattered
by the tumultuous sound of war whoops, accompanied by the clang-
ing of kettles, pots, and pans, coming from the direction of the river
camp which the emigrants had recently evacuated. The Mojave warriors had come back expecting to catch their quarry asleep and finish
them off with knives and war clubs. Finding that their intended prey
had flown the coop, they contented themselves by sorting through the
large quantity of loot left behind. This called for a victory celebration.
One wag, who still retained his sense of humor in spite of recent
events, suggested that perhaps the reason for all the merriment emanating from the Indians was because they had broken into Rose's med-
icine chest and found his eight-dollar-a-bottle brandy. Their great joy
with all the booty that fell into their hands is very likely the reason
why they did not pursue the fleeing wagon train.

Shortly after midnight the moon rose, casting just enough light
for the emigrants to resume their flight. All night and all the next day,
August 31, the weary survivors, driven by fear of what they might find
at the mountain camp, continued their torturous backward march.
Their anxiety to learn the fate of their comrades and loved ones motivated them to hurry on at the utmost speed. The day was scorching

hot, but there was little water or food for either man or beast. Pushed to its utmost limits, the mule team driven by Grandpa Jones and pulling the light ambulance with the wounded Lee Griffin inside, began falling farther and farther behind until it lagged almost a mile behind the others. The exhausted mules, acting mulish, resented the rough treatment, and they expressed their displeasure by stopping more and more often. Each time they stopped it took a greater effort to get them started again. Finally, neither the whip nor the sharp tongue of Grandpa Jones could get them to take a forward step. Grandpa Jones, alone except for the badly wounded Griffin, and doubtless under great physical and mental stress from events of the previous day, made an unfortunate and unwise decision. He unhitched the mules from the ambulance and turned them loose, thinking that they would discover water on their own and be recovered later after they drank their fill. He then caught up with the others who were nearing the mountain camp, leaving the ambulance and Griffin alone in the hostile desert. The mules were never seen again; both they and the ambulance with all its contents, except for Griffin, were a total loss. All the blame, however, should not attach to Grandpa Jones. Others in the group should have noticed when he began to fall behind and they should have gone back to help him, but they didn't.

When Ed Akey learned the ambulance was abandoned in the desert with Griffin inside, he determined to go back and rescue his friend. Although rather badly wounded himself, Akey, without waiting for his supper, went back to the desert alone to look for the ambulance and Griffin. After a long search in the dark he finally located the rig. The problem now was how to get Griffin back to camp. Griffin could hardly stand, much less walk. Both knew that to be caught in the desert by the Indians in such a vulnerable condition meant certain death. Self-preservation being a powerful force, the two devised a plan where Griffin would take a step forward by leaning heavily on Akey's shoulder, rest, then take another painful step forward. Repeating this process over and over again, the pair returned safely to camp. Thus, by the force of sheer determination, another life was saved.

Thomas Hedgpeth, who was probably the only man in the group who still possessed a mount, rode ahead of the others and was the first to make contact with the mountain camp. He was spotted by his father Joel Hedgpeth Sr., who was watching from a hilltop for signs of anyone coming from the direction of the river. They had been expecting the men to return with the work oxen to pull the wagons down to the river camp so they could join the Rose company. Just that day they had put the finishing touches to the road they were building and were eagerly looking forward to joining their comrades at the river and continuing their journey to California.

Joel Hedgpeth Jr., a youth of seventeen at the time, who was present at the meeting between father and son, describes their tearful reunion.

> The next day Brother Thomas came on ahead to bring us the news of the disaster. I well remember his arrival. Father had walked out to an eminence that enabled him to see down the road some distance. I was near him when we saw Tom coming. My brother was a splendid horseman—no Spanish cavalier of the olden times ever sat on his horse more knightly than he. But that day—Oh, that day! How different! He was riding the animal that he had risked his life to save the day before. He was sick from riding in the sun and weak from loss of blood. His left arm was swinging in a big white handkerchief, that had many blood stains on it. He seemed almost as limber as a wet dish rag. All his starch and usual knightly dignity were gone. Father walked on to meet him and exclaimed, "Well, Tom, I see something awful has happened. What is it? Are the rest killed?" Tom replied rather slowly, "No, only Mr. Brown is killed but a dozen or fifteen others are wounded, myself among them and the Indians have taken nearly all the cattle." The faith of my father's reply, like that of Job's, has been ringing in my soul all these years. Looking Tom in the face, Father said, "Well, thank God the boys are not killed. The Lord will take care of us somehow." Brother Thomas was helped from his horse and taken charge of by his wife and mother, perhaps the best friends that any man ever had—except the Divine Father. That night I heard Mother sobbing quietly and Father said to her, "Don't cry. Don't cry, Jane, the Lord will provide for us in some way."[24]

Soon the other survivors came into camp, and finding that all in the mountain camp were well, a joyous reunion was held. That night a well-cooked but frugal meal was enjoyed by all.

John and Emily Udell, circa 1867.
Courtesy C. Melvin Bliven.

Leonard John (L. J.) Rose. *Reproduced by permission of the Huntington Library, San Marino, California.*

Elizabeth Burgett Jones, wife of Ezra Jones, mother of Ed Jones and Amanda Rose, and mother-in-law of L. J. Rose. *Courtesy State Historical Society of Iowa, Des Moines.*

Amanda Markel Jones Rose. *Reproduced by permission of the Huntington Library, San Marino, California.*

Mary Baldwin Fox Brown, mother of Sallie Fox and wife of Alpha Brown. *Courtesy State Historical Society of Iowa, Des Moines.*

Sophia Frances (Franc) Fox, older sister of Sallie Fox. All the merchants in Fort Yuma wanted to marry her. *Courtesy Genevieve Thompson.*

Sallie Fox at age sixteen. *Courtesy Mrs. C. E. Crownover.*

Sallie Fox in later years. *Courtesy Robert Power, Nut Tree, Vacaville, California.*

Amanda Melvina Daly Holland, daughter of John Lucas Daly and Irene Morrow Daly and wife of Isaac Taylor Holland. *Courtesy Dorothy B. Wilbur.*

Madeleine Isabelle Adeline Daly Bucknam. She was married to Ezra Bucknam in Zuni, New Mexico, by John Udell. *Courtesy Dorothy B. Wilbur.*

Isaac Taylor Holland. *Courtesy Charles Holland.*

Mr. and Mrs. William Krug (Amelia Catherine Baley). *Courtesy Willetta Pokorny.*

Gillum Baley. *Courtesy Willetta Pokorny.*

Permelia Eleanor Myers Baley. *Courtesy Willetta Pokorny.*

Amelia Catherine (left) and America Frances Baley (right) left their names on Inscription Rock, El Morro National Monument, and later eloped with employees of the wagon train. *Courtesy Willetta Pokorny.*

William Right Baley and Nancy Funderburk Baley. *Courtesy Mary Lee Dugovic.*

Sarah Margaret Baley, eldest child of William Right Baley and Nancy Funderburk Baley. She carried her baby sister on her back from Albuquerque until relieved of her burden at the Gila River by the death of the infant. She was sixteen at the time. *Courtesy Willetta Pokorny.*

Ellen Grafton Baley McCardle as an adult. She was the little girl who was lost on the desert and later found. *Courtesy Willetta Pokorny.*

Joel and Jane Hedgpeth. Photo taken at St. Joseph, Missouri, on the way to California. *Courtesy Ray Hedgpeth.*

Thomas Riley Hedgpeth. *Courtesy Holt-Atherton Special Collections, University of the Pacific Library, Stockton, California.*

Reverend Joel Hedgpeth Jr. *Courtesy Ray Hedgpeth.*

William Pleasant Hedgpeth. He was the administrator of his father's estate. *Courtesy Joel W. Hedgpeth.*

CHAPTER 7

The Long Road Back

"This day all who were left alive of Mr. Rose's Party came into camp, bringing melancholy intelligence." This is how Udell began his journal entry for August 31, 1858. He then gives the details of the battle as related to him by the survivors. He quickly came to the conclusion that his own condition was worse than that of any of the others.

> I was in the worst situation of anyone in the company who had a family—my wife being sixty-five-years of age, and so feeble that she was not able to walk, and I had not an ox or hoof left, except an Indian pony which I had kept at my wagon, and he was so worn down he could scarcely travel or stand. The other families had an ox or two each, which they could have put together to haul their little ones who could not walk, and the small quantity of provision they had left, which they finally did, but there was not half enough provisions in the company to sustain us until we could reach white settlements, where we could get any, so that, in all human probability, at that time, we must all perish by the hands of merciless savages or by starvation— even if we could start from here. . . . At this time the scene in our camp was an awful one—the widow weeping and mourning for the loss of a beloved husband, and a loving daughter so mutilated by the savage arrow that her life was despaired of; the wounded still besmeared with their own gore—some lying helpless, some with an arm useless. Here were fathers, and brothers, and sisters, husbands and wives, and even an aged mother wounded by the barbed arrow of the unfeeling savage, and nothing but a premature death seemed to stare us in the face. Indeed, I almost envied the lot of those of our comrades who were left dead behind us—their lifeless bodies to be burned by the savage foe, as is the custom of these Indians. No wonder if

the tears streamed from every eye! I think that a heart like Pharaoh's would have melted in sympathy to have beheld our condition.[1]

Udell's gloom and doom were no exaggeration. Starvation and death now stared them in the face! Those who had remained at the mountain camp now had to make the same agonizing decisions that those at the river camp were forced to make—that is, what to take with them and what to leave behind. For the Baley company the choices were even more limited than they had been for the Rose company, for the Baleys did not have enough oxen to pull even one wagon. Everyone would have to walk, even mothers with infants in their arms.

The few oxen that remained would have to be used as pack animals until they either died or were butchered for food, and then the backs of humans would have to bear the load. As there was no immediate threat from Indians, the Baley company had time to cache the possessions they couldn't take with them. They spent three days preparing caches for their valuables.

Just when things seemed nearly hopeless, the weary survivors received news that gave them new hope. They learned that a large emigrant train from Iowa was encamped at Mountain Spring on the east side of Sitgreaves Pass, only a few miles back. Most likely, scouts from that party were the first to make contact.

Who could these strangers be? In their eagerness to find out, the anxious emigrants left the mountain camp that evening, September 3. They again crossed Sitgreaves Pass at night, and arrived at Mountain Spring early the next day. To the delight of the Rose company, this emigrant train also hailed from Van Buren County, Iowa, and some of its members were old friends of Rose. These gentlemen were John Bradford Cave, James Jordan, Robert Perkins, and Calvin "Cal" Davis.[2] They all had their families with them; Cave was the captain. There were three or four other families in this group. Most were driving a loose herd of horses and cattle with them. To help manage all these animals, they employed about thirty young men, probably grubstakers.

Also in this train, according to Udell, "Was an intimate acquaintance of mine, . . . John Hamilton is the gentleman's name; to him I repaired immediately for assistance for my old lady and myself—at least to carry our provisions for us."

This kind-hearted friend responded favorably to Udell's request, saying to him, "Yes, come, you and your old lady, and go with us; you shall fare with my family as long as I have an ox left, or anything." Unfortunately for Udell, there wasn't much that his friend could do for him other than to haul some of his provisions. Hamilton had lost two-thirds of his stock for lack of water and grass and from Indian depredations. He was forced to abandon five wagons, lacking oxen to pull them. In his one remaining wagon he had to carry his own large family and their provisions, as well as the family and provisions of his son-in-law, John Miller.

"He was ill able to haul his own large family," Udell writes, "yet his sympathy prompted him to take us in—while his companions in travel refused to take any except Mr. Rose and his men, although some of them had plenty of horses, mules, and cattle to take the whole company—but Mr. Rose was a monied man." This was not a fair assessment of the situation, for in reality, all had suffered greatly. Udell continues his discourse by stating, "I walked and my old lady rode my pony, and Mr. Hamilton carried our provisions as long as it lasted, which was not long after its being put into common stock."

The members of the Cave train shared what food they had with the unfortunates, even butchering some of their cattle so that the hungry emigrants could have fresh meat, but there was little nourishment in the carcasses of the half-starved animals. Cave and his party were nearing the end of their journey and were getting low on food, especially flour. They, too, had been harassed by the Cosninos (Hualapais) since leaving the vicinity of Peach Springs. Many of their cattle were killed or stolen.

After hearing all the gruesome details of the Mojave attack on the Rose-Baley wagon train, it didn't take much further convincing to persuade the Cave company to join the retreat, so they too turned back.

On the evening of September 4, the combined Rose-Baley and Cave wagon trains began their long march back to Albuquerque, New Mexico, a distance of nearly five hundred miles. As they continued their retrograde journey, they enacted a tale of hardship and suffering seldom equaled in the annals of westward emigration!

The season was early autumn, one of the hottest and driest periods of the year in the Southwest. Due to the intense heat, much of the traveling had to be done at night, but often the long distances between water holes forced the weary emigrants to travel both day and night. Although the days were hot, the nights were cold because they were in high desert country. Many of the unfortunates possessed only the thin summer clothing they had worn on the day of the battle; some lacked even a well-worn blanket to protect their frail bodies from the chill of night. All except infants, the infirm, and the seriously wounded had to walk. The rocky terrain quickly wore through the soles of their shoes, forcing many to walk barefoot. Trudging along over the sharp rocks and prickly cacti needles, their feet became swollen and infected, adding intensely to their suffering.

The rocky surface was equally hard on the feet of the animals; it wore their hoofs down to the quick, slowing the poor beasts considerably. The wagon train was now averaging only eight to ten miles per day over the same terrain where they had averaged fifteen to twenty miles per day on the outbound journey. To compound their problems, water was becoming more difficult to find; many of the water holes where they had found water previously were now dry. Feed for the stock was almost nonexistent. Many of the remaining animals died from starvation, forcing the abandonment of several of the Cave company wagons. Food supplies were almost gone, yet they were hundreds of miles from the nearest settlement. If these problems were not enough, they were now entering Cosnino (Hualapai) territory. These Indians now began a campaign of harassment even greater than the one waged against the emigrants on their outward journey. Sensing the weakened condition of the wagon train, the Indians felt the pickings would be easy. They would conceal themselves behind rocks and fire their arrows into the stock as the wagon train passed by. Udell wrote that an arrow was shot through the back part of his pony's saddle, but fortunately, no one was riding the animal at the time.

The rocky terrain, combined with the heat and the scarcity of food and water, soon began to take its toll on the unfortunate travelers. After crossing the Cerbat Mountains near present-day Kingman, Arizona, their water supply was nearly exhausted, yet they were still thirty miles from the nearest known source. Realizing they could not travel that distance without water, they sent fifteen young men ahead with the loose stock to the nearest known spring. While the animals were recruiting, water was to be carried back to the main party by a smaller group of young men following the first group.

When the latter group came within a short distance of the spring, they were startled by the sound of gunfire coming from that direction. Up ahead they saw only Indians and cattle at the spring. Seeing none of their comrades, they assumed the worst: a total massacre! They ran back excitedly to the main group and reported that the Indians had killed all the members of the advance party and taken possession of the spring as well as all the cattle. This was frightening news to the beleaguered wagon train, for without water they would all perish.

Udell and others hurried ahead to investigate this catastrophic report. When they arrived at the spring, they found that there indeed had been a battle, but again the emigrants had emerged victorious. The young men from the advance party had found a large number of Indians occupying the spring with the specific intent of denying its use to the wagon train. They expressed this intent with a barrage of arrows when the young men approached. Knowing that they must have water soon, the advance party charged the Indians and drove them from the spring. Two of the young men were seriously wounded, one from an arrow and the other from a musket ball. One of the Indians was seen firing a gun, so in all probability the gunshot wound was caused by hostile fire. This was the first time they had encountered Indians with firearms, which boded ill for the emigrants who, up to now, had been saved by their superior firepower. In addition to the two young men wounded, a fine horse also had been killed.

Savedra identified these Indians as Cosenenoes (Cosninos, or Cosniños), the name that early explorers applied to the Hualapai. This is about the only mention Udell makes of Savedra on the return trip. Savedra might not have been the most popular member of the wagon train at this moment; although no one blamed him for the Mojave attack, some were quite vocal about his shortcomings, especially his inability to find water. Anyway, there was little need for a guide now, since they had been over this route only a few days before.

Although the Hualapais were driven from the spring, their harassment did not cease. As the train traveled through Truxton (Truxtun) Canyon, the Indians fired arrows down at it from the top of the canyon.[3] Fortunately, no one was killed or wounded by these attacks, but several more precious cattle were killed or injured.

The emigrants decided to put a stop to these annoying tactics by sending a group of men to the top of the canyon to try to catch the culprits in the act. On the night of September 10, Gillum and William Right Baley, and six of the younger men, climbed to the top of the canyon where they hid behind rocks and waited for the Indians to appear. Early the next morning they surprised a group of warriors attempting to shoot arrows into the wagon train passing below. They fired at the Indians, killing three and driving the others away.[4] As souvenirs, the victors brought back a bloody scalp, a bow and some arrows. The women were horrified by the sight of these gruesome trophies, but after that the depredations ceased.

The wagon train moved slowly eastward through Truxton Canyon toward White Rock Spring, arriving there on September 12. At White Rock Spring the travelers were nearing the end of their endurance. Provisions were nearly exhausted; their only food was the meat from the cattle that had died on the road from starvation or thirst, or from both, and whose flesh contained little or no nourishment. Even this meager repast had to be consumed without benefit of salt or bread, as these two staples were almost gone.

Some of the emigrants gave up all hope and lay down by the side of the road to await death. The Rose-Baley and Cave wagon trains were rapidly going the way of the Donner party. As frequently happens when the going gets the roughest and the storm clouds are the darkest, it is the iron determination of the women that steadies the morale of the men and holds the group together. So it was with these emigrants. One little girl in particular refused to give up hope. She was seven-year-old Julia Brown, daughter of the slain Alpha Brown and Mary Brown, and a half-sister of Sallie Fox. Julia told her mother, "One thing assures me—the Lord will provide."[5] And provide, He did.

On the evening of September 13, while still camped at White Rock Spring, the emigrants observed strange objects slowly descending into the canyon and moving toward them. In the dim distance they resembled old-fashioned, high-crowned sunbonnets. What could they be? Could they be optical illusions caused by the effects of the thin air on half-starved bodies? Ironically, the first to see them was Sallie Fox, who had given the alarm when she saw the Mojaves sneaking up through the brush to attack the wagon train at the Colorado River. Sallie was still seriously ill from the arrow wound she had received in that battle, and due to a lack of proper medical care and adequate nourishment, her condition had worsened to the point where there was grave doubt about her recovery. When Sallie called attention to the approaching objects her mother thought that Sallie must be entering a period of delirium that often precedes death, and she feared for her daughter's life. But when her mother and others looked to where Sallie indicated, they too saw something on the far horizon moving in their direction. As the distant silhouettes approached nearer camp, the distinct form of covered wagons became discernible to the excited emigrants. Who could these newcomers be?

The new arrivals turned out to be members of a large wagon train hailing from Decatur, Macon County, Illinois, the joint property of E. O. and T. O. Smith. The Smiths were driving a large herd of cattle, horses, and mules that they hoped to sell in California. There were no women or children in the train. The Smiths had employed forty men as teamsters, blacksmiths, herders, etc., to assist in driving and managing this large herd. They also had encountered no problems with Indians until they reached the vicinity of Peach Springs, but at that location the harassment began. One of their men was wounded by an arrow shot at random into camp.

E. O. Smith (Edward Owen) was a forty-one-year-old native of Maryland, and of the two brothers, he was the one clearly in charge. The age of T. O. (Thomas O.) Smith is unknown, but he is believed to have been several years younger than his brother, who was a prominent businessman and an influential citizen of Decatur, Illinois. E.O. had built the first opera house in that city as well as an entire block of buildings in the business section of town. He was active in political affairs in the state of Illinois, having been a delegate to the convention that drew up the Illinois State Constitution of 1848. He was well acquainted with most of the political figures of the state, including Abraham Lincoln. He had successfully driven a large herd of cattle, horses, and mules to California in 1853 by way of the Southern Route. That venture proved to be most profitable; he hoped to repeat his success on this trip. An activist in political affairs in his home state, he had heard about Edward F. Beale's proposed survey for a shorter route to California, and wrote a letter to his congressman in February of 1858 requesting information on this new route. It is unknown just what information his congressman was able to provide him on this subject, but at Albuquerque he learned that two emigrant parties were already traveling the road. This was enough to convince him.

The Smiths proved to be good friends and good Samaritans. They not only shared their remaining food supplies to the last mouthful, but they also killed and butchered their dwindling herd of cattle to feed the starving emigrants. E. O. Smith was especially kind to the Widow Brown and her five children. That first night shortly after arriving at White Rock Spring, E. O. Smith sent some flour and beans to Mrs. Brown's tent. Writing about the overland trip many years later, Sallie Fox recalled, "No such beans were ever tasted before, even by a Boston epicure." Sallie thought that E. O. Smith was the handsomest man she had ever met. She vowed that if she married and had a son she would name him after E. O. Smith. True to her promise she named her only son, Edward O. Allen.[6] Without this fortuitous meeting with the Smiths, it is doubtful that many members of the Rose, Baley, and Cave companies would have survived the journey back to Albuquerque; slow starvation or death from an Indian arrow or war club would surely have been their fate.

Since the Smith train was composed only of able-bodied men, Udell argued that they were now strong enough to continue their journey to California.

> I thought as we were now one hundred and eighteen men strong, we could go on to California, and probably we could recover the most of our property from the Mojave Indians. I used every effort in my power to induce the company to go on to California, but a majority of those who had turned back represented the road as horrible and the Indians so numerous and warlike, that certain death to all would be almost certain to ensue. I argued that if twenty-five men had succeeded in driving the Indians from them, when the Indians had completely surrounded them in the brush, and had every possible advantage of them—if twenty-five men could do that, I thought that with one hundred and eighteen men and any kind of precaution, we could achieve the victory without the loss of one life. I pressed

my appeal so strong that some of the Iowa company became angry and began to curse me, so I didn't push the matter any further, as I was altogether dependent on others, go which way we would.[7]

Udell reckoned without the full knowledge and understanding of the psychology of fear and defeat. These emigrants were so imbued with it that for them there was no turning around and going westward again. Like a routed army, no persuasion, no matter how eloquently or logically presented, could stop their headlong flight or restore their forward march. Some of these same feelings of fear and defeat also rubbed off onto the members of the Smith train. E. O. Smith took a vote of his men as to whether they should return with the others or continue on to California, and whether they were willing to give up their seats in the wagons to the suffering women and children and share their food with them. All but two or three voted to retreat with the emigrants. Again, the rescuers elected to go with the rescued, and all turned back.

At White Rock Spring the emigrants were approximately two hundred and seventy-five miles from San Bernardino, California, but more than four hundred miles from Albuquerque. But a comparison of distances made little impression on the travelers, for all but Udell and a tiny minority had made up their minds to turn back.

The addition of the Smith train brought the total number of emigrants to 203 individuals, far too large a group to travel and camp together given the limited supply of water and grass. Again, they divided into two groups. Rose and his family, along with most of the Cave train, formed one section, while the remainder joined the Smith train. It was probably a good idea to have Udell and Rose in different sections since the two didn't get along well. It is interesting to note that the Widow Brown and her family were not included in the Cave group even though they had been with Rose all the way up until now. Perhaps because of Sallie Fox's wounds they could not travel as fast as Rose and the Cave train, which was in the vanguard. From White Rock Spring back to Albuquerque, the Rose-Baley wagon train could more properly be called the Cave-Smith wagon train since these two men were now the dominant members.

The Cave train, along with most of the Rose company, left the encampment at White Rock Spring on September 14, the day after the arrival of the Smiths. The now greatly enlarged Smith train spent the day organizing and left the following day. Night travel was still necessary due to the heat. Udell found the Smiths to be much more accommodating than were the members of the Cave train.

> The Messrs. Smith possessed quite different dispositions from the principal proprietors of the Iowa train. . .The Messrs. Smith furnished teams immediately for all those who had wagons, and wagons and teams to those who had none, so that all could ride, and they divided out their provisions among all alike, and their men rode horses and mules. I rode my pony. Mr. Hamilton and three other families from the Iowa train, who needed help traveled with the Smith train.[8]

With so many more mouths to feed, the food supplies which the Smiths had generously apportioned from their own dwindling larder began to run out. The Smiths butchered their cattle to feed the starving emigrants. "They killed their best," Udell wrote, "but they were feverish in traveling so far and suffering so much for water and food." They ate this meat garnished only with a few cracker crumbs because their salt and flour were again nearly exhausted. Smith vowed that as long as he lived he would always keep a good supply of crackers on hand.

To relieve the pressure on the diminishing provisions, about twenty to twenty-five of the young men decided to strike out on their own for California. Their plan was to travel about two hundred miles south through the desert and connect with the Southern Route. They were aware that the Butterfield Overland Mail was now carrying both mail and passengers between St. Louis, Missouri, and San Francisco, California over this route.[9] They believed they could get provisions from the relay stations and send word to the proper authorities about the desperate condition of the other emigrants. Several of the Smiths' best cattle were butchered and the meat jerked for their use on the way. Eloquent and emotional speeches were made in parting as both groups were still exposed to imminent danger and there was little expectation that they would ever meet again.

The expanded Smith train struggled on eastward until it reached the vicinity of Mount Floyd (Udell's Apache Peak). Other members of the party now referred to it as Picacho, probably confusing it with

Picacho Butte which lies a few miles to the south.[10] Here they caught up with the Cave train and the Rose company. Although no longer harassed by Indians, they still faced the threat of starvation. The food supplies brought by the Smiths were almost gone, and all were now living off the meat from the Smiths' feverish cattle. The emigrants realized that without help from the outside they could not survive much longer. At Picacho (Mount Floyd), they drafted the following letter to the commander at Fort Defiance, the nearest army post:[11]

> Picacho, Sep. the 22nd, 80 miles
> west of the St. Francisco Mountain
>
> To the Commander of Fort Defiance.
>   There are 8 companies of us here now, who started Beale road for California, consisting in all 23 men, 33 old and young ladies, and 47 children of all ages from the 2-week babe up— The first Company on the road reached the Colorado with 400 head of stock, wagons, provisions, and made presents to the Indians, and done all in their power to give no offence and please them, and know of no cause for offense that they gave— On the third day about 300 Mohave Indians, while some of the men were busy herding and preparing a raft for crossing the river, attacked the camp, and the men that were out, all at the same time, with the apparent intention of massacring all of them, but our wagons being in a good situation for defense, and all our men getting in that were out, they found it perhaps warmer work than they anticipated, and they contented themselves with taking all our stock except 19 head of cattle, and 11 horses, which were frightened by the attack, and ran up to the wagons, and had it not been for this, to us their lucky circumstances, we could never have got away, and that we did so is yet a mystery, and can only be explained by believing that they did not know of our departure, as we left in the night and only took 2 of our wagons to haul a little bedding and provisions for each—On the return of the first company to Colorado Springs [Mountain Spring] (24 miles from the Colorado) they met the second company, the [Cave company] and with what joy cannot be described, for starvation was already staring them in the face. They very generously delayed their train for several days, to the great injury of their stock, as they had no grass for them, and but scant water to help us over the mountains. They have also shared with everyone who needed with a generosity that is more rare and remarkable as they have taken it out of the mouths of

their own children, and divided it with others. Their waiting on
the first company and the scarcity of grass and water to here, has
been ruinous on them so much so, that out of nearly 500 head
there are now only 145 left, and they are all footsore and perfectly worn out, and have been 22 days coming thus far, and
would not be here now, if we had not met with the third
Company, [the Smith train] who have done all in their power,
and are doing all they can for the good of the whole. But our
stock is all worn down, poor, and what is worse their feet are
worn to the quick, and with cruel beating cannot make more
than 8 or 10 miles a day. Here the water will not last more than
a day longer, as it is rain water. It is 35 miles to Alexander
Cannon [*sic*], and 10 days ago there was no water there; from
there it is 30 miles to water, and 65 miles without water we can
never make with a wagon. We may possibly get some of our
stock, which will enable us to live until assistance can reach us,
and this will be all we have to live on, beef alone for some time
as our flour and all kinds of provisions are about gone. What
makes it still worse, the beef is very poor and sick, so that half of
us are more or less unwell, and very unfit to perform the labor
which is necessary, and walk along. Most of us are destitute for
shoes and warm clothing, many not even having a blanket and
ladies and little children who have always before been accustomed to plenty to eat, and comfortable homes, are trudging
along, crying, some from hunger, some tired with blistered and
bleeding feet—We hope you may help us—We pray you may
help us, for you not to help us is a thought blended with
death—We ask it not, as men, we could help ourselves, but for
our wives and little ones—We ask it as brothers of that order
whose emblem is the Square and the Compass, and we ask it still
more as men, belonging to one universal Brotherhood. May it
be possible for you to help us—In the fight with the Indians at
the river we had about 33 men in the engagement. The Cosnino
Indians have also been very troublesome, to the 2 last parties
going, and to all of us returning they have repeatedly shot at us
from hiding places and run off much stock, and should they
continue to follow us, then it would become a very serious matter for men are leaving us every day, leaving only the heads of
families, the weak, and wounded behind

We are respectfully Yours,

Signed: E. O. and T. O. Smith

Joseph Ferman   James H. Jordan

John Hamilton   J. B. Cave

J. McCoy	R. Rankins
J. Hobban	G. Baley
J. Miller	J. Daly
Mrs. Mary Brown	Joel Hedgpeth
Ezra Jones	Thomas Hedgpeth
Peter Allisons	Elizabeth Richard
L. J. Rose	Dr. Ralsie

It is unknown which member or members of the wagon train actually drafted the letter, but whoever it was, they possessed a better than average education for that period. The reference to the "Square" and the "Compass" pertains to the Masonic Lodge. The Masonic Lodge was, and still is, a prestigious fraternal organization. Many army officers belonged to it. From this emigrant train, Alpha Brown is known to have been a member, and there were doubtless others in the group who were members. It is interesting to note that John Udell was not one of the signers of the letter. The reason for the omission of his name is not known. Six of the young men volunteered to attempt delivery of the letter to Fort Defiance, nearly three hundred miles away. Unfortunately, the names of these six brave men are not recorded.

Udell, despite his sixty-three years of age, decided that he was the one who could rescue the wagon train from its imminent peril. His plan was to ride full speed ahead to the nearest Indian pueblo, Zuni, two hundred and fifty miles away, and send food back for the relief of the others. He remembered that they had been able to obtain corn from the Zuni Indians on the outward journey, and perhaps they could do so again. He also believed that he could get the Zunis to help deliver the food. If unsuccessful at Zuni, he would ride on another hundred or so miles to Albuquerque. The Smiths lent him one of their best horses to ride, as the only animal that Udell had been able to save from the Mojaves was his Indian pony which his wife now rode. By not being encumbered with a wagon or loose stock, he believed that he could make rapid progress and get help before it was too late.

He persuaded four young men to accompany him on his mission of mercy. They left camp at Mount Floyd on September 24, and traveled forty miles to Alexander Canyon where they camped for the night. They had found water here on the outbound journey. The next morning the four young men volunteered to go down into the canyon to search for water while Udell waited by the road for them to return. When they did not returned by nightfall, Udell, fearing for their safety, climbed down into the canyon to search for them. While there, he met Bradford Cave of the Iowa train, which was again traveling in the lead. Cave informed Udell that he had encountered Udell's companions earlier in the afternoon. The guide (presumably Savedra) told the young men he could pilot them across the hills by a route which would save them ten miles. They took the guide up on his offer and he led them out of the canyon and back to the road, but at a point some twenty miles ahead of where they had left Udell. Perhaps they thought Udell could either overtake them or would wait there for the wagon train to catch up with him. "Either would be a dangerous situation for me to be in, in a savage country," Udell wrote in his journal. He decided to camp where he was for the remainder of the night and get a fresh start in the morning without the company of his thoughtless companions.

The next day, September 26, Udell traveled thirty miles to Hedgpeth (Bear) Spring where he found Rose and his Iowa companions camped. Rose informed Udell that another small wagon train had come as far as Leroux Springs, but had turned back when they heard about the misfortune that had befallen the Rose-Baley wagon train. This new train carried some four or five hundred pounds of flour that the owners wished to sell. Udell started to ride on ahead to overtake this train, hoping to purchase a few pounds. At this point, Rose told Udell that he had already sent men ahead to purchase every pound that the train could spare. Udell states that Rose flatly refused to sell him a single pound:

> I begged of him to let me have some [flour], if it was not more than two or three pounds, for my old lady, as she was becoming sick from living on feverish beef alone. He positively refused to spare one pound, although I offered him three times as much as he had to pay for it. At the same time, the Iowa company, with which he traveled, had had flour all the way—while the Messrs. Smith's train and those of us who traveled with them had been living without any for a number of days.[12]

Rose suggested to Udell that if he would overtake this train, perhaps he could play on the sympathies of the ladies and persuade them to scrimp and let him have a pound or two.

Udell hurried on and overtook this train, which he found camped by a small stream. When Udell related his plight to the train's proprietor, Washington Peck, Peck told him that he had sold Rose's agents all the flour that he could spare, and that he would probably be short himself before his train got back to where they could purchase more. Moreover, he had sold the flour for exactly the same price that he paid for it, and did so with the understanding that it would be equally divided among all the sufferers. He was disappointed to learn that this was not done. After hearing Udell's tale of woe, the ladies of this emigrant train took pity on him and collected between fifteen and twenty pounds of flour which they gave to him without charge. With this stroke of good luck, Udell abandoned his plan of going on to Zuni and hurried back to his wife, "To share with her," he wrote, "the precious boon bestowed upon us by those generous-hearted people."

Apparently, after being so critical of Rose for his failure to share the flour he purchased from the Peck party with other members of the wagon train, Udell likewise failed to share his good fortune with the other members of his company. At least if he did so, he neglected to mention it in his journal, an omission not typical of Udell. However, he might be partially excused because the small amount of flour that he obtained, had it been equally divided among all members of the train, probably would not have amounted to much more than a slice or two of bread apiece. Besides, he had a sick wife to feed.

While Udell was traveling back and forth in his quest for flour, the Smith train reached Hedgpeth (Bear) Springs. This is where he found them camped when he returned with the flour. It was at this location that Thomas Hedgpeth killed a bear on the outbound journey. But now there were no signs of bear or any other game. Some nice fat bear meat would certainly have been a godsend. Any game that might have been in the vicinity during the summer months had by now disappeared, either off to a winter range or scared by the noise of such a large group of humans invading their habitat.

On September 30, Udell had more bad news to report:

> This day another alarm; three of those men who left us to go to California, a few days since, returned, and said they supposed the others had all perished for want of water. They traveled together, finding no water, until some of the party became

so famished they could travel no further. They then started in different directions to find water. Three of them succeeded, and returned to inform their companions. On their return they found guns, ammunition and provisions strewed along, but found no men. They then steered into camp as fast as they could, and found us fifty or sixty miles ahead of where they left us. We all supposed the other twenty had perished.[13]

On the evening of October 2, the Smith train arrived at Leroux Springs at the base of the San Francisco Mountains. This had been a very pleasant camp on the trip out, but now it was a camp of misery. The weather suddenly turned cold and rainy, causing the emigrants much discomfort due to a lack of food and proper clothing. Udell wrote of this camp, "My feeble old lady and myself suffered in being on the cold wet ground with wet clothes and nothing but clouds and one thin quilt to cover us." Leroux Springs, at an elevation of more than six thousand feet, gets heavy snowfall during the winter months.

The following day, the remainder of the young men who had attempted to take the Southern Route to California came into camp in an emaciated condition. Since they were presumed dead by their comrades, there was great rejoicing in camp upon their return. They related a story of incredible hardship and suffering. They had taken only a small quantity of water with them since they were confident of finding more along the way and didn't want to be burdened by carrying a large supply. Besides, they were in a hurry to get to California. When they failed to find water as expected, they had to abort their attempt to reach the Southern Route. They turned back to rejoin the emigrant train which had traveled some distance eastward in the meantime. The salty dried beef that was their only food greatly exacerbated their thirst, and soon their meager supply of water was exhausted. Some became so dehydrated they could travel no farther.

Three of the stronger young men set out to find water for the others. During their absence, one of the men who remained behind thought he recognized a canyon where he found water on the outbound journey. Leaving their belongings scattered along the way, the others eagerly followed their comrade to the supposed water hole. When they arrived at the spring, they discovered to their great disappointment that it was now dry. Driven by the utmost thirst, they traveled all night searching for water but failed to find any. They were about ready to lie down and await death when suddenly they came upon another water hole. Its water was so foul they could smell it from a distance. Living in the water was a kind of white worm about an inch long, but this was no deterrent to these thirst-driven young men. They simply pulled out their dirty handkerchiefs and strained the water through the filthy rags, declaring it the best water they had ever tasted! They spent the better part of the day at the water hole, resting and drinking their fill. They were still there when their three companions returned with water to where they had left them, only to find them missing. After refreshing themselves they caught up with the wagon train a couple of days later. Again, there was great rejoicing in camp upon their safe return.

The emigrants had now been more than a month on the road back to Albuquerque, but they had covered only about half the distance. They would have to do better! Soon winter would be upon them; already the first chills of the season were being felt. There was little actual danger of their being snowed in all winter as can happen in the Sierra Nevada, but winter in the high deserts of Arizona and New Mexico can be a miserable experience, especially for those who lack warm clothing and adequate food.

It soon became apparent that their only hope for survival lay in getting aid from the outside as soon as possible. Nothing had been heard from the young men who set out for Fort Defiance to seek help from the army. There was fear that they might no longer be alive. The young men who had attempted to reach the Southern Route were now back in camp in a starved and worn-down condition, a further drain on the rapidly diminishing food supplies. Again, another group of young men rose to the occasion and volunteered to go ahead to Albuquerque to seek help. They left Leroux Springs on the morning of October 4. Several more of the Smiths' cattle were butchered for their provisions.

With plenty of grass and water at Leroux Springs, the Smiths decided to remain there awhile to recruit their livestock so that they could better endure the trip across the desert where feed and water would be at a premium. Since there was not enough food to sustain such a large number of people at this camp, and relief was still uncertain, the Udells and several other families decided to strike out for Zuni, a distance of more than two hundred miles. There, they hoped to at least get some bread. They left Leroux Springs for Zuni on October 7, according to Udell:

> To-day my friend J. Hamilton, his son-in-law, John Miller, and Messrs. Hedgepeth [Hedgpeth] Mr. Daily [Daly] Mr. Holland and myself all started with our families to travel to Zuni, where we could get bread. As the Messrs. Smith intended to remain here [Leroux Springs] two or three weeks, to recruit their cattle, they furnished us teams to go on with and killed their cattle for our provision on the road. We traveled daily until the 20th of October, when we all arrived safe at Zuni, in a starving condition.[14]

Not mentioned by Udell are the two Baley families and Mrs. Brown and her family. They apparently remained at Leroux Springs with the Smiths. The reason is unknown, but it might have been because they had family members who were too ill to travel. The Zuni Indians again treated the emigrants with great kindness, furnishing them with bread, beans, and pumpkins. "All of which we ate so greedily for several days that we made ourselves quite unwell," Udell related.

Residing at Zuni at that time was an American merchant by the name of Ezra Bucknam. Through Bucknam's efforts the Daly and Holland families were able to obtain a large room in the pueblo. They then invited John and Emily Udell to move in with them. It must have been quite crowded with all of them living in one room, but at least it was better than sleeping on the cold, wet ground. Bucknam's kindness to the Daly and Holland families might have been partially motivated by his fondness for the Dalys' twenty-two-year-old daughter, Adeline (Madeleine Isabelle Adeline). On November 1, Udell recorded: "Today I joined Mr. Ezra Bucknam and Miss Adaline Daily [*sic*] in the sacred bonds of matrimony." Bucknam cast covetous eyes toward Adeline on the outward journey, but there was not enough time for him to strike up a relationship with her. The marriage reduced the size of the wagon train by one person.

On October 30, a large army wagon loaded with provisions for the hungry emigrants arrived at Zuni. The letter that the emigrants wrote back at Mount Floyd pleading for help had finally borne fruit. The six young men who attempted to deliver the letter to Fort Defiance had been unable to do so because of the Navajo war that broke out in the vicinity of Fort Defiance.[15] Eventually, after great difficulty, they succeeded in getting through to Albuquerque, where they delivered the letter to a Major Backus, then in command at that post. Backus drafted an order to a Lieutenant L. W. O'Bannon authorizing the following commissary stores to be immediately dispatched to the emigrants:[16]

> Lt. O'Bannon, 3rd Inf.
> Headquarters, Albuquerque, N.M.
> A.A.C.S. October 12, 1858
>
> Sir:
> It appears by good evidence that a party of Californians have been attacked by Mohave, and other Indians, near the Colorado River—lost three men, four women, and two children, and the party is now returning in a starving condition. It is on Beals [Beale's] trail beyond Sunia [Zuni]—They have sent in for relief, and I propose to send a six mule wagon tomorrow to meet them at or near Sunia—I wish you to send the following subsistence stores, by said wagon, and file this paper as your voucher.
> Viz. 600 — six hundred pounds of flour.
> 400 — four hundred pounds bacon
> 100 — one hundred pounds of coffee
> 200 — two hundred pounds of sugar
> 8 — eight quarts of salt
> 4 — four gallons of vinegar
> Major Tucker will have a team in readiness tomorrow morning, by which the stores may be sent without delay to Mr. L. J. Rose, one of the men of the suffering party—A small escort will go out with the party to Zunia, including six of the Californians.
>
> I am, Most Respectfully
> Your Obidt. Servt.
> E. Backus
> Major, 3 Infry. Comdg.

The order for four gallons of vinegar was crossed out in the original letter; apparently vinegar was in short supply at the post and couldn't be spared. The six Californians referred to in the letter as forming part of the escort might have been the six young men who delivered the letter to the army. The U.S. Army is not in the habit of giving food to civilians, and when it does, usually in cases of an emergency, it must justify the act with proper authorities. Colonel B. L. E.

Bonneville, then in charge of the Department of New Mexico, sent this letter to army headquarters in New York City.[17]

> Headquarters, Dept. of New Mexico
> Santa Fe, N. M.
> Nov. 6th, 1858
> Lieut. Colonel L. Thomas
> Asst. Adjt. General
> Headquarters of the Army
> New York, City
>
> Colonel:
> In continuation of my communication of the 23rd of October, I have the honor to enclose for the consideration of the General in Chief, the following copies of reports received from Colonel Miles and his subordinates in the Navajo Expedition, showing operations in that country up to date, viz.:
> (A) Report of Lieut. Col. Miles 3rd Infry
> (B) Report of Bvt. Major Brooks 3rd Infry
> (C) Report of Captain McLane R.M.R.
> (D) Supplementary report of Bvt. Captain Hatch R.M.R.
> (E) Report of Lieutenant Howland R.M.R.
> (F) Copy of my instructions to Col. Miles on the above report.
> Major Backus's column is in the field since the 24 ultimo, but has not been heard from.
> A large party of emigrants who had taken Beale's route to California was totally defeated with the loss of all their stock, provisions, etc., by the Mohave Indians at the crossing of the Colorado River, and must have starved had not fortunately on their return, met another party traveling about eight miles behind them. In a short time all were reduced to the most destitute and deplorable condition, having nothing to eat but the few work oxen left, and hundreds of miles away from the settlements or assistance. They succeeded in informing Major Backus, then in command of Albuquerque, of their situation, and he sent out a supply of commissary stores, sufficient to bring them into the settlements. In consideration of their perfect helplessness, being amongst a people not able to appreciate their condition, and speaking a different language, I found it indispensably necessary to give them additional assistance, there being a large number of women and children left perfectly destitute.
> I am, Colonel, very respectfully

Your obedient servant.
B. L. E. Bonneville
Colonel, 3rd Infantry, Commanding.

The arrival of the army commissary wagon in Zuni (there may have been more than one wagon) was cause for great rejoicing for it now appeared that the worst of the ordeal was over. On November 1, there was more good news. The Smith train with the remainder of the emigrants arrived in Zuni. The Smiths decided not to stay two to three weeks at Leroux Springs recruiting their cattle as they had first planned. The physical condition of some of the emigrants traveling with the Smith train might have prompted them to hurry on toward the settlements.

The government provisions were divided equally so that each family had enough food to get to civilization, one hundred and fifty miles away. The army also sent a small escort of soldiers along to protect the emigrants against any Navajos who were still at war. The army hauled all of those who had lost their teams, so that none had to walk.

Meanwhile, Rose and his fellow Iowans who were traveling with mule teams, forged farther and farther ahead of the others and reached Albuquerque on October 28.

The trip back from Zuni to Albuquerque was slow, but it was made in relative comfort when compared to the ordeal that they had gone through. There was food enough for everyone and enough wagons to haul the whole group. They again camped at Inscription Rock, but this time none of the emigrants carved his or her name on the rock; they were all too intent on getting back to Albuquerque. On November 10, the Smith train arrived at the Indian pueblo of Laguna. That evening they listened to a sermon preached by the Elder Gorman, the same Elder Gorman who preached to them on the way out. Udell described the sermon as, "A discourse very applicable to our misfortunes and present circumstances." Gorman not only provided the emigrants with spiritual comforts but also gave them money, flour, clothing, and vegetables to the amount of twenty-five or thirty dollars, according to Udell. This timely aid, combined with that provided by the army, enabled them to reach Albuquerque on November 13, 1858, nearly two and one-half months after being attacked by the Mojave Indians at the Colorado River.

CHAPTER 8

A Cold Miserable Winter

T own citizens and the army did everything in their power to ease the emigrants' suffering after their arrival back in Albuquerque. Some of this outpouring of good will was no doubt motivated by guilty feelings on the part of the army and the local citizenry for having encouraged these emigrants to travel Beale's uncompleted wagon road; nevertheless, this aid was a godsend to the weary, starving survivors.

The army issued a soldier's ration daily to each person, including children, for a period of thirty days. This was no trifling gesture when one remembers the great distance from which most supplies had to come. These rations consisted mostly of flour, salt pork, bacon, jerky, sugar, and coffee—nothing gourmet, but these everyday foods were a big treat for people who had been eating nothing but the flesh of starving cattle. The bachelor officers and others without families on the post voluntarily gave up their quarters to those sufferers who lacked shelter. The army employed many of the men as teamsters and herders, while the townspeople contributed clothing, blankets, items of furniture, money, and whatever else they could spare to lessen the privations of these unfortunates.

Of the returning travelers, the Udells were the most fortunate, for on the outward journey Udell struck up an acquaintance with Judge Samuel Winslow, a man of considerable wealth and influence in Albuquerque. This friendship now paid off handsomely. Word of the disaster at the Colorado River had preceded the emigrants back to Albuquerque. Judge Winslow and his wife, having heard about the plight of the wagon train, prepared a comfortable room in their own spacious home for the Udells. They fed them from their own table and provided them with garments from Winslow's clothing store. Udell was properly grateful for this assistance, for he recorded in his journal, "Such benevolence and hospitality will, I trust, be rewarded by that great and good Being who rewards all according to their works."

The Udells remained as house guests of the Winslows until November 23. On that date Udell wrote, "I have engaged to herd and feed the government beef cattle, for fifteen dollars per month and a soldier's rations of provision." Winslow, a sutler for the army, might have used his influence in securing a job for Udell. With a promise of employment, Udell was able to rent a comfortable room in town for himself and Emily. "We thought that with this we could support ourselves through the winter, and not trespass on Mr. Winslow's hospitality any longer," Udell recorded. The good citizens of Albuquerque donated a few housekeeping articles to make the Udells a little more comfortable. Some of the army officers also helped by donating money. Udell specifically mentions money donations from Captain John Trevett, Major G. H. Fry and his lady, and Colonel D. S. Miles and his lady; enlisted personnel also helped with donations of money. "Sergeant Morrison and Private Haywood made me a present of five dollars each, in cash," wrote Udell. Considering that a private's pay at that time was only eleven dollars per month, this was a significant amount. Soon after the Udells moved into their room, Emily became quite ill. Udell remained by her bedside and was unable to start his job as a herder for the army. Udell records that Mrs. Winslow was very attentive to Emily, as were the daughters of Gillum Baley. His journal entry for November 24, stated, "My wife considered dangerous," and for November 25, he again reported, "My companion is no better." For the next two days he continued to report no improvement, "My dear wife is no better; may the Lord bless the means for her recovery. "But for November 28, he had good news to report: "My companion is much better, thanks be to God for mercy and favor." And in the next two days, more good news: "My wife's health improving slowly."

For December 1, Udell reported: "I commenced herding government stock, employed by Commissary Hannon, at fifteen dollars per month, and a soldier's rations of provisions." He is silent about his friends, the John Lucas Daly and Isaac Taylor Holland families, but they might have been among the families who were quartered by the army that winter. Edward Warren Holland, in his autobiography, states that his father, Isaac Taylor Holland, obtained employment as a blacksmith at one of the army posts.[1] He doesn't say what his grandfather, John Lucas Daly, did that winter in Albuquerque, but since Daly was known to be an experienced teamster, it is probable that he also was employed as a teamster by the army.

Rose was another of the more fortunate emigrants. Although he had suffered the heaviest financial loss, he still had a little money left. He rented a small adobe for his extended family (his own family and his in-laws, the Joneses) in Albuquerque, then began looking around for some type of business that he might acquire with a minimum down payment, but he was unable to find anything. To conserve what was left of his dwindling bankroll, he started searching for employment commensurate with his abilities. None of those teamster or herder jobs for him! According to his son, L. J. Rose Jr., the only job his father could find was as a waiter at one of the local restaurants. It was menial labor and far below his expectations, but it did offer him an opportunity to learn something about the restaurant business without investing any money.

It didn't take long for Rose to tire of waiting tables, and as soon as he had saved a little money he left Albuquerque and moved to Santa Fe. He had formed a very favorable impression of Santa Fe on the outbound trip. He believed that it had much more to offer in the way of business opportunities than did Albuquerque. Since he could find no suitable housing, he moved his family into a tent on the outskirts of town and began making inquiries with real estate agents about local business ventures. He soon learned that one of the principal hotels in town, The Exchange Hotel (formerly the U. S. Hotel) was on the market. The down payment, however, was considerably more than his meager bankroll. Not one to let a good business opportunity slip through his fingers, Rose wrote a letter to his brother-in-law, Harvey K. S. O'Melveny, asking him for a loan to cover the balance of the down payment. O'Melveny was a prosperous young attorney in Cairo, Illinois.[2] He promptly forwarded the necessary funds enabling Rose to purchase the Exchange hotel. Rose called his hotel simply La Fonda (*la fonda* means an inn, tavern, or boarding house in Spanish). A luxurious La Fonda Hotel occupies the same site today.

Santa Fe at that time had the reputation of being a wide-open town with gambling and prostitution running rampant. La Fonda was a rundown, one-story, flat-roofed adobe, but it was favorably located near the plaza in the center of town. It was not the hotel part of La Fonda that appealed to Rose, according to his son, L. J. Rose Jr., but rather the bar and gambling business. The son describes his father as a first-rate poker and seven-up player. Although managing the enterprise required most of his time and effort, Rose would occasionally engage in high-stake poker games, usually with very profitable results. Whether it was entrepreneurial skill, or just good luck, Rose's venture in the hotel business was a big success. When he sold La Fonda shortly before the outbreak of the Civil War, he realized a net profit of $14,000 after paying off all debts. In a period of a little more than one year, Rose had recouped almost half of the loss he had suffered at the hands of the Mojave Indians at the Colorado River. After closing his business dealings in Santa Fe, Rose moved to southern California where Lady Luck continued to smile on him.

Fate was not as kind to the other emigrants as she had been to Udell and Rose. The condition of one group is perhaps best expressed by the petition that Gillum and William Right Baley filed with Congress for reimbursement of their losses to the Mojave Indians. The concluding paragraph of their petition reads as follows:

> Your petitioners further state they are now in Albuquerque, New Mexico, with their families in a destitute situation, unable to procure work or means to proceed on the Southern Route to California or go back to Missouri, and they are now living in the houses and on the bounty of the officers of the Army at this place.[3]

The petition also states that Gillum had a wife and nine children, and that William Right had a wife and eight children, making a total of twenty-one Baleys, the largest family group in the wagon train. It is difficult to imagine how so many people could be crowded into the small quarters allowed single officers in a frontier post. It is probable that some of the emigrants, particularly the older children, were quartered in tents lent to them by the army

Like many of the other emigrants, the Baleys had sold their farms back in Nodaway County before leaving for California and had no place to return to in Missouri. The proceeds from the sale of their farms had been invested in livestock for a later resale in California, and for the expenses of the trip across the plains. Now that this was lost, they were forced to live on the bounty of others. Unlike Rose, they had no wealthy relatives from whom they could borrow money or receive extensive aid. The brothers stated in their petition that they were unable to obtain employment, but since the petition was dated November 19, they hadn't yet had much time to look for work. They, too, were eventually employed by the army.

The Hedgpeths, like the Baleys and others, arrived back in Albuquerque in a destitute condition. The plight of the elder Hedgpeths was particularly severe due to their advanced ages. Jane Hedgpeth's health had begun to deteriorate during the return trip. The long overland journeys seemed to be particularly hard on elderly women. The Hedgpeths also were housed by the army and given employment as herders and teamsters.

In the spring of 1859, Thomas Hedgpeth and his family returned to Missouri. They had seen enough of the Elephant! Thomas became a minister in the Methodist Episcopal Church, South, and spent the remainder of his life doing the Lord's work in his native state of Missouri.

The individual who probably suffered most from the long ordeal was Mary Brown, the widow of Rose's foreman, Alpha Brown. She not only lost her husband in the battle with the Mojaves, but her thirteen-year-old daughter, Sallie Fox, had been seriously wounded during the attack. The members of the local Masonic Lodge did everything in their power to aid the unfortunate widow and her children. Alpha Brown had been a member of the Freemasons back in Iowa, and when the wagon train stopped in Albuquerque on the outward journey, he made it a point to visit the Albuquerque chapter and get acquainted with his Masonic brethren there. They did everything possible to comfort and aid the widow and children of their departed brother.

If fate hadn't already been cruel enough to Mary, she now dealt the hapless widow yet another blow. Her five-year-old son, Orrin, became seriously ill and died. Every effort was made to save the little fellow, but the effects of malnutrition and disease were too much for the medical technology of the time. His tiny coffin was hauled by wagon to the small burial ground set apart for the Americans living in Albuquerque. After it had been lowered into the ground and covered with dirt, well watered by tears, the mourners gathered stones and placed them on the grave to prevent wolves from digging up the body. As the grieving mother turned to take one last look at her son's final resting place, an agonizing cry burst from her lips: "Oh my boy, my boy! How can I leave him there?"[4] The blow was somewhat softened by a promise from the local Freemasons to look after the grave.

All the emigrants were deeply saddened by the little boy's death, but outside of his immediate family, none took the death harder than did E. O. Smith, who was particularly fond of Orrin. The little fellow would summon Smith to such meals as they had by calling out, "Smiffy, come to beans [dinner]." Smith would respond with a smile on his face and come leading the small messenger by a forefinger. Orrin's half-sister, since become Sallie Fox Allen, clearly recalled this incident when she attended the funeral of E. O. Smith in San Jose, California, many years later. As she paused by his casket and looked down upon his kindly face for the last time, the words, "Smiffy, come to beans," seemed to ring in her ears. She wondered if, perhaps, somewhere out there in the great beyond, the two of them might be walking hand in hand to the promise of a far richer repast than they had ever envisioned while together on Earth.[5]

The date of the little boy's death is not recorded, but it might have occurred soon after the return to Albuquerque; he possibly become ill while on the way back. While we cannot be sure of the disease that claimed the little victim, we can be sure that whatever it was, hunger and exposure played its deadly part. Poor Mary Brown, to preserve her sanity, her family reported, would unravel one stocking at a time and then reknit it, repeating the process over and over again until her fingers became numb and swollen from the effort!

Shortly after their return to Albuquerque, the emigrants held a meeting at Gillum Baley's residence, at which time they elected officers, adopted a preamble, and drew up certain resolutions, which they forwarded to government officials in Washington, D.C. These were printed in the *Santa Fe Gazette* on December 4, 1858, and copied by other newspapers:

At a meeting held at Gilham Bailey's [Gillum Baley's] residence in Albuquerque New Mexico, on the 20th day of November 1858, by the returned emigrants who were going to California on Lt. Beale's route and were driven back to this place by the Mohave Indians from the Colorado River, E. M. Jones was appointed chairman and John McCord Secretary, when the following preamble and resolutions were unanimously adopted:[6]

Whereas, When we arrived in Albuquerque on our road to California last spring, the officers of the army and American citizens of this place received us in the most friendly manner and furnished us all the information in their power as well as paying a part of the expenses of our guide for crossing the plains; and whereas, when we were driven back from the Colorado river to this place by the Indians, ourselves and families nearly famished on the road for want of provisions; and whereas, an express was sent by us to Fort Defiance informing the officers in command at that point of our deplorable situation, which express could not reach them on account of the war with the Navajo Indians, but went directly to this place; and whereas, the moment our distress was made known by our express to the officers in command at this place they immediately relieved our wants by sending us three wagons loaded with provisions, and also an escort of soldiers to protect us from the depredations of the Indians, and also to haul in the more unfortunate who had lost all their teams; and whereas, after our arrival at this place the officers of the army gave us a part of their own quarters to shield us from the chilling blasts, and also provisioned us for thirty days after our arrival and treated us on all occasions in the most kind and gentlemanly manner. Therefore be it

Resolved, That we are not master of language sufficiently strong to convey to the officers and citizens of this place and Santa Fe our heartfelt thanks for the kindness they have shown us—a kindness which time never can obliterate from our memory.

Resolved, That the proceedings of this meeting be signed by all the emigrants present, and that a copy be sent to the Missouri Republican, St. Louis, Mo., also another to the Santa Fe Gazette N.M. with a request that they publish the same.

E. M. JONES, Chairman	John M. Dailey [John Lucas Daley]
John McCord, Secretary	Columbus Holbrooks
Robert Perkins	Joseph Storm
Leonard J. Rose	Henry C. Davis
Lewis J. Hedgpeth	Wm. H. Reed

Joel Hedgpeth   John A. Walker
Wm. Garton   Robert Dinwiddie
Wm. Z. Baley [William Right Baley] John Billings
John Hambleton [John Hamilton]   Richard T. Barnes
John Udell   John Miller
Thomas R. Hedgpeth   M. J. Bixley [7]

On the evening of December 9, 1858, a second meeting was held by the emigrants at the Atlantic and Pacific Railroad Hotel in Albuquerque. They were joined at this meeting by a delegation of local citizens who had much to gain financially by keeping the emigrant routes open and unobstructed by Indian attacks. At this session an emphatic demand was made to the government for the establishment of two new military posts to better protect this new overland route to the West Coast. One of these posts was proposed for the Canadian River crossing on the eastern portion of the road to protect emigrants from Comanche and Kiowa Indians. Although the Rose-Baley wagon train was not molested by either of these tribes, other emigrants were not so fortunate.

The second post demanded by the delegates was for a strong fort to be established at Beale's crossing of the Colorado River where the Rose-Baley wagon train had so recently suffered its devastating attack from the Mojave Indians. Copies of the resolutions adopted at this meeting were forwarded to various newspapers and prominent officials.

Meanwhile, there was nothing the emigrants could do but make themselves as comfortable as possible under the circumstances while awaiting the coming of spring and warmer weather. Udell gives us some idea of the severity of the weather that winter in Albuquerque. His journal entry for December 2 read, "High wind and cold rain. Quite uncomfortable for an aged man to be out, but necessity compels me to do it." It was necessary for him to be out in such severe weather because he had just started his job as a government herder the day before. For December 3, he recorded, "Snow six inches deep, and hard freezing weather." Udell's journal entries for this period are quite short, usually one brief entry covering a period of several days. He was probably too tired from working all day to do much writing when he got home at night. The winter of 1858–59 was apparently colder than usual for Albuquerque.

In his December 12 entry, Udell made an exception to his short journal entries. On that day he wrote at some length about a religious ceremony he witnessed at the local Catholic church in celebration of Our Lady of Guadalupe. Each year on that date the locals reenacted a dramatic play called *La Aparicion,* in which a vision of the Virgin Mary appears to a poor Aztec convert to Christianity. Udell's puritanical upbringing and his lack of education and understanding of other cultures prevented him from appreciating the beauty and significance of this pageantry. He summarized his impression of the performance by writing, "Such doings frequently transpire among this people, under the title of sacred or sanctimonious. To me it is perfectly ridiculous and blasphemous."

The period between December 14 and 24 must have been a dull time in Albuquerque. Udell wrote, "Nothing worthy of note." Apparently there were no Protestant churches in town at that time, for had there been, Udell would certainly have attended services there and reported that fact in his journal. Instead, he and some of the other emigrants attended Christmas Eve and Christmas Day services at the local Catholic church. As one might expect, Udell found much to criticize at these services.

> Dec. 25. Christmas. Last night and To-day the Mexican (Catholics) made themselves very ridiculous in the eyes of us Americans, in their attempts to celebrate the Birth of Christ. At night they claimed to have the Child (Jesus) born in their large Church. They presented the images of the Virgin Mary, the Apostles and many others, to a very large audience of spectators, and passed the ceremonies of having the Babe born in the presence of all, and had persons to talk and act the part of those who are recorded in Scriptures in relation to it. After the ceremony is over, all pay adoration and reverence to those images. To American Christians, it was considered most blasphemous mockery. The conduct of the day was very similar to that on the 12th.[8]

Apparently nothing newsworthy happened during the last week of the year 1858, for again he recorded in his journal, "Nothing worthy of note." But on the last day of the year he described another of those events that so aroused his puritanical wrath.

Dec. 31. This day a new scene among the Mexicans was presented to my eyes and ears. A rough, ragged, ugly-looking young man was traveling from door to door through the village [Albuquerque] with a box about one foot in length and six inches in width, containing a small coarse-looking image, apparently made of wood and painted white, with a glass over it; he would make a long prayer to the so-called Saint at every door, in behalf of the family, to be taken direct to Heaven, as they supposed, by the Saint which the image represents. He then receives a gift from the inmates of the house. All the parties seem to express as much sincerity and faith in that prayer to the little wooden image as I ever saw in a Protestant when praying to Almighty God. I was informed that this was a grant from the Priest to some devoted poor people to get their bread, and the Catholics dare not refuse to give them something.[9]

Udell recorded no New Year's Eve or New Year's Day celebration on the part of the American emigrants in Albuquerque. Perhaps they felt that they had little to celebrate other than simply being alive. The weather he reported as "Hard freezing nights, and cold, windy days; snow on the ground yet." Sometime between January 21–25, the Udells received a letter from their son, Oliver, in California. The Butterfield Overland Mail was now in full operation and it was possible to receive mail in Albuquerque on a regular basis. They received another letter from Oliver on January 27; this one contained a check for fifty dollars, a gift much appreciated by the elderly couple.

Udell's journal entries for the month of February, 1859, are mostly about the weather. He reported that, "Ice has frozen here this winter from ten to twelve inches thick." The cold weather was hard on the sixty-three-year-old man who had to work outside every day herding cattle, and then come home and cut wood and help his invalid wife with the cooking and the washing.

Since there was no Protestant church in town, Udell and other emigrants organized a Sunday evening worship. Both he and Gillum Baley were lay preachers and probably took turns conducting the services. Udell's journal entry for February 6 stated, "Our Sunday evening meetings continue with increasing interest. This evening I preached to a large and attentive congregation, principally officers and soldiers of the American Army." Since the campaign against the Navajos was recently concluded and a peace treaty signed, many officers and soldiers were returning to their posts after having been gone for several months.

On March 3, exciting news reached Albuquerque: Edward F. Beale arrived in town. Beale had just completed improvements to the Fort Smith, Arkansas, to Albuquerque, New Mexico, branch of the road. Accompanying him was a large group of engineers, topographers, explorers, soldiers, teamsters, laborers, and others.

Beale was anxious to get started on the second phase of the project—improving the road between Albuquerque and the Colorado River. He had spent the summer of 1858 in Washington, D.C., completing his reports and drawing maps of his proposed new wagon road. When completed, he presented them to his superior, Secretary of War John B. Floyd, who was greatly impressed with Beale's work. He sent the reports to the House of Representatives along with a cover letter urging its speedy approval. Congress, too, was impressed with the project, for it quickly appropriated $100,000 for further road work and an additional $75,000 for the construction of bridges along the route, in essence making Beale's Wagon Road the first federally funded interstate highway in the Southwest.

CHAPTER 9

California at Last

W hen Beale arrived back in Albuquerque on March 3, 1859, he was surprised to learn that several emigrant trains had attempted to travel his proposed wagon road. He never envisioned emigrants using the road until the government established a military post at the Colorado River (Beale's Crossing) to protect them from the Mojave Indians. He also had planned to do a considerable amount of road work as no roadbed existed over much of the route, and in many places the route was almost impossible to find. While in Washington, D.C., he secured an appropriation to build bridges over the larger streams, and to construct dams on some of the seasonal watercourses to ensure a more reliable water supply.[1] He felt compassion for the emigrants who suffered so severely in their attempt to travel this new route, but there was little he could do to help them.

Beale felt special pity for the Joel Hedgpeth and John Udell families due to their advanced ages and the fact that they had no means of leaving Albuquerque on their own. In conversations with army officers and local townspeople, he learned of the delicate health of both Mrs. Hedgpeth and Mrs. Udell. His sympathy for the two elderly couples was so aroused that he decided to take them with him on his road-building expedition from Albuquerque to California, although he had no authorization to do so and no allowance for their expenses. For these reasons neither couple is mentioned by name in his official journal. It is believed that he paid their expenses from his own pocket. He provided each family with a wagon and a team of mules so that they would not have to walk. The Hedgpeths had their four younger children, Lewis, William, Joel Jr., and Elizabeth traveling with them. Their eldest son, Thomas Hedgpeth, and his family had returned to Nodaway County, Missouri, as previously noted.

From March 3–8, Beale was busy preparing for his road-building expedition. He replenished his supplies and hired additional men as teamsters and laborers. Among this group was at least one member of the Rose-Baley wagon train, William Garton, one of the young men who had accompanied the Baley company.[2] There might have been others. Beale was delighted to learn that the Butterfield Overland Mail was now in full operation over the Southern Route, and it was now possible to travel by stage from Albuquerque to Los Angeles. He took advantage of this new mode of transportation by sending his chief clerk, Fred Kerlin, to California with a message for Beale's business partner, Samuel A. Bishop, at their Tejon ranch. The message requested that Bishop meet him near the Colorado River with a load of provisions since Beale intended to carry only enough supplies to reach that point.

Beale left Albuquerque on March 8, 1859. Udell described the train as, "Consisting of nearly fifty men, fourteen wagons, and probably one hundred mules and horses. . . . We crossed the Rio Grande and proceeded the same route we traveled last year—Mr. Beale's business being to improve that route, under the instruction, or employ of the United States government."

Udell described the weather as sunny and windy with night time temperatures below freezing. For March 13, he recorded: "Ice one inch thick this morning, and freezing all day. Cold for old people camping out." The expedition approached the Continental Divide over the Zuni Range of the Rocky Mountains at an elevation of approximately eight thousand feet.

At Agua Fria the expedition laid by a few days to let the men do some roadwork. "The road just as you ascend to the top of the Rocky Mountains wants some work which the hands have been doing," wrote Dr. Floyd, the expedition physician in his journal.[3] While encamped at this location Beale sent two wagons under the command of his brother, George Beale, ahead to Zuni to see if the Indians there had any spare corn to sell. "They either sell readily and for little or nothing, or not at all," Beale wrote in his journal, "and are as capricious in their disposition as possible."[4]

After completing the roadwork over the Continental Divide, the expedition moved on to the famed Inscription Rock campsite. To the Hedgpeths and Udells, Inscription Rock was becoming a familiar sight, this being their third trip there in the last eight months. The rock was also an old friend to Beale, but to some members of the group, camping at the rock was a new experience. One of these first-time visitors was Dr. Floyd who was greatly impressed with the vista spread before his eyes. His journal entry for Monday, March 21, 1859, read:

> We left camp this morning early and after a most windy, somewhat cold and very disagreeable day of it, we made the celebrated camping ground known as Inscription Rock. It has many names, some of them so early as 1639 and from that down to the present day. Those of the early Spaniards are mostly well done, those of the Americans mostly scrawl, many with very obscene remarks attached, thus perpetuating as far as they could their blackguardism.[5]

Floyd might have been impressed with Inscription Rock, but as far as we know he did not leave his name on the monument; if he did it, was obliterated before it was recorded or photographed. Beale's name appears on the rock but is undated. He probably carved it on his first trip in 1857. At least three members of Beale's 1859 expedition carved their names on Inscription Rock. The names of E. P. Long, F. Engle Jr., and P. Gilmer Breckinridge, with the date 1859, appear in bold lettering on the south side of the rock. All three were members of Beale's road-building expedition. Frederick Engle Jr. was Beale's second in command on this expedition. E. P. Long's name was written in flowing script, followed by the name of his hometown, Baltimore, Maryland. The names F. Engle Jr. and P. Gilmer Breckinridge, engraved in sharp square letters, appear to have been made using professional tools.[6]

The expedition left Inscription Rock on March 20, and headed for Zuni, camping that night on a branch of the Zuni River. The next day they met Beale's brother, George, whom Beale had sent ahead with two wagons to try to purchase corn from the Pueblo Indians at Zuni. George Beale brought good news: He found the Pueblo Indians in a trading mood and bought some corn from them. Later that day, the expedition was caught in a severe dust storm. "This day was very disagreeable," Beale wrote, "with a high wind blowing dust in every direction, reminding us of Washington City in a winter gale."[7]

Little time was spent in Zuni because there was no grass nearby for the animals. Camp had to be made some distance from the pueblo. Beale went into town to pay a courtesy call on the Zuni governor, Pedro Pino (Laiiujitsailu). Pueblos were usually headed by governors rather than chiefs or alcaldes, a condition originally imposed upon them by the Spaniards. "The old Indian met me in town with many compliments and congratulations," Beale wrote, "and bearing in his arms a box containing my 'artificial horizons' (instrument used in taking altitudes) that I had left with him in passing last winter. He told me the charge had been a great burden on his mind and he was glad to be rid of the responsibility."[8] They then went to the governor's residence for further talks. The governor had a long list of grievances against the American government that he wanted to get off his chest. The United States, he told Beale, had persuaded him into an alliance against the Navajos. In that war his warriors fought side by side like brothers with the Americans, explained the governor. But then the American government had found it convenient to make peace with these longtime enemies of the Zunis, and he now feared retaliation from his old foes.

Beale's advice was blunt and very unsympathetic, and not at all exemplary of a man who would one day become a U.S. diplomat. "I told the old fellow I thought it served him right for meddling in things which did not concern him, and warned him for the future to avoid all entangling alliances."[9] The old governor probably wished that he could take back some of the compliments and congratulations that he had so generously bestowed upon Beale at the beginning of their meeting. Before leaving Zuni, Beale gave some presents to the Indians and was successful in trading for some cornmeal. He then rode back to his camp with the dust storm still raging.

Because of the severe weather, the expedition remained in camp the following day, March 28. The next morning conditions weren't much better except that snow had now replaced the dust. Udell reported, "Hard freeze again last night; snow fell about two inches deep, freezing all day; cold traveling for the women [Mrs. Hedgpeth and Mrs. Udell]; I walked; we came to Jacob's Well—twenty-eight or thirty miles."

They laid by the next day to do some roadwork, although the weather was still bad. The following morning, March 31, they left camp at 7:00 a.m., and traveled ten miles to Navajo Springs (also called Mud Springs). Dr. Floyd gave a good description of these springs in his journal:

> We passed today 6 miles from Jacob's Well the Navajo or Mud Springs as they are called. They are most curious, surrounded by a range of low hills or rather a basin in the great plain. They run all the year and several of them apparently force up mud along with water until their rims are several feet, from 3 or 4, above the level of the basin or the other and running springs. The mud is very deep, a camel was mired in one over his hump and had to be drawn out with ropes. This morning they were frozen over and Mr. Beale, in attempting to walk over one of them, broke in up to his waist. I was near and gave him a helping hand. He got out without difficulty but was very muddy. Scarcely half an hour afterwards, an old woman, Mrs. Hedgpeth, with the curiosity of a woman and the gawkyness of a green one, popped into the same place. She screamed painter and Tucker pulled her out. She never would have got out without help.[10]

This is almost the only reference to either emigrants or camels in Floyd's journal. Beale, for obvious reasons, doesn't mention emigrants, and by now, neither Beale nor Floyd thought that camels were oddities. They considered these humpbacked animals just as important and necessary as their horses and mules. At least twenty-five camels were sent to Beale from Camp Verde at the beginning of the road-building expedition. The remainder of the camels used on the 1857 survey expedition had been left at Fort Tejon in California under the tender care of Hadji Ali (Hi Jolly), one of the Arab camel drivers who came over from Asia Minor with the camels. Among those camels left at Fort Tejon was Old Seid, Beale's favorite riding camel. Udell seemed totally unimpressed by the camels, for he made only one unimportant reference to them in his journal.

On April 2, they reached the Little Colorado. The weather, Udell noted, was windy, cold and freezing. "We have to keep large fires to be comfortable all night." The journals of both Beale and Dr. Floyd verify the inclement weather. For the Hedgpeths and the Udells, these discomforts were mild when compared to the hardships and suffering the two elderly couples endured on their return trip to Albuquerque after the battle with the Mojave Indians. They now enjoyed the luxury of warm clothing and a sheltering wagon instead of sleeping on the frozen ground with only a thin blanket to cover them. The larder, too, was now much better stocked. Instead of meat from half-starved cattle served without the benefit of salt or bread, they now dined on fresh mutton from the large herd of fat sheep that the expedition was driving as a mobile commissary. There were now plenty of salt and other condiments to make the fare more palatable, as well as a good supply of corn and flour for bread. To vary the diet, Beale's guides and hunters, Little Axe and Dick the Delaware, were able to supplement the menu with game, including such delicacies as beaver, duck, venison, antelope, and elk.

The expedition arrived in the vicinity of the San Francisco Peaks on April 12, 1859. The weather was still cold, Udell noted in his journal. On the night of April 15, they camped at Leroux Springs where the Rose-Baley wagon train had camped for several days the previous summer. Here, the expedition left the broken-down horses and mules along with some of the wagons and excess baggage. The animals would be recruited and picked up on the return trip. Two men were left to guard them. "Light frost last night, pleasant day," Udell recorded. "We came seven or eight miles and camped near plenty of wood and water; no water here last summer."

Slowly moving westward, the expedition camped at Hedgpeth (Bear) Spring on April 18. While digging a larger basin for the spring so that it could accommodate more animals drinking at one time, one of Beale's men looked up and observed a strange sight. Looking down the valley in the far distance, he saw two men mounted on camels rapidly approaching the spring. Since the sight of two men racing across the Southwest desert on camels wasn't exactly an everyday event, the man called Beale's attention to the apparition. As the two figures came nearer, Beale recognized one of the riders as his business partner, Mr. Samuel A. Bishop, astride Old Seid. The other rider was Hadji Ali (Hi Jolly). Bishop brought forty men with him, along with the remainder of the camels and some provisions. He had received Beale's message delivered by Fred Kerlin stating that Beale was bringing only enough provisions to last until he reached the Colorado River and asking that

Bishop meet Beale there with fresh supplies.[11] There was great joy in camp with their arrival. Udell could not resist the temptation to take a parting shot at his former traveling companions for their timorous decision to turn back after the battle with the Mojave Indians. He recorded in his journal:

> . . . Our fears of the Indians were dispelled; Mr. Bishop, with forty men, had fought his way through the Mojave Indians, after being surrounded by them, and had effected his crossing of the main Colorado without the loss of a man. See what men of composure and courage can do! I wonder what our one hundred and eighteen men will think when they hear this?[12]

Udell was incorrect when he wrote that Bishop fought his way through the Mojave Indians. Bishop, with his forty men, attempted to force a crossing of the Colorado River at Beale's Crossing, but found his way blocked by a large number of hostile Mojave warriors. Fearing to divide his small force, he wisely withdrew to Pah-Ute Creek where there was plenty of water and grass. He attempted to get help from the army post at Fort Yuma, but when this failed he took a route to the north of the Mojave Villages that had been used by Francois X. Aubry in 1853 and 1854. There, he was able to cross the Colorado River unmolested. This route, however, was too rocky and too rough to take wagons over. Bishop packed what provisions he could on the backs of his camels and mules and went on to a rendezvous with Beale. The supplies that he was unable to take with him he cached at Pah-Ute Creek for future use. He sent the wagons and remaining men back to civilization.[13]

When Udell saw Beale and Bishop riding camels, he decided that he, too, would like to add camel riding to his résumé. According to Joel Hedgpeth Jr., a lad of eighteen who witnessed the event, Udell communicated his wishes to Beale, who completed all the necessary arrangements to accommodate him.

> "Certainly, certainly you shall ride a camel," Beale then called to his Turkish camel driver, Hadji Ali. "Bring us Old Seid and let Mr. Udell have a ride." The camel was brought and caused to kneel down and the old man vaulted into the saddle. When at the command of the Turk, Old Seid moved forward and backward and upward and the old man became alarmed

but Hadji Ali admonished him, "Hold on tight." As the camel moved off in that long swing trot, the old man's alarm became terror, as shown by his face, and he lustily calls out, "Stop the beast," greatly to the amusement of the boys. When the camel had trotted off a hundred yards or so he came back and kneeled down. Mr. Udell was prompt to dismount, thankful that he was still alive.[14]

This frightening experience very likely had something to do with Udell's lack of enthusiasm for camels and his failure to write anything about them in his journal.

With Bishop were several members of the Central Overland Mail Company which had a contract from the U.S. government to carry mail over Beale's Wagon Road, but because of the hostile Mojave Indians, the mail company was unable to cross the Colorado River on their initial eastbound trip. With the union of Bishop and his crew plus the men from the Central Overland Mail Company, the expedition made good progress on its journey westward. By April 23, they reached Peach Springs. Udell reported weather conditions as "windy, cold, and uncomfortable." Several new springs had been discovered, and new alignments were made to the road to take advantage of these new sources of water.

The expedition now entered the territory of the Hualapai Indians, and as with the Rose–Baley wagon train of the previous year, the Beale expedition began to suffer from Indian depredations. A mule was stolen at Truxton Springs; a short time later an arrow was shot at Mr. Carrington, one of Beale's men. Fortunately, the arrow hit a rock before reaching its intended victim. The next day another mule was stolen and arrows were shot into camp during broad daylight. At Savedra Spring yet another mule was taken and another one shot, dying a short time later. Beale wondered if there might be some way of circumventing these malicious acts. He hit upon the same idea that the Baley company used the summer before. After supper was cooked and darkness descended, camp was silently moved some distance away. The mule that had died was left in plain view at the first camp. Several men concealed themselves behind rocks, knowing full well that the Indians would steal into camp to claim the carcass after the fires had died down.

Sure enough, just before daybreak, several Indians sneaked into camp to take the dead mule. The men concealed behind the rocks opened fire on the intruders, killing four and driving off the others. The fallen warriors were relieved of their scalps, and the bloody trophies, along with some bows and arrows, were brought into camp the next morning as vouchers. Beale described the event as, "Altogether a pretty good practical joke—a merrie jester of ye white man and ye Indian."[15] No more Indian depredations were reported.

On April 29, the expedition arrived at Mountain Spring at the eastern base of the Colorado (Black) Mountains. This was the same place where the Rose-Baley wagon train camped the previous year and where they met the Cave train on the retreat to Albuquerque. They camped here for several days while the construction crew did a considerable amount of work on the road to, and over, Sitgreaves Pass. While the road builders were busy, Udell, Joel Hedgpeth, and several others paid a visit to the mountain camp where the emigrants had cached their valuables the previous summer. To their great disappointment, they found that the property that they had so carefully buried had been dug up and carried away, presumably by the Mojaves. Even the wagons had been burned.

The expedition camped here while Beale and twenty men went ahead to the Colorado River to ascertain whether they could cross peaceably. To their great surprise, five white men met them on the trail. These men were American soldiers belonging to the command of Lieutenant Colonel William Hoffman.[16] They informed Beale that Hoffman had arrived at the Mojave Villages on April 20 with a force of nearly six hundred men and had forced the Mojaves to sign a peace treaty. Beale and the members of his expedition were happy to meet fellow Americans, but they were disappointed in not getting a chance to battle the Mojaves. "We were all disappointed," Udell wrote, "for we were prepared and willing to punish these savages for their outrages upon us emigrants last summer."

When he heard the news that a peace treaty had been signed, Beale called in all of his advance scouts, "much to their disappointment and intense disgust," he wrote.[17]

After concluding a peace treaty with the Mojaves, Hoffman returned to Los Angeles for supplies. He left Major Armistead, two companies of infantry, and a detachment of artillery at Beale's Crossing for the purpose of establishing a permanent post to protect other emigrant parties as per his instructions from the War Department.[18] Hoffman called the post Camp Colorado, but Armistead changed the name to Camp Mojave and later to Fort Mojave.[19] The fort was built on high ground on the Arizona side of the Colorado River within a few hundred yards of the site where the Mojaves had launched their surprise attack on the emigrants the previous August. Iron axletrees, burned wagons, broken boxes and kegs, torn books blood stained and scorched, were still found on the battlefield when the fort was established.[20]

The resolutions that the emigrants had drawn up back in Albuquerque in November of 1858 had borne fruit. They were published in the *Santa Fe Gazette* on December 4, 1858, and in the *Daily Missouri Republican* on December 29. Copies also had been sent to prominent military and civil authorities, both in the East and in the West. News of the Mojave attack on the Rose-Baley wagon train had been published in the *Santa Fe Gazette* as early as October 16, 1858, and reprinted in other newspapers, including the *Los Angeles Star* on November 18, 1858. There was no way that the U.S. government could ignore the attack on the emigrants. When the War Department learned of the battle with the Mojave Indians, Secretary of War Floyd ordered Brigadier General Newman S. Clarke, in charge of the Military Department of California, to mount a punitive expedition against the Mojaves.

General Clarke wasted no time in dispatching a sufficient force under the command of Lieutenant Colonel William Hoffman to chastise the Mojaves and establish a permanent military presence in Mojave territory at Beale's Crossing. Hoffman carried out his orders (halfheartedly, some thought), concluded a treaty with the Mojave nation, and established a military post at Beale's Crossing. Seeing that resistance would be futile, the Mojaves submitted to the rule of the American government and ceased to be a major problem.

Maps printed after 1859 no longer showed the place name of Mojave Villages at Beale's Crossing, instead showing the name Fort Mojave. Fort Mojave was deactivated at the beginning of the Civil War because its soldiers were needed for the battlefields in the East. However, in 1863 it was reactivated and manned by units of the California Volunteers. After the Civil War it was again manned by the regular army. It remained in service until 1890 when it was deactivated and turned over to the Bureau of Indian Affairs for use as a Mojave Indian school. It was used for this purpose until its final closure in 1930. Today, only a few foundation stones mark the spot where the fort once stood.[21]

When Beale reached the Colorado River, he learned that the large supply of provisions that Bishop had cached for him on the California side of the river had been dug up and stolen, allegedly by some of Hoffman's soldiers.[22] Beale had counted heavily on these supplies. Without them, he was faced with a food shortage. There was only one thing he could do—go to Los Angeles, the nearest source of supply, and bring back fresh provisions. Beale, his brother George, Samuel Bishop, and some of their key men set out for Los Angeles immediately. All of the workers left behind, except for a few men employed as herders, were sent back to do construction work on the road from Sitgreaves Pass to the Colorado River.

Since he was in a hurry to get supplies back to his men, Beale could not take the Udells and Hedgpeths with him to Los Angeles. He left them camped near Major Armistead's troops at Fort Mojave where they were well protected from any possible Indian raids. Udell wasn't pleased at being left behind. The weather was hot and oppressive, and the air was filled with dust that made his eyes sore. "To add to our troubles," he wrote, "our camp was in sight of our last year's battleground, and the Indians were visiting us in large numbers every day and annoying us. To remain thirty days in such circumstances, anxiously longing to get home, was not very pleasant." However, Udell reported that they were well treated by the army. "I would here note," he recorded, "that the officers at this post have shown us much kindness. From Major Armstead [Armistead], the commander, I received good reading material; the soldiers were also very kind."

Beale arrived in Los Angeles on May 12, where he wasted no time in purchasing the necessary provisions for his work crew and the emigrants waiting at the Colorado River. He was thoughtful enough to purchase two ladies' saddles, one for Mrs. Udell and one for Mrs. Hedgpeth, knowing that they would be riding pack mules back to Los Angeles. Udell in his journal acknowledges the thoughtfulness of Beale in providing for the comfort of the women.

Beale assembled a pack train of forty mules, loaded them with supplies and sent them back to the Colorado River. He obtained the animals from Phineas Banning, the owner of a large transportation company in southern California. The pack train was driven by Mexicans, probably Banning's employees. Neither Beale nor Bishop accompanied the pack train back to the Colorado, but went instead to Fort Tejon. They also visited their ranch while in the area.

The pack train arrived back at the Colorado River on June 1 with its welcome load of provisions. It had been only twenty-eight days since Beale left for Los Angeles, but to those waiting at the Colorado it must have seemed like an eternity, as they had been on short rations all the while. The very next day, the pack train headed back to Los Angeles under the supervision of William Tucker, one of Beale's most trusted assistants. With it went the Udells and the Hedgpeths—for them, it was California at last!

The trip across the California desert was no picnic. This section of the journey was over desert more arid and with fewer water holes than any of those in New Mexico or Arizona. But now they were traveling with a well-organized pack train with experienced and competent men in charge. What a difference that made! Because of the high temperatures, between 100 and 130 degrees, much of the traveling was done at night. Udell's journal entry for June 6 read, "Remained in camp to rest, our old ladies much fatigued, having rode nearly all night." Udell doesn't say so, but it is a safe bet that the "old men" were fatigued too. The route taken was what later became known as the Mojave Road by way of Pah-Ute Creek, Marl Springs, Soda Spring and over Cajon Pass to San Bernardino and then on to Los Angeles.

On June 11, they arrived at Mr. Highman's ranch, meeting the first white settler they had encountered since leaving Albuquerque. "Mr. Highman has an excellent stock ranch here," Udell wrote. "Fine large springs of good water. He gave us a good supper and breakfast, gratis."

On June 14, they traveled thirty-five miles, "a fatiguing journey for aged ladies under a hot sun," wrote Udell. "We are now in the white settlements of California [San Bernardino]."

Shortly before reaching Los Angeles they were met by Bishop, Beale's partner, who was on his way back to the Colorado River to supervise the road building. Bishop, on behalf of Beale, presented Udell with a check for fifty dollars, ". . .which paid expenses of my wife and myself to the end of our journey," Udell recorded. Beale also included letters of introduction to some of the most influential people in Los Angeles. Udell would put this windfall to good use. Whether these same considerations were extended to the Hedgpeths is unknown, but Beale, being a fair-minded gentleman, probably did so.

The weary travelers entered Los Angeles on June 15 and camped near the plaza. Udell was quick to take advantage of his letters of introduction. The first person he presented one of them to was Phineas Banning, the transportation king of southern California. He met with instant success. ". . . Mr. Banning furnished us a room and provisions for eight days, while we were awaiting the arrival of a steamship to convey us to San Francisco, and he conveyed us twenty-five miles to the ship, [at San Pedro] free of charge," Udell recorded. The name of their ship was the *SS Senator.* The price of the fare to San Francisco for the two of them was sixty dollars, but Udell was able to get the fare reduced to just forty dollars. After a two-day voyage up the coast of California, during which they both suffered from seasickness, the Udells arrived in San Francisco on June 26, 1859. It being a Sunday, there was no steamer service to Sacramento until Monday evening. Again Udell called forth his power of persuasion and obtained free lodging for himself and Emily. "Mr. Weygant not only kept us free of costs," Udell wrote, "but he came down to the office of the steamship 'Eclipse,' and we related our misfortunes. They gave us free passage to Sacramento, a stateroom and our meals." Udell certainly knew how to evoke the sympathy of strangers.

The destination of the Udells was Silveyville, a small farming community near Sacramento where their sons Henry and Oliver lived. Udell and his wife arrived at the end of their long, perilous journey on June 30, 1859, after being fourteen months and twenty-one days on the road. Udell wrote of the event: "We hope to spend the few remaining days of our pilgrimage on earth in the society of our children and Christian friends in this country, where health, and peace, and plenty reign." Udell ended his journal with a note of high praise for Beale's Wagon Road as a potential railroad route. With the exit of Udell the narrative loses its diarist, but the drama continued to unfold.

The Udells and the Hedgpeths parted company in Los Angeles at the plaza, where they had camped together. The Hedgpeths were headed for Visalia, an inland settlement in the San Joaquin Valley; they might have had friends or relatives living there. In his recollections, Joel Hedgpeth Jr. was silent on this point and he didn't reveal what route they traveled to reached their destination. Most likely they traveled by way of the Butterfield Overland Mail Route past Fort Tejon and over Tejon Pass, as this was the most direct route between Los Angeles and Visalia. The Butterfield Overland Mail also carried passengers over this route, but it is unlikely that the Hedgpeths, a family of six, could have afforded to travel in this manner. Probably they joined a pack train and all walked except those too ill or too infirm.

After arriving back in Albuquerque, many of the young men employed as teamsters or herders gave up hope of ever getting to California and returned to their former homes in Iowa and Missouri. It is uncertain what happened to some of the members of the Cave company after their return to Albuquerque, but we do know that James H. Jordan returned to Iowa where he became a prosperous and well-respected citizen.[23] In an Indian depredation suit that he filed in 1891 (U.S. Court of Claims, Suit No. 3487), John Bradford Cave gave his address as Sacramento, California. Calvin "Cal" Davis settled in Sebastopol, California. It is unknown what happened to Robert Perkins or to Udell's friend, John Hamilton.

One company of the returned emigrants, the Smiths, did not wait for Beale's return to Albuquerque or the coming of spring to continue their westward journey. They grew restless during the winter and decided to continue to California at the earliest possible moment. They persuaded four of their former employees to go along and help drive what was left of their once vast herd of livestock. They set out from Albuquerque for California in late January of 1859. To avoid the cold and the heavy snows of the San Francisco Mountains, as well as the treacherous Mojave Indians, they chose to travel the Southern Route.

The Smiths had always shown much compassion for Mrs. Brown and her fatherless children. They resolved to take the widow and her family to California with them. Little Sallie Fox's wounds had healed sufficiently for her to travel. Thanks to the Smiths, Mary Brown and her four surviving children became the first members of the Rose-Baley wagon train to reach California, arriving in Los Angeles in the spring of 1859 (the Hedgpeths and Udells didn't arrive until June 16, 1859). Mrs. Brown had a brother, George Baldwin, living in Placerville. He was single and had written to his sister inviting her to come to Placerville and keep house for him. He also promised to pay for their passage. E. O. Smith agreed to accept two hundred dollars to cover his expenses in bringing Mary Brown and her children to California; it would be payable at the end of the journey. Mary Brown also had a sister, Lavinia De Golia, living in Placerville, and another sister, Julia Allison, living near Vacaville, California.

Although the Southern Route avoided the hostile Navajo, Hualapai, and Mojave Indians, it passed through territory inhabited by a tribe of Indians considered even more fierce and warlike—the dreaded Apaches. This route went through an area controlled by the Chiricahua tribe of the Apaches who were led by their great chief, Cochise. From his stronghold at Apache Pass, Cochise and his warriors kept a close watch on all traffic that passed their way; no one, not even the Butterfield Overland Mail, passed through Chiricahua country without his knowledge and approval. Because E. O. Smith and his small train were traveling without a military escort, they must have felt some trepidation as they approached Apache Pass. According to Edith Allen Milner (Sallie Fox Allen's daughter), they didn't have to wait long.

> Sure enough, one afternoon—I think near "Apache Pass"—Cochise and his warriors suddenly appeared in Camp as if they had sprung out of the ground. But Mr. Smith and his bald head seemed to hit their fancy and they started to get acquainted instead of "Shooting them up" as the Mojaves had done. They thought Mr. Smith had been scalped and had survived. He gave them beads and trinkets and Cochise was delighted. He said he was "Wayno (Bueno) Indian" and told his horsemen to "Vamoos" but he was going to stay all night in camp. His warriors disappeared as suddenly as they came. They were just "swallowed up," and Cochise stayed on to the consternation of Mama [Sallie Fox] and her family. Mama was sure they would all "wake up dead" and wished that the bear which had come into camp some time previously and had bitten off the ear of the "Iron Gray Mare" would come again that night and bite off all their heads so that the Indians would not get them. But Mr. Smith tried to be hospitable and made such a hit with Cochise that that Indian really was as "Bueno" as he said he was, and let them go through undisturbed in his territory, and they had no trouble with the Apaches.[24]

Fortunately for the Smith train, Cochise had not yet declared war on the Americans; he did so in 1861 as the result of the Bascom Affair.[25]

One evening while playing along the edge of the Gila River, Sallie picked up three or four black walnuts that had been washed up on the bank of the river. She wondered where they came from because she could see no walnut trees growing along the river. Perhaps, she thought, the walnuts had been washed down during high water from some place farther upstream. They reminded her of the walnut trees she had seen growing back home in Iowa. She put them in her apron pocket where they remained until she arrived in California. She knew her Aunt Julia and Uncle Josiah Allison lived on a ranch near Vacaville. Upon arrival there, she would ask her Uncle "Si" to plant them for her. Maybe one of them would sprout and someday grow into a big walnut tree just like those back home in Iowa.[26]

On the trail one day, a few miles west of the present Painted Rock State Park between Tucson and Fort Yuma, the little emigrant party came upon a grave site marked by a headstone. Upon it were engraved the words, "Sacred to the Oatman family," which little Sallie misread as "Scared to the Oatman family." There were still some of the hubs and other remnants of the Oatman wagons lying about. The tragic story of the Oatman family had been told and retold around emigrant campfires at night. The graves contained the bodies of Royce Oatman, his wife Mary Ann, and four of their seven children. The discovery of these graves must have brought back to Mrs. Brown and her family painful memories of the Bentner family. There were several similarities between the fate of the Oatman family and that of the Bentners. Both were attacked by hostile Indians while traveling alone across the desert. Both families had been warned that such solitary travel in Indian country was dangerous. Both ignored the advice and paid with their lives.

The Royce Oatman family had been members of an emigrant party headed for California in 1851 by way of the Southern Route. The other members decided to spend more time at a Pima Indian village before continuing their journey. The Oatmans, in a hurry to reach California, decided to push on for Fort Yuma on their own. One evening while camped on a bluff overlooking the Gila River, they were attacked by a group of Yavapais warriors. Both parents and four of their children were brutally murdered by the Indians. Their fourteen-year-old son, Lorenzo, was repeatedly clubbed over the head and left for dead. Two of the daughters, sixteen-year-old Olive and eight-year-old Mary Ann, were taken captive by the Yavapai and later sold to the Mojaves as slaves. Lorenzo, despite the severity of his wounds, managed to find his way to a friendly Pima Indian village where he told his ghastly story. Mary Ann died while in captivity, but Olive was eventually ransomed from the Mojaves and reunited with Lorenzo. While a captive, Olive's face was permanently tattooed by the Mojaves. The town of Oatman, Arizona is believed to be named for his hapless family.[27]

In later years both Olive Oatman and Mary Brown lived in San Jose, California. Olive sent word to Mary that she would like to meet her, but according to Edith Allen Milner, Mary's granddaughter, Mary refused the invitation because she feared she could not stand the ordeal of talking about both of their harrowing experiences. The two never met.[28]

After crossing the Colorado River on a ferry at Fort Yuma, Mary Brown and her children set foot on California soil at last. They must have presented quite a bedraggled appearance, because, according to Edith Allen Milner, the storekeepers at Fort Yuma took pity on them and out-fitted them from head to foot with new clothes at no cost.[29] Sallie's older sister, Sophia Frances (Franc) Fox, was about fifteen at the time and very pretty. All the merchants in Yuma wanted to marry her. Mary Brown had her hands full in getting Franc out of Yuma still unwed.

Eventually the little band of emigrants arrived safely in Los Angeles, which they thought was the fairest city in all the land. The exact date of their arrival is not recorded, but it must have been late March or early April, 1859, since they reported the hills around Los Angeles "green with spring." Sallie always remembered the lovely rose geranium in the garden at San Gabriel Mission.[30] In Los Angeles Mary Brown was met by her brother, George Baldwin, who had come to take the family to his home in Placerville. George then tendered to E. O. Smith the two hundred dollars that Smith had agreed to accept for bringing Mrs. Brown and her children to California, but Smith is said to have responded, "Oh no, I never intended to take any pay. I only made that arrangement so that Mrs. Brown might be easy in her mind on the way." This was the kind of man that E. O. Smith was.[31]

It is not known how or by what route George Baldwin transported his sister and her family to his home. They might have gone up the coast by ship as far as San Francisco as John and Emily Udell had done. Edith Allen Milner in her manuscript stated that when her grandmother, Mary Brown, caught her first view of the Pacific Ocean after many months of privation, her only comment was, "Thank God, there's enough of it!"[32]

Before going on to Placerville, Baldwin took Mary Brown and her family to visit their sister, Julia, and her husband, Josiah Allison, in Vacaville. When they arrived, Sallie presented the walnuts that she had picked up on the banks of the Gila River to her Uncle "Si" for him to plant for her. She went with him and helped him plant the walnuts. Sure enough, one of them did sprout and it eventually grew into a huge tree. It fronted the main road between Sacramento and San Francisco and afforded shade to passing travelers.

One summer the Allisons grew a surplus of black figs and decided to put a small fruit stand under this black walnut tree. The figs sold quickly and soon other fruits were added to the list. Ice water and lemonade were also provided. The venture proved so successful that a restaurant was soon added. The Allisons decided to call their restaurant and fruit stand the Nut Tree since Sallie's black walnut tree dominated the site. The business grew and grew. Today, the Nut Tree is one of the largest amusement parks in California, complete with its own airport, post office, bakery, and other amenities.[33]

Sallie's walnut tree survived until it was toppled by a storm in 1952. Before it expired, a walnut from the grand old monarch was planted near the plaza of the amusement park by Josiah Allison's great-great-granddaughter.

The Baleys and the Daly and Holland families also reached California in 1859. Since they left no diaries or other written accounts, not a lot is known about their journeys. What little is known comes from recollections of family members, oral histories, vital statistics extracted from family Bibles, biographical sketches from county histories, church records, obituaries, newspaper accounts, and interviews with descendants.

It is not known if these families traveled together in the same wagon train to California, but the few facts available and the time frame of their journeys suggest that possibility. Evidence indicates that these families also chose the Southern Route to California. Not even the knowledge that an army post (Fort Mojave) had been established at Beale's Crossing on the Colorado River could convince these emigrants to travel Beale's Wagon Road a second time. Fear of the Mojave Indians and the painful memories of Beale's route from the year before were still vividly etched in their minds.

According to Paul Vandor's *History of Fresno County*, the Baley families made two separate attempts to reach California from Albuquerque in 1859:

> A search there [Albuquerque] for new equipment was almost a failure, but they finally secured a few thin cattle and started again for the West. Soon the cattle gave out and were killed and eaten by the little band of almost starved emigrants. Again they were forced to return to Albuquerque, this time driven by pangs of keenest hunger. Their condition was pitiable in the extreme. Footsore and starving, they finally landed in the town where comforts were procured for the suffering crowd. It was remarked by all that the women of the party had endured all of the hardships of this memorable journey without uttering a word of complaint; the frightful sufferings were endured with a patience born of true heroism, nor did they give up in despair although it became necessary for them to walk the entire distance to California.[34]

A few provisions were obtained and a small number of animals procured for a third attempt to reach California. This time they were successful, but not without great hardship. One story which has been handed down by family tradition is that Sarah Margaret Baley, the seventeen-year-old daughter of William Right and Nancy Baley, carried her little one-year-old sister, Mary Patience, on her back until relieved of her burden by the death of the little child at the Gila River. This little girl was born at the mountain camp shortly before the battle with the Mojave Indians. The cause of death is not recorded, but there can be little doubt that malnutrition played its part. The tiny body was buried by the side of the road, family tradition says, and the site was obliterated by running wagons back and forth over the grave so that it would not be found and disturbed by Indians. The William Right Baley family Bible gives her date of death as 12 October 1859.

All was not hardship and suffering on the road to California. Two of the girls in the wagon train brightened things up a bit, at least for themselves, by discovering romance during the 1859 attempt. Twenty-year-old Amelia Catherine and eighteen-year-old America Frances, daughters of Gillum and Permelia Baley, fell in love with two employees of the wagon train. These were the same two girls who had left their names on Inscription Rock the year before. Amelia Catherine fell in love with William Krug, while her sister, America Frances, chose August Block. The long winter of forced idleness in Albuquerque afforded the young people ample opportunity to get better acquainted with each other. There was just one problem standing in the way of marriage for the love-smitten foursome, but it was a formidable one—the girls' father objected to the marriages and refused to give his consent. Gillum's blessings were not forthcoming because both prospective bridegrooms were recent German immigrants and worst of all, he suspected that one or both might be Catholic! Being a lay Southern Methodist minister, Gillum was in no way going to allow his daughters to marry German papists. Never!

Cupid, however, is not easily deterred, as Gillum Baley soon discovered. The lovers eloped by walking twenty miles to a Presbyterian mission (probably Laguna) where they were married without Gillum's consent.[35] When presented with the *fait accompli*, Gillum Baley bowed to fate and accepted the two Germans as sons-in-law, if not with joy, at least with civility. As far as it is known, they got along all right.[36]

The little train of weary emigrants arrived at Fort Yuma in late October of 1859. Here they could at least replenish a few of their supplies. With several eligible young ladies in the party, they were probably well treated by the merchants there. However, they managed to escape without losing any of the young ladies to the wife-seeking businessmen. After crossing the Colorado River at Fort Yuma, the Baleys were at last in the Promised Land of California. But they still had a distance of over two hundred miles to travel, much of it over a burning desert, before reaching Los Angeles, a thriving metropolis of five thousand people. Most emigrants traveling between Fort Yuma and Los Angeles during this time followed the road used by the Butterfield Overland Mail. A favorite stopping place on this route was Warner's Ranch. That was most likely the way the Baleys came.

The immediate destination of the Baleys was Visalia, a settlement in the San Joaquin Valley where their friends and fellow wagon train travelers, the Hedgpeths, were living. Whether or not this was their original destination is unknown. They might have had relatives living in Visalia. In his Indian depredation suit against the U.S. government, Gillum Baley based the value of his livestock lost to the Mojave Indians on what they would have been worth on the California market. In his deposition he stated he was familiar with livestock prices in California during that period because he had a brother and a brother-in-law living in California with whom he had regular correspondence. The 1860 U.S. Census reveals the name of a Burchard Baley living in Visalia. Since Baley spelled without the letter *i* is a rather uncommon way of spelling the name, it is quite possible that this might have been the brother in California that Gillum made reference to in his deposition.

The Baleys arrived in Visalia in early December of 1859, badly in need of rest and sustenance. Two members of the company, William Right Baley and the newlywed August Block, obtained employment as teamsters and settled there with their families temporarily.

The other Baley brother, Gillum, hearing stories about recent gold mining successes on the San Joaquin River above Millerton, decided to go there and again try his luck as an argonaut. In Millerton he was unable to find a house for his large family, which included his newlywed daughter, Amelia Catherine, and her husband William Krug. Gillum went a short distance up the river to Fort Miller, where he moved his family into the commissary rooms of the old abandoned fort. The Krugs settled themselves next door in the headquarters building.[37] Squatting in abandoned buildings was a common practice in those days.[38]

Like the Baleys, not much is known about the 1859 journey of the Daly and Holland families from Albuquerque to California. The only documentation that has come to light is a short, unpublished autobiography by Edward Warren Holland, the second child of Isaac Taylor Holland and Amanda Melvina Daly Holland. Since he was only three years old in 1858, it is unlikely that he would have retained much personal knowledge of the trip. Any information in his autobiography about the emigrant journey of 1858–59 would have had to come from what he heard from his parents and others. The autobiography deals mostly with his later life. Holland states that his family and the Dalys lost all of their livestock in the battle with the Mojave Indians. This forced them to abandon both their wagons (the Daly wagon and the

Holland wagon) and destroy all of their personal belongings except what they could carry on their backs, a small quantity of flour, and some bedding that could be loaded into the one remaining wagon (the Rose wagon) that had to serve the needs of all the emigrants.

According to Holland, his two-year-old twin brothers, Tom and John, both died of starvation on the same day during the 1859 trip. They were buried together in a common grave. After arriving back in Albuquerque, Holland's father (Isaac Taylor Holland) obtained work as a blacksmith at the government post, where they remained for eight months before resuming their journey to California. Edward didn't mention any other families in the train, but he did present the general route that they followed:

> This time we traveled the Southern Route by way of Tucson, Maricopa Wells, Gila Bend, and Fort Yuma. We arrived in San Bernardino, Calif., about the first of October, 1859, and late in December we resumed our journey to Tuolumne County, Calif., which was our original destination. We arrived there, at Sawmill Flat on Jan. 3, 1860.[39]

L. J. Rose and his family (including his in-laws, the Joneses) were the last members of the Rose-Baley wagon train to arrive in California. Rose remained in Santa Fe operating his hotel, La Fonda, until he sold the business for a good profit in late 1860. In addition to having a keen business mind, Rose also possessed an excellent sense of timing; just a few months later the Civil War broke out, greatly reducing the amount of trade passing through the area and reducing the need for hotels.

According to his deposition in his Indian depredation suit, Rose and his family arrived in Los Angeles County in late November of 1860. They came by way of the Southern Route and crossed the Colorado River at Fort Yuma. From Fort Yuma they traveled the Butterfield Overland Mail Route by way of Warner's Ranch. Despite it being winter when Rose arrived in the San Gabriel Valley, he was so impressed with its beauty and serenity that he decided to pause there for a while.

With the arrival of the Roses in California, all the families of the Rose-Baley wagon train except for the Bentner family, massacred by the Mojaves, and the Thomas Hedgpeth family, which returned to Missouri, were now in the Promised Land. It was nearly two and one-half years after they started their journey in April of 1858.

Edward F. Beale as surveyor general
of California, 1862. *Courtesy California
Historical Society, Amelia R. Neville
Collection.*

E. O. Smith proved to be a kind
friend and a good Samaritan.
Courtesy Terry Feist.

The camel driver, Hadji Ali (Hi
Jolly) and his bride at Tucson about
1880. *Courtesy Arizona Historical
Society, Tucson.*

Brevet Brigadier General B. L. E.
Bonneville, who, while still a
colonel, was in charge at
Albuquerque in 1858. *Courtesy the
Library of Congress.*

Brevet Major General Daniel H. Rucker. As Major Rucker, he gave L. J. Rose a letter at Albuquerque in 1858 attesting to the fine quality of Rose's livestock. In 1891 he gave a deposition in support of Rose's Indian depredation suit. *Courtesy the Library of Congress.*

Colonel William Hoffman (Old Hoffy). He forced the Mojaves to sign a peace treaty. During the Civil War he served as commissary general of prisoners. *Courtesy the Library of Congress.*

Inscription Rock, El Morro National Monument, New Mexico. *Author's collection.*

Miss A. C. (Amelia Catherine) Baley's name on Inscription Rock, El Morro National Monument, New Mexico. The inscription is badly eroded. *Courtesy National Park Service, El Morro National Monument.*

Miss A. F. (America Frances) Baley's name on Inscription Rock at El Morro National Monument, New Mexico. The letter "F" is sometimes mistaken for the letter "E" because of a crack in the rock, making identification difficult because there was no Miss A. E. Baley in the wagon train. *Courtesy National Park Service, El Morro National Monument.*

John Udell's signature on Inscription Rock at El Morro National Monument, New Mexico. *Photograph by Harry C. James; courtesy Southwest Museum.*

Sarah (Sallie) Fox's name on Inscription Rock at El Morro National Monument, New Mexico. *Courtesy Dorothy Leland.*

Isaac T. (Taylor) Holland's signature on Inscription Rock, El Morro National Monument, New Mexico. *Courtesy National Park Service, El Morro National Monument.*

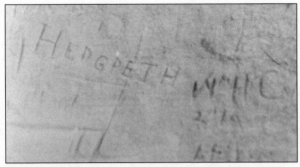

The Hedgpeth name on Inscription Rock, El Morro National Monument, New Mexico. *Courtesy of Joel W. Hedgpeth,* who states that the name was carved by William Pleasant Hedgpeth on the morning of 8 July 1858.

P. H. Williamson's inscription on Inscription Rock at El Morro National Monument, New Mexico. Williamson was one of Rose's hired men but traded places with Tamerlane Davis, one of Udell's men. *Courtesy National Park Service, El Morro National Monument.*

Gillum Baley's signature at Register Rock No. 4 in Canyon Diablo. *Courtesy Jack Beale Smith.*

East side of Black Mountains near Sitgreaves Pass. Notice the rocky terrain in the foreground. *Author's collection.*

"Mojave Indians" as they appeared to the Whipple railroad survey party in 1854. From Lt. Amiel W. Whipple et al., *Reports of Explorations and Surveys, to Ascertain the Most Practicable and Economical Route for a Railroad from the Mississippi River to the Pacific Ocean,* vol. 3.

Dress worn across the plains by Permelia Baley. Modeled by author's daughter, Carol Baley. Dress in possession of Wiletta Pokorny. *Author's collection.*

The dress that Sallie Fox wore on the day of the Mojave attack and the small rubber doll that she carried with her on the journey to California. Note the arrow hole in the upper part of the dress. Sallie's mother shortened the dress to get material for making Sallie a sunbonnet. *Courtesy Vacaville Museum, a Center for Solano County History.*

S.S. Senator, the coastal steamer that took John and Emily Udell from San Pedro to San Francisco. From an oil painting signed and dated, "Joseph Lee, 1875." *Courtesy California Historical Society.*

The pueblo of Zuni as it appeared in 1890. *Photograph by Ben Wittick; courtesy Museum of New Mexico.*

Pedro Pino, governor of Zuni. Photograph by John K. Hillers; *courtesy National Anthropological Archives, Smithsonian Institution.*

CHAPTER 10

The Legal Battle

Having been assured by the army and the citizens of Albuquerque that all the Indians living along Beale's proposed wagon road were friendly and peaceful, the members of the Rose-Baley wagon train were unable to understand why they had been so treacherously attacked. Lieutenant Colonel Hoffman, in his negotiations with the Mojaves, made no attempt to ascertain from them the motive for their vicious attack. Without an official explanation from the army or other government authorities, it was natural that the emigrants would theorize among themselves why they had been so brutally assaulted, and how they could seek redress.

There was some speculation that perhaps the Mormons stirred up the Mojave Indians against the Americans. Because of the problems that then existed between the Mormons and the U.S. government (the Mormon or Utah War of 1857–58), it is easy to understand why some of the blame might be directed toward that religious group. Fresh in the emigrants' minds was the Mountain Meadows Massacre in southern Utah in September of 1857, when a group of Mormon militia, Indians, and southern Utah Mormon officials murdered 120 members of a wagon train from Arkansas. Among the victims who were shot, clubbed or knifed to death were men, women, and about thirty-five children.[1]

The Mormons had sent agents among the Mojave and other Colorado River tribes in 1857 and early 1858.[2] Whether these agents encouraged the Mojave and neighboring tribes to attack American emigrant trains is uncertain, but it is a well-known fact that the Mormons sought alliances with various Indians tribes in the Southwest and counseled them to take sides with the Mormons against the Americans.[3]

In fairness to the Mormons, it should be noted that they faced a desperate situation in their ongoing dispute with the U.S. government. President James Buchanan had sent troops to Utah to install a new governor and other officials for the purpose of enforcing the laws of the United States. The Mormons feared they might be driven from Utah and forced to seek a new haven outside the boundaries of the United States. This was not an unreasonable fear; before settling in Utah, they were driven out of both Missouri and Illinois. If forced to leave Utah, one of the options they were considering was resettlement in northern Mexico. To get there they would travel the Mormon Trail south to a point near present-day Las Vegas, Nevada, and then continue south to the Colorado River, which they would follow all the way to Mexico. To do so, they would have to pass through territory occupied by various Colorado River tribes, including the Mojaves. It made good sense for the Mormons to send envoys among these tribes and attempt to establish good relations with them. Since it has not been proved that the Mormons incited the Mojave Indians to attack the Rose-Baley wagon train, they are at least entitled to the benefit of the doubt.

The only known Mojave account of the attack on the Rose-Baley train is a reminiscence by an old Mojave, Jo Nelson (mature Mojave name—Chooksa homar), who was about fifteen years of age at the time of the attack. In 1903, he told his story of the battle to A. L. Kroeber, a well-known anthropologist. According to this old Indian, the Mojaves were persuaded to attack the emigrants by five young firebrands who had recently returned from Fort Yuma. While there, the young warriors learned something about the ways of the white man. They heard tales from other Indians about the mistreatment of Native Americans by the whites. The five believed that the best way to prevent this from happening to their people was to keep the whites out of Mojave territory, and to attack and annihilate the whites should they be bold enough to enter. The elders and other Mojaves were at first opposed to the attack, according to the old Mojave. They said to the five young warriors: "Well, if you want to fight, go fight. But we will not help you. If you think you can fight them [successfully], go ahead." The five young warriors answered:

> If we let the whites come and live here, they will take your
> wives. They will put you to work. They will take your children

and carry them away and sell them. They will do that until there are no Mohave [Mojave] here. That is why I want to stop them from coming, want them to stay in their own homes. The eastern Indians, I hear, that is what they [the Whites] did to them there: they took their children and said to them: "You are not to see your parents." And they keep birds eggs and coyotes and bears and every kind [of animal]: maybe they will keep you all [confined] in a place too. As for me, I do not want them to do that to me. The whites will not listen to the Mohave. If you tell them to do something, they say No.[4]

After being harangued by the young firebrands, the elders and the others were gradually persuaded to go along with the plan. Their head chief, Arateve (probably Irreteba), who might have been able to prevent the attack, was away at Fort Yuma at the time. According to this account, the Chemehuevi, neighbors of the Mojaves on the west side of the Colorado River, also were induced to join the Mojaves in the attack. The old Indian stated in his reminiscence that a small number of the Chemehuevis swam the Colorado River and attacked the emigrants from the west, while the Mojaves were attacking from the east. Some of the Chemehuevi arrows, the old Indian stated, overshot their intended targets and landed among the Mojaves, and at least one of the Mojave warriors was wounded by those projectiles. None of the emigrant accounts mentions being attacked from two sides simultaneously, but the arrows were flying so thick and furious that the emigrants might not have observed a Chemehuevi attack. Later, in peace talks with Lieutenant Colonel Hoffman, the Mojaves tried to blame the attack on the Chemehuevis and neighboring tribes.

This account would explain why the Mojaves repeatedly asked the emigrants their destination and if they intended to settle in Mojave territory. The Mojaves knew that the country around them was a vast, barren desert where no crops grew, while their little green strip along the Colorado River grew lush crops without much effort, thanks to the annual spring flooding of the Colorado River. They perceived their little oasis to be the garden spot of the world and the envy of surrounding tribes. Surely such a treasure must be coveted by the white men, whose homeland, as far as the Mojaves knew, might also be a desert. Therefore, it was incumbent on them to defend their little paradise with all their might.

This might have been the first time that the Mojaves had ever seen white women and children. All previous contacts with whites were with soldiers, priests, or explorers. The Mojaves thought that since these new strangers were bringing their families with them, they must be planning to settle in Mojave territory. And weren't they cutting down trees along the river to use in the construction of their houses?

Regardless of the reason or the motivation for the attack, what the emigrants desired most was to replace their losses and proceed unmolested to their destinations so that they could get on with their lives. They reasoned that since Indian affairs were the responsibility of the federal government, and since they had been advised by the agents of their government that it was safe to travel Beale's Wagon Road, the United States should indemnify them for their losses.

One of the first things the emigrants did upon returning to Albuquerque was to file claims for their losses against the U.S. government and the Mojave Indians, as specified by Congress. This they did by filing verified petitions before Judge Kirby Benedict, chief justice of the supreme court for the territory of New Mexico, listing the value of each item lost in the attack and the total loss for each claimant. Although the losses occurred in what is now Arizona, this area at that time was part of the New Mexico Territory. Arizona became a separate territory in 1863 and a state in 1912.

Rose was the largest property owner and had suffered the greatest loss. His petition claimed a loss of $27,932.76. The petition of Gillum and William Right Baley totaled $7,400. Joel Hedgpeth's claim was for $4,340, and that of Thomas Hedgpeth, $1,644. Rose's petition was supported by affidavits of several of his employees as witnesses. For additional evidence, he presented letters signed by two army officers in Albuquerque on the outward journey testifying to the superior quality of his livestock. The Baley and Hedgpeth petitions were supported by the affidavits of five of their employees. After these petitions and affidavits had been subscribed and sworn to before Judge Benedict, they were forwarded to Washington, D.C., where Congress acted on them in its usual prompt and efficient manner.

Indian depredations had long been a problem on the western frontier of the United States. To deal with the situation, Congress had passed the Intercourse Act of June 30, 1834, which gave the commissioner of Indian affairs the authority to hear and to award claims in Indian depredation cases. This act states in part:

> Any Indian belonging to any tribe in amity with the United States, shall not take or destroy the property of any person lawfully in Indian country or passing through Indian country. Such citizen himself or his agent may make application to the proper superintendent or agent, who, when being furnished with the necessary documents and proofs, shall under the direction of the President make application to the nation or tribe to which the offender shall belong for satisfaction, and if such nations or tribe shall refuse or neglect to make satisfaction in a reasonable time, not exceeding 12 months, it shall be the duty of such superintendent or agent to make return of his doings to the Commissioner of Indian Affairs that such steps may be taken as shall be proper to obtain satisfaction.

The usual procedure was for the superintendent or agent to submit and read the claim to the defendant Indians in council. If the defendant Indians sitting in council rejected the claim, the superintendent or agent reported this fact in writing to the commissioner of Indian affairs. If the commissioner still thought such claim was justifiable after hearing the response of the Indians in council, he was empowered to withhold the amount of the claim from the annuities or other monies owed to the tribe by the United States, or to withhold other rights to the land they had ceded. In many instances, Indians received food rations from the government for living on reservations and giving up their ownership of hunting rights to certain lands. These benefits could be reduced to settle a claim against the group. A state of amity was usually interpreted to mean that a treaty existed between the United States and that tribe or nation. There were no provisions in this act for the United States to pay these damages if said Indians had no annuities or other monies due them. Indian tribes or nations with whom no treaty existed were not covered by this act.

Another treaty that applied to Indian depredations was that of July 1, 1852. Article 7 provided for free and safe passage for the people of the United States through the territory of the Apache Indians in the Southwest.[5] The problem with this treaty was that it did not adequately identify just who the Apaches were, nor did it precisely delineate the boundaries of their territory. The Apaches at that time were a large group of closely related Indians divided into several tribes and sub-tribes. They had no chief or council who could speak for or bind all of them. The Apaches primarily gained their sustenance by hunting and gathering, though they also raided other Indian villages and sometimes plundered the settlements of Mexicans and Americans. They were noted for being superb horsemen. The Apaches ranged over a large part of the territories of New Mexico and Arizona as well as the Mexican states of Sonora and Chihuahua. No anthropological studies had yet been made of the Indians of this area; their linguistic, ethnic, and cultural backgrounds were poorly understood by most Americans. There was a tendency to lump together under the term Apache all Indians living in the Southwest who could not be assigned to any other known tribe. Even less was known about the Indians living along the Colorado River. It was a common practice for government authorities in the 1850s to include these Indians under the Apache umbrella, although they had little in common with the Apache.

Despite their reputed fierceness, some of the Apache tribes entered into treaty relationships with the United States. Knowing this, and knowing that the Mojaves had sometimes been included under the Apache label, the members of the Rose-Baley wagon train had every reason to believe their petitions came under Article 7 of the Treaty of July 1, 1852. They also believed the Mojave Indians were in amity with the United States. After all, hadn't army officers in Albuquerque described these Indians as friendly? Hadn't they recommended this route to the emigrants as a safe road to travel? And hadn't Beale himself described the Mojaves as "fat and jolly?" But convincing the government and collecting damages would prove to be a different matter.

The emigrants' petitions were presented to the Thirty-fifth Congress (1857–59), second session. No action was taken on these claims by this congress before its term expired in 1859. The first session of the Thirty-sixth Congress (1859–61) took up the matter of the emigrants' claims, referring them first to the House Committee on Claims and then to the Senate Committee on Indian Affairs. The Committee on Indian Affairs sent the claims to the commissioner of Indian affairs for an investigation and a written report. Commissioner A. B. Greenwood made a written report on February 3, 1860, to the

Honorable W. K. Sebastain, chairman of the Senate Committee on Indian Affairs, in which he stated:

> The practice of this department seems to have required the existence of a treaty between the government and a tribe of Indians before they could, under its construction, be considered in amity. The Indian tribes are treated in many respects as if they were independent nations, and if so considered, they certainly could not be termed strictly and legally in amity with us without these formal steps. If that view be a correct one then of course I can have no jurisdiction, as no articles of agreement and convention were ever entered into with these Indians [Mojaves].
>
> Moreover, it does not appear that these claims were ever submitted to the Indians in council, that they might be heard in their defense. It may be said that in the condition of affairs, that would have been mere formality, resulting in nothing, if there were no obstacles to prevent its being done altogether, but the law demands that it be done, and as an executive officer, I have no equity power to give relief against its positive requirements.
>
> There is another requirement that seems not to have been fulfilled, it no where appearing that the parties claimant have ever sought private satisfaction or revenge for the injuries inflicted upon them. Believing as stated above, that I have no jurisdiction over these cases, as presented, I beg leave herewith to return the papers.[6]

With this adverse report from the commissioner of Indian affairs, the emigrants' claims never got out of committee. On February 19, 1861, the Senate Committee on Indian Affairs discharged the claims from further consideration, thus dooming any chance for them to be voted on by the Thirty-sixth Congress. Lacking the financial resources to hire legal counsel, the Baleys and the Hedgpeths could take no further action on their claims at that time. Rose, however, was in a more favorable position to press his claim. He had a brother-in-law, Harvey K. S. O'Melveny, an attorney in Cairo, Illinois, who could keep him informed on legal matters affecting his claim. This was the same O'Melveny who had lent Rose the money to purchase the La Fonda Hotel in Santa Fe.

In 1864 Rose again submitted his claim to Congress. Again it was referred to the Senate Committee on Indian Affairs and again sent to the commissioner of Indian affairs for his recommendations. Again the commissioner gave an unfavorable report and the claim was discharged from committee and no further action was taken.

Nothing more happened on Rose's claim until January, 1870. At that time, O'Melveny wrote a letter to his congressman, T. W. McNeely of Illinois, asking if there now existed any treaty or law by which redress could be obtained. Congressman McNeely forwarded O'Melveny's letter to E. S. Parker, the new commissioner of Indian affairs. Commissioner Parker replied to McNeely that there was no other law except the one on which the Senate Committee on Indian Affairs, headed by W. K. Sebastain, based its decision of February 3, 1861 (the Intercourse Act of June 30, 1834), and that the Mojave Indians had no annuities or other monies from which the claim could be paid, even if found true and admitted by the Mojaves.[7]

In early May of 1870, O'Melveny addressed a letter to Governor Anson P. K. Safford of the territory of Arizona, requesting any help he might be able to offer on Rose's claim. This action was probably taken by O'Melveny to satisfy Commissioner Greenwood's criticism that no private satisfaction had been attempted to satisfy the claim. Governor Safford replied that the Mojaves probably committed the depredations (a fact that O'Melveny and Rose already knew) since they lived along the Colorado River, and that O'Melveny should contact George L. Andrews, superintendent of Indian affairs for the Territory of Arizona, as he lived near these Indians and was well acquainted with them.[8] Andrews replied that he was powerless in the matter.[9]

These negative responses in no way discouraged Rose in his quest for justice. An act passed by Congress in 1872 gave him new hope. This was an act of Congress approved on May 29, 1872 (Stat. 17, p. 190). This act provided for a reexamination of Indian depredation claims that had been before Congress and were rejected, or had not been acted upon by that body. The act provided for the filing of Indian depredations directly with the Department of Interior, rather than with Congress. The secretary of interior would then send the claim to the commissioner of Indian affairs, his subordinate, for his recommendations. If approved by the Interior Department, the claim would then be sent to Congress for its approval. The method of collection and the requirement that the defendant Indians be in amity with the United States remained unchanged.

Rose took advantage of this act and withdrew his claim from Congress, where it had been gathering dust, and filed it with the Interior Department on February 17, 1873. To press his claim more vigorously, Rose hired a Washington, D.C. attorney, A. T. Britton, of the law firm of Britton and Gray. Rose's brother-in-law and previous legal counselor, Harvey K.S. O'Melveny, had moved to California and was elected county judge in Los Angeles County. It was probably O'Melveny who advised Rose to hire a Washington, D.C. attorney. A lawyer who knew his way around government circles and could deal with bureaucrats was in a much better position to press a claim against the government than was an attorney in a distant location.

The acting commissioner of Indian affairs, H. R. Clum, returned the papers to his superior, the secretary of the interior, with the following comments:

> This claim has been heretofore the subject of action by this office and the Interior Department, and it has also been adversely reported upon by the Committee on Indian Affairs of the U.S. Senate. There being no additional or new testimony submitted, this office is of the opinion that the case cannot be taken up and again reported to the Department of Interior.[10]

With a recommendation like this, Secretary of the Interior Columbus Delano had little choice but to return the papers to Rose's attorney.

Undaunted by this rebuff, Rose and his attorney on June 20, 1874, resubmitted the claim, along with additional evidence, to the Interior Department. Acting Commissioner Clum this time accepted the claim and put the proper legal machinery into motion. The first step was to submit the claim to the Mojave Indians gathered in council. The claim never went this far before. In a letter from the Colorado River Indian Reservation to the Commissioner of Indian Affairs dated February 12, 1875, U.S. Indian Agent J. A. Tonner reported:

> I have submitted the case to the Mojave Indians on this reservation assembled in council and have fully explained to them the nature of the claim and all its particulars; they assure me that the depredation was committed by the branch of the tribe resident in the neighborhood of Fort Mojave and that there are but two persons now on the reservation who were

present at its occurrence. These latter inform me that they were boys at the time and that they recollect the attack of their people upon a large train, presumably that of the claimant, that a good many Mojaves were killed, that one horse was captured and several cattle killed, not many they say, but when further asked admitted that probably many other animals were stampeded. This is all the information I could obtain on the matter. I did not demand any satisfaction for the claimant as the people (with the exception of those two individuals) denied any participation in the outrage complained of by Mr. Rose.[11]

Commissioner Clum recommended to his superior, the secretary of the interior, that the sum of $13,819.88 should be enough to fully indemnify Rose for his losses. This amount turns out to be exactly one-half the requested sum of $27,639.76. Clum justified his Solomonic solution on the grounds that Rose presented no clear proof in his petition as to the superior value of his livestock. Knowing claimants sometimes have a tendency to overvalue their property, Clum probably figured fifty percent would be about the right amount. The secretary of the interior must have felt the same way for he sent the claim to Congress without making any changes. Again Congress failed to act on Rose's petition.

Rose's claim remained dormant until some minor changes were made to the law covering Indian depredation claims by an act of Congress approved March 3, 1885 (Stat. 23 p. 326). This act provided the sum of $10,000 to the secretary of the interior for the purpose of investigating certain Indian depredation claims. It further directed the secretary of the interior to make a complete list of all claims previously filed with the Interior Department which had been approved in whole or in part and remained unpaid, and those which had not yet been examined. These would be presented to Congress at its next session. The act still retained the provision that the Indian nation or tribe whom the claim was against be in a treaty relationship with the United States. The act also empowered the secretary of the interior to make additional investigations and take further testimony as deemed necessary to determine the value of the property taken or destroyed. Since Rose's claim had been approved in part by the Interior Department in 1875, he was eligible by this act to submit his claim for reexamination, which he did in July of 1885. This time, however, the Interior Department viewed his claim much differently than it had in 1875. Acting Commissioner of Indian Affairs A. B. Upshaw (there seems to have been a high turnover of acting commissioners in those days) rejected the claim in whole on the grounds that the Mojave Indians were not in amity with the United States at the time that the depredation occurred. He was sustained in his opinion by the secretary of the interior who sent the claim to Congress with the recommendation it be disallowed, which it was.

Rose's claim appeared dead, but again a bill passed by Congress breathed new life into his claim. This piece of legislation was an act of March 3, 1891, titled, "An Act to Provide for the Adjudication of Payments of Claims Arising from Depredations," (Stat. 26 pp. 851–854) This act made major changes in the way Indian depredation cases were to be handled. It allowed those with unpaid claims to sue the United States and the Indian tribe or nation responsible for the depredation in the U.S. Court of Claims. If judgment were obtained by plaintiff and the defendant Indians had no annuities or other monies due them from the United States, the claim would be paid from the United States Treasury. The judgment, or the balance thereof, would then become a lien against any future annuities or monies owed to the defendant Indians by the United States. This act also waived the statute of limitations for claimants, allowing Rose and the other emigrants the right to file suit in the Court of Claims even though their claims were now thirty-three years old.

Rose filed his petition in the U.S. Court of Claims on June 3, 1891, claiming damages of $27,639.76 (Case No. 21760).[12] In his petition Rose listed his address as San Gabriel, California. Because of the long time that had elapsed since the filling of his original claim, he was able to list the name and address of only one of his witnesses. This witness was Gillum Baley, who was living in Fresno, California. All his other witnesses were either dead or had drifted away to places unknown. Later, Rose's attorney was able to locate Major D. H. Rucker, one of the two officers who had inspected Rose's livestock in Albuquerque on the outward journey in 1858 and who had given Rose a letter attesting to the excellent quality and fine condition of the animals Major Rucker had survived the Civil War and was now a retired brigadier general living in Washington, D.C. He was past eighty years of age and his memory had begun to slip, making his deposition of limited value.

It is unknown whether Rose persuaded Gillum Baley to also file an Indian depredation suit in the Court of Claims or whether Baley filed his suit independently of Rose. What is known is that Gillum Baley filed a suit in the Court of Claims (Case No. 8214) in 1892, claiming damages of $7,400. He listed himself and his deceased brother, William Right Baley, who died in 1881, as plaintiffs. Also filing suit at the same time and place was William Pleasant Hedgpeth. He filed as the administrator of his father's estate, Joel Hedgpeth Sr. (Case No. 8373), who died in 1874. The Hedgpeth suit sought damages of $4,340. William Pleasant Hedgpeth gave his address as Tollhouse, Fresno County, California. The heirs of Thomas Hedgpeth, who died in 1877, did not file a suit.

The legislative act of March 3, 1891, allowed for depositions to be taken locally. Gillum Baley, William Pleasant Hedgpeth, and Joel Hedgpeth Jr. journeyed to Tulare, California, by train in July of 1893 to give their depositions in support of the Baley petition. Gillum Baley and Joel Hedgpeth Jr. then gave depositions in support of the Hedgpeth petition. Their counsel was Edward Warren Holland. Counsel for the government was Thomas Ball. As it was in Rose's case, all of the witnesses who had signed affidavits for the Baley and Hedgpeths claims back in Albuquerque in 1858, were now either dead or their whereabouts unknown.

Holland had been a member of the Baley company of the Rose-Baley wagon train, although he was only three years old at the beginning of the trip. Holland was a son of Isaac Taylor Holland and Amanda Melvina Daly Holland. He was now a successful attorney in Tulare, California. This was the reason why Gillum Baley and the two Hedgpeths traveled fifty miles from Fresno to Tulare rather than giving their depositions in Fresno before an attorney who had no first-hand knowledge of the case. In Edward Warren Holland they knew they would be represented by counsel who had actually shared the hardships of the wagon train with them. To represent them in the Court of Claims, both Gillum Baley and William Pleasant Hedgpeth hired the Washington, D.C. law firm of John Wedderburn to represent them as attorney of record. Wedderburn selected A. L. Hughes, one of his law partners, to prosecute the case.

Rose, Baley, and Hedgpeth all based their claims on the Intercourse Act of June 30, 1834, and the July 1, 1852, treaty, which provided for safe passage of white settlers through Apache territory, and on the act of March 3, 1891, which provided for the adjudication and payment of claims arising from Indian depredations. Proving that the attack took place and was committed by the Mojave Indians, and proving the amount of the damages, could be done by the affidavits and depositions of witnesses. But proving that the Mojave Indians were a branch of the Apaches and were in amity with the United States would be a different matter. In an attempt to show that the Mojaves were a branch of the Apaches, claimants in their petitions quoted from the reports of Indian agents dating back to the 1850s in which the Mojaves had been referred to as a "Branch of the Apaches in blood and belonging to them generally." In an attempt to prove the Mojaves were in amity with the United States at the time of the attack, claimants quoted statements made to them by army officers and citizens in Albuquerque on the outward trip in June of 1858, in which they were assured that all Indians living along Beale's Wagon Road were friendly and peaceful. Claimants also stated in their petitions they had done nothing to provoke the Mojave Indians or give them cause for the attack. Quite to the contrary, they stated they had acted in a friendly manner toward the Mojave Indians at all times and had distributed gifts valued at between one hundred and two hundred dollars to these Indians.

The interest of the United States was defended by the office of the U.S. Attorney General. Acting Assistant Attorney General Charles W. Russell and Assistant Attorney W. H. Robinson were assigned to the case. The Mojave Indians did not hire separate counsel but relied upon Russell to represent them. The United States, in a brief filed July 1, 1891, in answer to the claimants' petitions, quoted in part from a report written by Special Agent Bailey who stated in his report, "The term 'Apache' seems to be generic and is applied indiscriminately to all the tribes living on or near the thirty-fifth parallel from the Tontos on the west to the Mescaleros on the east." (Senate document, 2nd session, Vol. I, 1858–59, pp. 557–58)

The brief goes on to recite the reports of previous commissioners of Indian affairs who had rejected the claims on the grounds that the Mojave Indians were not in a treaty relationship with the United States at the time of the attack, and therefore the Interior Department had no jurisdiction in the matter. The government contended that the Mojaves were a separate and distinct tribe and were not in amity with the United States at the time of the attack on the Rose–Baley wagon train on August 30, 1858. The government claimed that the Mojaves were not brought into a treaty relationship with the United States until the conclusion of military operations which Lieutenant Colonel Hoffman began on January 9, 1859, a full six months after the attack. The brief concluded with the following statements:

> From all the evidences which have been cited it appears that at the time of the depredation these Indians [the Mojave] were nothing more and nothing better than the most savage wild Indians, caring nothing for the Government of the United States, not dependent upon it, not cared for by it, in no way subject to its control and to be feared just as a man might fear a wild beast, and to be slain without compunction just as one would kill a rattlesnake or a mountain lion.
>
> It is therefore respectfully submitted that this plea must be sustained and the suit dismissed for want of jurisdiction.
>
> Charles W. Russell
> Acting Assistant Attorney General
>
> W. H. Robinson
> Assistant Attorney[13]

The Court of Claims took its time in deciding the case. More briefs were filed and more motions were put forward by both sides. Finally, on March 21, 1898, the court announced its decision. It rendered a judgment of dismissal in all three suits (Rose, Baley, Hedgpeth) on the grounds that the defendant Indians (the Mojave) were not in amity with the United States at the time of the attack, and that the Court of Claims lacked jurisdiction in these cases. Section 7 of the act of March 3, 1891, stated that the judgment of the Court of Claims on Indian depredations was final and could not be questioned unless a new trial or a hearing was granted.

Rose, Baley, and Hedgpeth filed motions to set aside the judgments and grant new trials on the grounds that the court erred in dismissing the cases and that the findings of fact were contrary to the evidence. The motions for new trails were all dismissed. The only legal remedy left to the claimants was to appeal to the U.S. Supreme Court. Rose filed an appeal with the Supreme Court in 1899, but because of financial constraints, Baley and Hedgpeth did not. The U.S. Supreme Court in 1900 refused to hear Rose's appeal, thus ending one of the longest Indian depredation cases in United States court history.

By then, all the original claimants were dead.

CHAPTER 11

The Later Years

All the members of the Rose-Baley wagon train who settled in California became useful and productive citizens of their
adopted state. Some were elected to political offices while others occupied positions in the business world or in churches, but most followed
more mundane vocations such as farming, mining, blacksmithing,
teamstering, and the like. All died relatively poor, although L. J. Rose
and Gillum Baley accumulated considerable wealth at points in their
lives. Most enjoyed good health and a reasonably long life span. One,
Elizabeth Burgett Jones lived beyond the century mark. All were true
pioneers of the Golden State.

John Udell's journal ended with his arrival at the homes of his
sons, Oliver and Henry, in Silveyville, Solano County, on June 29, 1859.
We know little about his later years. We do know that he spent some
time editing his journal because it was published in 1868 by the
Ashtabula Sentinel Steam Press in Jefferson, Ashtabula County, Ohio,
where he had previously lived. The same publisher in 1856 published
Udell's first book, *Incidents of Travel Across the Great Plains.* The press also
published the local newspaper, the *Ashtabula Sentinel.*

Udell's little book did not make the best seller's list; only a few
copies were sold. If Udell had expected the profits from his literary
efforts to sustain him and Emily in their declining years, he must have
been deeply disappointed. Today, fewer than a dozen copies of this book
are known to exist—each now worth a king's ransom. Fortunately, the
journal was reprinted in 1946 (courtesy of the Huntington Library) by
N.A. Kovach in Los Angeles, California, with an introduction by Lyle
H. Wright, as one of its California Centennial Series. However, even
this edition is becoming difficult to find.

It is likely that John and Emily Udell had to depend on the bounty of their two sons for much of their sustenance during their twilight years. Udell might have regaled his friends (strangers, too, if they would listen) with tales of danger and hardships that he had encountered during his four transcontinental journeys. These stories might have earned him a few free meals or other gratuities.

John Udell and his two sons, Oliver and Henry, are listed in *The Poll Lists of the Election District of the County of Solano, for 1867* as voters in the Silveyville district, according to Lyle H. Wright's introduction to the 1946 reprint of Udell's journal. He credits his information to Miss Mabel R. Gillis, a librarian at the California state library. After the railroad bypassed Silveyville in favor of Dixon, many of Silveyville's residents moved to Dixon and other nearby settlements. The Udells might have joined this exodus. Melvin Bliven of Wedderburn, Oregon, a descendant of John and Emily Udell, states that Emily Udell died April 19, 1868, in Dixon, Solano County, California, and that John Udell then married Mrs. Clarinda Anderson on January 15, 1871, in Sonoma County, California.[1] John's son, Oliver Udell, died December 11, 1872. His obituary, printed in the *San Francisco Examiner* for December 17, 1872, and copied in the *Solano Democrat* for December 21, listed his father, John Udell, as one of his survivors but did not give an address for him. John Udell's name then disappears from the records of Solano and Sonoma counties.

John Udell died June 30, 1874, six days after his seventy-ninth birthday, according to Melvin Bliven, who found the record in a family Bible.[2] He is buried in the Paskenta Cemetery, Paskenta, Tehama County, California. He had a daughter, Caroline Wood, who was living in Tehama County at the time. He might have been living with her at the time of his death. We do not know what happened in Udell's subsequent marriage; his second wife is not buried in the Paskenta Cemetery. Although the details of his death and later years are unknown, his little journal is a fitting monument to the accomplishments of a pioneer who crossed the western plains four times before the advent of the railroad.

As for the other family Beale brought with him to California, the Joel Hedgpeths, their new home did not turn out to be the Promised Land they had hoped for. Shortly after the family's arrival in

Visalia, Jane Hedgpeth fell ill and died. She had been in poor health since the forced return to Albuquerque. The exact date and the cause of her death are unknown, but most likely, the hardships and privations of the overland trip to California played a part in her early demise. Jane Hedgpeth was fifty-one years old at the time of her death in 1859. She was buried in the Lone Oak Cemetery, near the town of Ivanhoe, Tulare County, California. The cemetery was abandoned and untended for many years, during which time vandals plundered the site and removed many of the headstones, including Jane Hedgpeth's. Therefore, her exact grave site is unknown. Annie R. Mitchell, the well-known and respected historian of Tulare County, stated in a letter to the author that during the 1930s a Mrs. Sadie McGinnis Connelly, who had family members buried there, compiled a list of burials in the cemetery from the headstones still in place at the time. The name Mrs. Joel Hedgpeth was on this list. These names were later placed on a marker at the cemetery by the Tulare County Historical Society.[3] Today the site of the cemetery is surrounded by a citrus grove.

Joel Hedgpeth later married Ruth Enloe in Visalia on December 9, 1861.[4] We know little about this marriage except that he was living in Millerton, then the county seat of Fresno County, when he died on June 12, 1874. With him at the time of his death was his good friend and fellow member of the Rose-Baley wagon train, Gillum Baley.[5] Joel Hedgpeth was buried at the old Fort Miller cemetery which is now under the waters of Millerton Lake.[6] Like that of his first wife, Jane, his grave site also was lost. Descendants of the couple erected a memorial stone to their memory at the Academy Cemetery at Academy, Fresno County, California, where several of their descendants and fellow wagon train members are buried.

Three of the sons of Joel and Jane Hedgpeth, Thomas R. (Riley), Lewis J. (Johnson), and Joel Hedgpeth Jr. became ministers in the Methodist Episcopal Church, South. Thomas R. Hedgpeth, the eldest son, spent the remainder of his life in Missouri serving his God as a minister of the gospel. His obituary appeared in the Church Minutes for the Missouri Conference for 1887 and stated in part:

> Thomas R. Hedgpeth departed this life at the residence of
> his son, Rev. Henry Hedgpeth in Rockport Atchinson County,
> Mo., on the 24th day of March 1887, aged about fifty-seven years.

His funeral service was preached on the following Sabbath at Salisbury, Chariton County [Missouri], C. I. Van Deventer, officiating. . . . With a vigorous and inquiring mind, and by diligent application to Study—especially to the Holy Scriptures— Brother Hedgpeth attained to more than average ability as a preacher of the Gospel, one whom the people generally heard with interest and edification. . . . He lived the life of the righteous, was greatly comforted and blessed of God in his affliction, and his end was peace. . . .[7]

The church minutes for 1917 reported the death of his widow, Eliza Jane Hedgpeth:

Mrs. Eliza Jane Hedgepeth [*sic*] died Tuesday morning, April 10, at 8:30 o'clock, at the home of her son, Dr. C. E. Hedgepeth, 301 1–2 Illinois Ave, Rockport, Mo.[8]

Lewis J. Hedgpeth served as a circuit rider in the San Joaquin Valley of California during the 1860s. Because of poor health (probably tuberculosis) he was transferred to Phoenix, Arizona, where he served for a number of years as chaplain for the Arizona Territorial Legislature. He died December 18, 1912, in Phoenix, Arizona.[9] There are descendants still living in Arizona.

Joel Hedgpeth Jr. better known as Joel Hedgpeth, D.D. (Doctor of Divinity), served in the Pacific Coast Conference of the Methodist Episcopal Church, South, holding pastorates in the San Joaquin Valley and the gold rush country. He was the author of a recollection entitled *A Trip Across the Plains in 1858–1859*, which revealed many details of the Rose-Baley wagon train. He died June 12, 1922, and was buried in the cemetery at Academy, California.[10]

William Pleasant Hedgpeth was the only one son of Joel and Jane Hedgpeth who did not choose the ministry for a career. Instead, he became a farmer and cattle rancher near Tollhouse in the foothills of the Sierra Nevada in Eastern Fresno County. He was chosen to be the administrator of his father's estate, probably because he was the only one of the sons who wasn't a minister and therefore more likely to be settled in one place. Methodist ministers in those days were (and still are) frequently on the move. It is interesting to note that he was not appointed the administrator of his father's estate until 1892, eighteen years after his father's death. This suggests that his father left no estate at the time of his death and that William Pleasant was appointed the administrator for the sole purpose of pursuing the heirs' possible rights in the Indian depredation suit.

Of all the members of the Rose-Baley wagon train, none suffered more grief or sorrow than Mary Brown. During the overland journey she lost her husband, Alpha, her only son, Orrin, and her daughter, Sallie Fox, was severely wounded by Mojave arrows. After her arrival in California, she kept house for her brother, George Baldwin, in Placerville until he died there some years later. While living in Placerville, Mary Brown married her third husband, Judge James Johnson. She and Johnson had two sons and a daughter: Edward (Ned), Eugene, and Lila Johnson. According to Edith Allen Milner, Mary Brown's life was always a struggle financially and otherwise. The Promised Land of California never quite panned out for her. But in spite of a hard life, she lived to the age of seventy-five, dying in Alameda in 1899.

After arriving in Placerville, Sallie Fox went to live with her mother's sister, Lavinia, and her husband, Darwin De Golia. Sallie's older sister, Sophia Frances (Franc), lived with Mrs. Brown's other sister, Julia, and her husband, Josiah Allison, in Vacaville where Sallie had planted her walnuts before going to Placerville. This helped to relieve some of the financial pressure on Mary Brown. It is unknown where Sallie's two half-sisters, Relief (Liefy) and Julia Brown, lived during this period, but they probably stayed with Mary Brown.

The De Golias both taught elementary school in the gold rush country, and from them Sallie developed an interest in teaching and became a school teacher. Her first teaching job was at Spanish Dry Diggings near Georgetown in El Dorado County. She also taught at Coloma and in Placerville. Later, the De Golias moved to San Francisco, taking Sallie with them. She taught elementary school in that city for three years. While living in San Francisco, Sallie earned extra money by working as an artist coloring photographs for studios. She also painted and sold oil paintings.

In 1870 Sallie took a trip back to the land of her early childhood in Iowa. She took along a souvenir of the battle with the Mojave Indians, the little dress that she had worn on the day of the battle, with the arrow holes clearly visible in the front of the garment.

While relating the story of the Indian attack and describing how she was wounded, a little boy in the group excitedly asked, "And did you live?" The little dress with the arrow holes in it is now preserved at the Harbison House Museum on the grounds of the Nut Tree Amusement Park near Vacaville, California.

Sallie married Oliver Perry Allen in San Francisco on August 17, 1873. Allen was a graduate of the naval academy and had served as a naval officer during the Mexican War. After the war he resigned from the navy and entered the banking business, working his way up until he became an officer with the Anglo-Californian Bank. They lived most of their married life in Berkeley, California. Sallie and Allen had three children: a son, Edward Oliver Allen; a daughter, Edith Mary Allen; and Julia, who died in infancy. Edward was named after E. O. Smith, just as Sallie said she would do if she ever married and had a son.

The Allens gave their children a good education. Both graduated from the University of California, Edward with a law degree and Edith with a degree in music. After Oliver Allen's death in 1901, Sallie and Edith went to Europe where Edith studied music in Berlin. Edith married Charles Milner in 1914. They had one child who died in infancy. Edith was always interested in the stories about the journey to California, carefully recording her mother's talks about the trip across the plains with the Rose-Baley wagon train. It is from these accounts that we learned many of the details of Sallie's life.

Sallie Fox Allen died at the age of sixty-seven at the Masonic home in Napa, California, on February 7, 1913, (her husband had been a Mason). She was buried in the Allen family plot at Mountain View Cemetery in Oakland, California.

Sallie's older sister, Sophia Frances, usually called "Franc," married William Randolph Galleher in El Dorado County in 1862. They reared six children and lived most of their married life in the vicinity of Lotus, El Dorado County, where Franc died October 10, 1896, at the age of fifty-three. She was buried at nearby Coloma, the site where gold was first discovered in California. Sallie's half-sister, Relief (Liefy), who was an invalid all her life, died before reaching maturity. She was the daughter of Alpha Brown from his first marriage. (There was also an older daughter from this marriage, Mary Ann, who did not make the trip west with the Rose-Baley wagon train.)

Sallie Fox's other half-sister, Julia Brown (daughter of Alpha and Mary Brown, and the sister of Orrin Brown), married Arthur J. Foster of San Francisco. They reared two children and lived most of their married life in the Bay Area. Julia Brown Foster died October 21, 1927, at her home in Berkeley, California, at the age of seventy-seven. She is believed to have been the last surviving member of the Rose company of the Rose-Baley wagon train.

Mary Brown and her family were always grateful to E. O. Smith for having brought them safely to California and for his noble act in refusing payment for their passage. E. O. Smith, despite the heavy financial losses that he incurred while playing the part of the good Samaritan, was not dispirited or overwhelmed by his adversities, but rather retained a cheerful and positive attitude. He frequently stated to his friends, "A man should be willing to sacrifice half of his property for the pleasure of making his home in the Sunset state."[11] He lost more than half of his livestock on the trip, but he still believed there was a future for him in California. After fattening and selling the remainder of his once vast herd of cattle, he began making plans to return to the Midwest to purchase more livestock. He knew that if he could get them safely to California, he could sell them for a hefty profit.

In the autumn of 1860, E. O. and T. O. Smith and six associates, left Los Angeles for Texas where they intended to buy horses and then drive the animals back to California for resale. They believed that horses would be more profitable than cattle. The party traveled the Southern Route, for they were still fearful of Beale's Wagon Road and the Mojave Indians.

While passing through Apache country, they were attacked by a group of about thirty Apache warriors. They were able to repel the attack but lost several of their horses to the Indians. They encountered many more hardships, including an eighty-six-mile stretch without water. At last, they arrived safely in El Paso, where they planned to rest and relax for a few days. But they noticed something strange about the place! The Stars and Stripes was not flying from the flag pole, and in its place flew the Lone Star flag of the Republic of Texas. All one heard was talk of war and secession. The Smiths and their companions learned that Texas had seceded from the United States and was about to join a new nation called the Confederate States of America.

Realizing this was not a propitious time to launch a new business venture, the Smiths and their associates canceled their business plans and hurried to their homes.[12]

Back home in Decatur, Illinois, E. O. Smith was eagerly greeted by his family and friends. Shortly after his arrival, his fellow citizens elected him mayor of Decatur. His tenure of office coincided with the Civil War, making the duties of the office especially important. Smith applied himself diligently in helping his country prepare for war. Decatur raised and fed regiment after regiment of soldiers for the Union Army. Although a Democrat, E. O. Smith was a firm believer in the Union cause and in President Abraham Lincoln, who was a personal friend. Smith's first wife, Harriet Krone Smith, died in 1867. In 1869 he married Mrs. Catherine Hillman of Elmwood, Illinois. She was a well-educated woman and was very active in the feminist movement

Unable to forget his pleasant memories of California, E. O. Smith and his family returned to the Golden State in 1870. This time the trip west was made on the newly completed transcontinental railroad, and it was a much more comfortable journey than his previous trips by oxen and covered wagon. He settled near San Jose, where he became a wealthy and successful farmer. He was actively involved in civic affairs and local politics, and was elected a delegate from Santa Clara County to the California state constitutional convention of 1879, thus having played a part in drafting the constitutions of two states—Illinois and California.

E. O. Smith died at his home in San Jose from a sudden heart attack on March 8, 1892. A memorial sketch containing many eulogies was printed by the *San Jose Mercury*, March 12, 1892. Among those attending the funeral, according to the memorial sketch, were two members from the Rose-Baley wagon train: Mrs. O. P. Allen (Sallie Fox) and Mrs. Julia Foster (Julia Brown).

E. O. Smith should certainly be considered one of the heroes of the Rose-Baley wagon train. Although not a member of this group until he joined them at White Rock Spring in the retreat to Albuquerque, the assistance he rendered the starving emigrants made it possible for them to reach the settlements of New Mexico. He could just as easily have given them a small handout of food and continued on his way to California, but instead, he turned back with them, sharing their misery and nurturing them from his own dwindling larder. This unselfish act saved many lives.

Little information is available about T. O. Smith (Thomas O. Smith), the younger brother of E.O., except that he accompanied his brother on the cattle-driving expedition to California in 1858–59. He was closely involved in his brother's various business enterprises. E. O. Smith's memorial sketch states that Thomas O. Smith married Evaline Hillman, a daughter of E. O. Smith's second wife, Catherine Hillman Smith. The article also states that they lived in San Jose. There is a Thomas O. Smith buried in section one, block 115, of the Smith family plot at the Oak Hill Cemetery in San Jose. His age is given as fifty-five on the headstone, and his date of death is given as February 10, 1875.

Another hero of this ill-fated wagon train was Gillum Baley. His slaying of the Mojave chief leading the attack against the wagon train might have saved the emigrants from total massacre. The disaster at the Colorado River, with the loss of his wagons and livestock, was a serious blow to his dreams and aspirations, but like E. O. Smith, Gillum Baley viewed his losses as only a temporary setback. He still believed that California was the land of opportunity. After all, he had his family and his health; what more did a man need? Having experienced some success as a forty-niner, he decided to try his luck once more as an argonaut. Gold was still being found in some quantity along the San Joaquin River above Fort Miller and along the nearby Fresno and Chowchilla Rivers. After moving his family into the commissary quarters of abandoned Fort Miller, he began mining along the San Joaquin River. He did not have much success on that stream, but the Fresno and Chowchilla Rivers proved more fruitful, enabling him to purchase a few head of cattle.

During the summer of 1861 Gillum Baley attempted to establish a home on the Chowchilla River at a place ever since known as Bailey (Baley) Flat, but the great floods of 1861 and 1862 washed everything away, putting an end to his dreams of a cattle ranch on the Chowchilla.[13] Undaunted by still another reversal, he continued his mining activities, never giving up on his plans for acquiring land and cattle in California. A small break came his way in 1862 when he was appointed justice of the peace. This position provided him with a small income from fees collected on civil cases as well as some prestige and visibility in the community.

Gillum Baley was elected a county judge in 1867. This was the highest judicial office in the county under the 1850 constitution. (There was a district judge on a higher level, who had jurisdiction over several counties.) He served as county judge for twelve years, gaining a reputation as an honest and incorruptible jurist. It has been reported that not a single case of his was ever reversed on appeal.[14] It was during his tenure of office that the county seat was moved from Millerton to the newly created town of Fresno (1874). The Central Pacific Railroad had been completed through the San Joaquin Valley in 1872, and Millerton was now off the beaten path.

One of the first things Judge Baley did after moving to Fresno was to organize St. Paul's Methodist Episcopal Church, South. This was the first church established in the city of Fresno. It was started with just seven members, five of them from Judge Baley's own family. The first services were held in a room upstairs over a saloon. Later, a small wooden structure was built at the northeast corner of L and Fresno Streets.

Politically, Judge Baley was an active member of the Democratic Party. His only fraternal connection was with the Independent Order of Odd Fellows (I.O.O.F.), in which he held various offices.

In 1879 California adopted a new state constitution which made major changes in the judicial system by combining the offices of district judge and county judge into a new court known as the superior court. Judge Baley was a candidate for the new position, but lost his bid in the primary election. The county was growing more populous and its citizens were becoming better informed; voters might have felt that the new office required someone with a law degree and more formal training than the frontier education possessed by Judge Baley.

Although he was now sixty-seven years old, Judge Baley was not one to take it easy or think about retirement. In 1881 he opened a grocery store in Fresno in spite of the fact that he had no previous experience in the grocery business. As the business grew, he took in his son-in-law, James M. McCardle, as a partner. McCardle was married to Ellen Baley, the little girl who had been lost in the desert during the overland trip to California. Later, he bought out McCardle's interest and brought in his son, George, as a partner.

In 1884 Judge Baley was persuaded by his friends to reenter the political arena, this time as a candidate for the office of county treasurer, to which he was easily elected. He continued the operation of his grocery business while serving as county treasurer. Apparently the strain of both jobs was too much for him, for he did not seek reelection in 1886 (the term of office for county officers, except for judicial officers, was two years in those days).

Because of declining health, Judge Baley sold his grocery business in 1888. Now seventy-five years of age, he still retained his full mental vigor and remained active in church and political affairs. He had great faith in the future of Fresno County and made many investments in local enterprises. He is listed as a capitalist in both the 1891 and 1892 Fresno city directories. Both the city and the county grew rapidly during the decade of the 1880s. It appeared that he and Permelia could look forward to financial security in their twilight years. But it wasn't to be! The Panic of 1893, although bad throughout the nation, was especially hard in Fresno County. All the local enterprises in which he had invested failed. What had promised to be the golden years for Judge and Permelia Baley suddenly became a period of despair. To keep a roof over their heads and creditors away from their door, they were forced to turn their home into a boarding house. Nearing their eighties, the aged couple now had to cater to the whims of paying guests in their home.

Their only hope now lay with the successful outcome of the Indian depredation suit which had been filed in the U.S. Court of Claims. It was this hope that Judge Baley took with him as he boarded the train and journeyed to Tulare to give his deposition in July of 1893. But as the case dragged on, even this faint glimmer of hope began to disappear. He never lived to see the conclusion of the case.

Judge Gillum Baley died at his Fresno home after a short illness on November 11, 1895, at the age of eighty-two. His obituary, which appeared in the *Fresno Morning Republican* for November 12, 1895, carried this caption: "GILLUM BALEY DEAD. A Life of Honor and Without Reproach." The *Fresno Daily Expositor* for this date captioned his obituary: "A GOOD MAN IS GONE. JUDGE GILLUM BALEY IS NO MORE." The *Fresno Daily Expositor* ran an editorial in its November 13, 1895, edition which read in part:

Judge Gillum Baley, whose death last Wednesday night was noticed in the EXPOSITOR of the 14th inst, was esteemed by all who knew him as being as honorable and as high minded a man as ever lived in Fresno County. He seems to have had no enemies but to have won the esteem and love of all. . . . He was not a trained lawyer, but his excellent judgment and incorrupt-ible fairness in dealing with people made him pre-eminently the man for the place. Though on the bench for a dozen years, not a single decision of his was reversed.

The Fresno County Bar Association passed a series of resolu-tions honoring Judge Baley on November 12, 1895. They were pub-lished in the *Fresno Daily Expositor* on November 13, 1895, and captioned, "A MOST JUST JUDGE." A similar series of resolutions was adopted by the Fresno County Board of Supervisors.

His funeral, attended by an overflow crowd, was held on November 12, 1895, at St. Paul's Methodist Church, South, which he had organized in 1874. The next day the body was taken by horse-drawn carriage to the pioneer cemetery at Academy where he was laid to rest beside his two sons, William Moses and Lewis Leach Baley.

Permelia Baley lived until December 8, 1906. Her funeral was also held at St. Paul's Methodist Church. She was buried at the Academy cemetery beside her husband, following one of the last horse-drawn funeral processions held in Fresno. Her obituary in the *Fresno Morning Republican* was captioned: "OLD RESIDENT PASSES AWAY. Death Closes Useful Life of Mrs. P. E. Baley." The obituary read in part:

> Mrs. Permelia E. Baley, one of the oldest and most respected residents of Fresno County died yesterday morning at 10 o'clock at the residence of S. J. [Stonewall Jackson] Ashman [her grandson] 154 Abby Street. In the passing of Mrs. Baley, the community loses one who was beloved and honored by all as a woman of noble character, whose life has been spent in assisting to build the county. . . .

Ernestine Winchell devoted her weekly column "Fresno Memories" to Permelia Baley in the Sunday, November 29, 1925, edi-tion of the *Fresno Morning Republican*. It was entitled, "An Eventful Life."

The relationship between the two brothers, Gillum and William Right, was always close. They were together in California during the gold rush, had farmed near each other in Nodaway County, Missouri, and had shared the dangers, the privations, and the suffering during the long and tragic overland journey to California with the Rose-Baley wagon train. They parted company at the end of the long journey only because of dire necessity. Gillum went to Fort Miller to mine gold. William Right remained in Visalia where he had found employment as a teamster hauling supplies from Stockton down to the mining camps in the Sierras and back to Visalia.

This job kept him on the road for long stretches of time. Growing tired of being away from home and family so much, William Right yearned to get back into farming and cattle raising. In 1864 he and Nancy purchased one hundred and sixty acres on Big Dry Creek in Fresno County, near the property of their daughter and son-in-law, Sarah Margaret and John G. Simpson. The property was located at the beginning of the Sierra Nevada foothills and was suitable only for dry farming and cattle raising. He grew grain on the acreage and used the grain to fatten hogs for the market. He also grazed sheep on public lands in the San Joaquin Valley near where the city of Fresno now stands.

William Right Baley helped establish a private school at Big Dry Creek. Because of its high quality of education, it soon became known far and wide as the Academy. Eventually the community of Big Dry Creek began to be called Academy instead of Big Dry Creek, and Academy it is today on the map of Fresno County.

He and Nancy were actively involved in establishing the Methodist Episcopal Church, South, at Academy. He was one of the trustees of the church at the time the church building was erected in 1876. This is the oldest church building in Fresno County and it is still used on special occasions by the nearby Clovis United Methodist Church.

William Right Baley died November 18, 1881, at the age of sixty-two. His obituary appeared in the *Fresno Weekly Expositor* on November 23, 1881:

> DEAD—William Wright [Right] Baley, an old and esteemed citizen of this county, died at his home on Big Dry Creek last Friday night after being seriously ill for some weeks. He was a brother of Hon. Gillum Baley, of this place, and has resided in this County for a number of years, where he has reared a family of children. He was a native of Missouri, and at the time of his

death was in the sixty-first year of his life. His remains were interred at the cemetery near his home last Sunday, being followed to their last resting place by a large concourse of mourning friends and relatives.[15]

Nancy Margaret Funderburk Baley died March 6, 1900, at the age of eighty, and is buried next to her husband in the cemetery at Academy. Her obituary appeared in the *Fresno Morning Republican* on March 7, 1900:

> MRS. BAILEY DEAD. Passing Away of a County Pioneer.
>
> Mrs. Nancy Bailey, [Baley] a native of Academy [she was actually a native of Tennessee], died yesterday at Academy. She was a member of one of the oldest families that settled in this County when Academy was a thriving village and before Fresno was in existence. Mrs. Bailey was a sister-in-law of the late Judge Gillum Bailey. Her husband died several years ago. Several children, among them John and Henry Bailey, survive their parents, and the Simpson boys are grandchildren.
>
> The death of "Grandma Bailey" as the deceased was familiarly and affectionately known, will be mourned by the whole neighborhood.

The Daly and Holland families also entrusted their futures to the new state of California. After arriving at Saw Mill Flats in Tuolumne County, in January of 1860, John Lucas Daly and Irene Morrow Daly settled on Turnback Creek near the village of Summersville, which has since been merged with the town of Tuolumne. Apparently they lived quiet lives and left very little information about themselves in the records of Tuolumne County. Their names do not appear in the indexes for either the 1860 or the 1870 U.S. census for Tuolumne County. In the December 15, 1877, issue of the *Tuolumne Independent*, there appeared this brief obituary:

> DIED: Near Summerville [Summersville], Irene Daly, a native of Kentucky, age 64 yrs. Missouri and Oregon papers please copy.

No follow-up article appeared in later editions of this newspaper. The reference to Oregon newspapers indicates that the Dalys might have lived in Oregon for a time during the 1860s and the 1870s.

This would account for their names not being listed in the 1860 or the 1870 census for Tuolumne County.

The name John Lucas Daly appears in the 1879 and 1880 voter registration lists for Tuolumne County. He first registered on August 30, 1873. He gave his age at the time of registration as sixty-four, his place of birth as Kentucky, his occupation as farmer, and his place of residence as Turnback Creek. The 1880 census (Page 6, Dwelling No .89, Family No. 89) lists a John L. Daly as living in the household of Isabella (Isabelle) Bucknam. His age is given as seventy-one, his occupation, farmer, and his place of birth as Kentucky. This is consistent with what is known about John Lucas Daly. His relationship to Isabelle Bucknam is given as father. It appears, then, that John Lucas Daly went to live with his daughter Isabelle after the death of his wife Irene in 1877. It was a common practice in those days before Social Security for aged parents to live with one of their children. According to Hart Ralph Tambs, a great grandson of Isabella Bucknam, the Isabella Bucknam listed as the head of household in the 1880 census is the same person as the Adaline (Udell's spelling) Daly that John Udell united in matrimony to Ezra Bucknam in Zuni, New Mexico, on November 1, 1858.[16] Her full name, according to a short biographical sketch of her written by Tambs, was Madeleine Isabelle Adeline Daly Bucknam. She was known as Madeleine by friends and family members.[17]

Tambs stated that the Bucknams did not come to California with the Dalys and the Hollands in 1859, but remained in New Mexico where Ezra was employed by the U.S. government as an Indian agent. Later, Ezra was transferred to Texas. In 1868 the Bucknams moved to California and settled near the Dalys at Summersville where Ezra engaged in farming and mining. Being unhappy in this type of work, Ezra studied law in his spare time and was successful in passing his bar examination. He began a law practice and became a successful attorney. Because of a lack of opportunities in the legal profession in a small place like Tuolumne County, he moved to Oakland in 1877 to further his legal career. Madeleine refused to move to Oakland with him because she didn't like city life. She preferred to remain on their ranch with their children in Tuolumne County. They agreed to a separation and later to a divorce.[18] After a few years in Oakland, Ezra moved to Tulare, Tulare County, where he established a law practice and an insurance business. The divorce is the reason why Madeleine was listed as head of household in the 1880 U.S. census.

In the January 15, 1887, edition of the *Tuolumne Independent*, there appeared this brief obituary:

> DIED: In Summerville [Summersville], January 12th, John Lucas Daly, a native of Kentucky, age 78 years.

Again there was no follow-up in the newspaper and no death recorded at the courthouse in Sonora.

Madeleine spent the remainder of her life on her ranch in Tuolumne County, living in a primitive log cabin built by Ezra before he went away to Oakland. She reared their six children at this ranch. Madeleine never remarried, but Ezra did. He married Sarah M. Enloe Ketcham at Visalia, California, on October 27, 1880.[19]

Madeleine was killed in an accident on November 27, 1913. She was struck by a trolley car while waiting for a train at Lodi, California, where she had gone to visit friends. She was seventy-seven years old at the time of her death.[20] The *Sonora Union Democrat* carried a detailed account of the accident in its December 6, 1913, edition. John Lucas Daly, Irene Morrow Daly, and Madeleine Isabelle Adeline Daly Bucknam are all buried in Carters cemetery near Tuolumne, California.

Isaac Taylor Holland and his wife, Amanda Melvina Daly Holland, son-in-law and daughter of the Dalys, also spent the remainder of their lives in Tuolumne County. Isaac did some placer mining when the family first arrived, but after a few months he returned to his regular trade of blacksmithing, working for the firm of Ford, Haskel, and White in Columbia.[21] The 1860 U.S. census for Tuolumne County shows the family living in Township Two, which included Sonora and Columbia. In 1868 the family moved to Eucher Flat which is near Summersville. Here, Isaac engaged in farming and blacksmithing. This location was also near the Daly ranch. The 1880 census for Tuolumne County shows the family living at Italian Bar, which is on the south fork of the Stanislaus River near Sonora and Columbia.[22] Isaac's age was forty-eight and his wife, Amanda Melvina, was forty-nine, Isaac's place of birth was given as Tennessee; Amanda Melvina's birthplace was given as Missouri. Isaac's occupation was listed as blacksmith. The census reported six children in the family. The two older sons, Hiram and Edward Warren, were no longer living in the household. Hiram, now twenty-six, was listed as single and the head of his own household. Edward Warren, age twenty-four, might have been living out of the county or out of the state at the time.

Isaac Taylor Holland was killed in an accident near Sonora on September 15, 1892, when he was run over by his own wagon while attempting to halt a runaway team. The details of the accident were reported in the *Tuolumne Independent* in its September 17, 1892, edition.

Isaac was sixty years of age at the time of his death. His obituary appeared in the *Union Democrat* of Sonora for September 17, 1892:

> I. T. Holland was an excellent man, industrious, temperate and upright. He leaves a large family to mourn the sad facts of a kind and affectionate husband and father.

A lengthier obituary written by his son, Edward Warren Holland, appeared in the September 24, 1892, edition of the *Union Democrat*.

A second tragedy struck the Holland family only a few weeks later when Hiram, the eldest son of Isaac and Amanda, died on October 11, 1892. Hiram was four years old when he left Missouri with the Rose-Baley wagon train. His death was reported in the *Tuolumne Independent* for October 15, 1892, in its "Sonora News" column. Note the graphic language which was common in those days:

> Constable Hiram Holland, who resides near Summersville, has been ill for some time past. On Tuesday morning he had a severe hemorrhage of the lungs and died a few moments afterwards. He arose from his bed and rushed into another room where his sister Mrs. Lawrey was. As he opened the door the blood gushed from his mouth in volumes and Mrs. Lawrey was frightened into spasms. When she came to, her brother was dead.

Holland's widow Amanda died in Summersville, Tuolumne County, on February 11, 1901. Isaac Taylor Holland, Amanda Melvina Daly Holland, and Hiram Holland were all buried in Carters Cemetery in Tuolumne.

Edward Warren Holland was only two years old when he left Missouri with his parents for California. He grew up in Tuolumne

County, and after trying his hand at several different trades, he decided to become an attorney. He studied law under the guidance of his uncle, Ezra Bucknam, in Tulare, California. In those days one did not have to go to law school to get a law degree. He successfully passed the bar in 1889 and opened a law practice in Tulare. It was to him that Gillum Baley and William Pleasant Hedgpeth turned for legal counsel when they filed their Indian depredation suit against the U.S. government in 1892. He also served as city attorney in for the city of Tulare and helped draft the first city ordinance. Later he served a term as justice of the peace in Tulare. He married Nettie L. Carkeek in Tulare on September 18, 1894.

In 1890 he moved back to Tuolumne County and opened a law office in Sonora. He was appointed district attorney of Tuolumne County in 1905 to fill an unexpired term, and in 1906, he was elected to a full four-year term. In 1908 he won the Democratic nomination for Congress in the first district, but because the district had a 7,000 member Republican majority, he was defeated in the general election. He then returned to private practice.[23]

In 1912 he and his family returned to Tulare, where he practiced law until he retired in 1934. Judge Edward Warren Holland died in Oakland, California, on February 8, 1940. He is buried in the Tulare cemetery next to his wife, Nettie, who died in 1932.

Unlike the other emigrants of the Rose-Baley wagon train who arrived in California in a more or less destitute condition, Rose and his family arrived with a bankroll of $14,000 from the sale of their hotel in Santa Fe. After settling his family into a comfortable home in the San Gabriel Valley, Rose began looking around southern California for property to purchase, but he found nothing that appealed to him as much as the San Gabriel Valley. In 1861 he acquired 1,300 acres near the eastern boundaries of the San Pasquel land grant for a price of little more than one dollar per acre. Today, the beautiful city of Pasadena covers much of this area. At that time most of the land was still in a primeval state consisting of large oak trees and other native flora. Rose went to work clearing the land and planting orchards and vineyards. He called his estate Sunny Slope. It soon became the showplace of southern California.[24]

He constructed a winery for crushing his own grapes and also crushed grapes from other growers. At that time the wine industry in southern California was in its infancy; there were only a few vineyards in the area, all cultivating the Mission grape, a variety named for the missions where it was cultivated by Spanish and Mexican padres. As a wine grape it was only mediocre. Rose found that by growing his grapes without irrigation he could improve the quality of his wine. Not completely satisfied with the product, however, he began experimenting with cuttings from Europe until he found varieties that produced a superior quality of wine. Soon other growers began to follow his example. Lacking money for expensive crushing machinery which had to be shipped out from the East, Rose crushed his grapes by having workers stomp on them with their bare feet.[25] This time-honored method of making wine did not lessen the quality in any way; some believed it might improve the quality by giving it that human touch. Later, Rose added a distillery for distilling some of his wine into brandy. Because of the superior quality of his products, he found a ready market on the East Coast. In 1879 Rose produced 125,000 gallons of brandy. The Internal Revenue Service taxed him $112,500 on the brandy alone.[26]

Rose had gone heavily into debt in developing Sunny Slope, but his investments began to pay off. He now felt free to indulge in one of his lifelong ambitions—horse breeding and racing. Long an admirer of fine horse flesh, he purchased the finest breeding stock on the market and began building barns and practice racetracks at Sunny Slope. He hired the best horse trainer that he could find, a man by the name of Walter Maben. Soon Sunny Slope was noted for its fine stable of trotting horses, of which the best was known as Stamboul the Great. This great thoroughbred was three times voted the best in show at Madison Square Garden in New York City. Later, Rose extended his investment to racing horses. He entered his horses in races at county fairs from San Diego to San Francisco, and he usually won.

As Rose's name became well known in southern California, his friends urged him to get into politics. He yielded to the suggestions, and in 1886 he was elected to the state senate representing Los Angeles County on the Democratic ticket. After serving a term in the state senate, his supporters persuaded him to run for a seat in the U.S. Congress. His opponent at the Democratic convention was George S. Patton, father of the famed World War II general, George S. Patton Jr.

Wining the Democratic nomination in Los Angeles County in those days was tantamount to winning the election. The two became so deadlocked in the balloting that neither could garner the necessary number of votes to secure the nomination. The convention then chose a compromise candidate, Charles Barlow, who won the seat at the general election. This ended Rose's political career.

In 1887 Rose sold his Sunny Slope ranch to an English syndicate for more than one million dollars. He then purchased nine hundred and forty acres just south of Sunny Slope. Rose christened his new estate Rosemead, or Rose's meadow (*mead* is an archaic English term for meadow). At Rosemead he devoted most of his time to horse breeding and horse racing, having divested himself of his winery and distillery interests. Later, the city of Rosemead came into being at this location.

By 1892 Rose had grown tired of the horse-breeding business and sold off his entire stable of race horses at public auction. He then turned over the management of Rosemead to his son, Harry, who developed the acreage for fruit growing. Rose began speculating heavily in real estate, buying and selling so many parcels of land that it is difficult to ascertain just how much property he owned at any one time. He built a fine Victorian mansion in Los Angeles at Fourth and Grand streets for himself and his family. When the house was torn down in 1937, parts of its interior were used as sets for Hollywood movies.

Rose began to diversify his investments to include a copper mine and a smelter in Arizona, a hotel in Ventura, and an opera house in Pasadena. Then, like a bolt of lightning, the Panic of 1893 hit the nation! It caught Rose short of cash and greatly overextended. The value of his investments plummeted while his creditors began pressing him. More and more he began looking to the successful conclusion of his Indian depredation suit as a means of easing some of his pressing financial problems. It must have been quite a disappointment to him when the U.S. Court of Claims dismissed his suit.

On May 18, 1899, Los Angeles newspapers reported that Senator L. J. Rose had taken his own life. He left a note addressed to his wife stating that he had grown weary of his burden of indebtedness. He was seventy-two years old.[27]

He left a legacy as an innovator and a man of great integrity and vision. Rose's meadow, Rosemead appears as the name of a city and as a boulevard on today's maps of Los Angeles County. His wife, Amanda, was named in the will as executrix of the estate. It was she who filed the unsuccessful appeal of her husband's Indian depredation suit with the U.S. Supreme Court. Amanda Rose died in Los Angeles in 1905 at the age of seventy-nine.

The last adult member of the Rose-Baley wagon train to die was Elizabeth Burgett Jones, the mother of Amanda Rose and the mother-in-law of L. J. Rose. She died in Los Angeles on February 26, 1909, at the advanced age of one hundred and five.[28] The last surviving member of the Rose-Baley wagon train, as far as can be ascertained, was Nancy Jane Baley Greenup, daughter of Gillum and Permelia Baley, who died at Clovis, California, on December 10, 1947, at the age of ninety-one.[29] She was just two years old when the wagon train left Nodaway County, Missouri, in 1858.

The young men employed by the Rose-Baley wagon train scattered to various parts of the country after returning to Albuquerque. Consequently, we have little information as to what happened to most of them. But thanks to J. W. Cheney, who interviewed Edward Akey in Van Buren County, Iowa, in 1915, we know something about the later lives of four of the young men who worked for Rose: William Harper, William Stidger, Edward Akey, and Lee Griffin (Leander St. Clair Griffin). William Stidger was one of the young men (the other was Edward A. Young) whom Rose sent back to the previous camp to look for the Bentner family, and in the process discovered the mutilated body of one of the Bentner girls. Edward Akey and Lee Griffin were the two herders who were caught out in the open by the Mojave Indians at the beginning of the battle. They were able to fight their way back to camp, but both were wounded by Mojave arrows; Griffin was seriously wounded.

Cheney's interview with Akey was published in the *Annals of Iowa* in July, 1915, under the title "The Story of an Emigrant Train" (previously cited in this book). Unfortunately, neither the *Annals of Iowa* nor the Iowa Historical Society provided any information on J. W. Cheney. Cheney reported:

> In the spring or summer of 1859 Harper and Stidger returned to Iowa, and at the beginning of the Civil War in 1861, Harper was a teacher and Stidger a student in Daniel Lane's justly celebrated Keoosauqua Academy.

Harper enlisted in the first company raised in Van Buren County, Company F, 2nd Iowa Infantry, and was a second lieutenant when killed in his regiment's famous charge at Fort Donelson, February 15, 1862. Stidger enlisted as a private in Company E, 15 Iowa Infantry, was slightly wounded in the leg and thigh at Corinth. He served nearly four years and was promoted until he became adjutant of his regiment. He died at Red Oak, Iowa in 1880.

In the Civil War, Lee Griffin became a Confederate "bushwhacker," was captured, made his escape and armed himself, was pursued and overtaken, refused to surrender and was shot down, but continued to fight as long as he could handle his two revolvers.

After getting back to Albuquerque, Mr. Akey remained in the Southwest a year or two before returning to Iowa. He is now 83 years old and well-preserved for his age.

Edward Akey died March 16, 1922, just a few days short of his eighty-ninth birthday. His rather lengthy obituary appeared in the *Keosauqua Republican* on Thursday, March 23, 1922.

As previously noted, two of the young men employed by the Baley company became full-fledged members of the wagon train by marriage. These two were August Block, who married America Frances Baley, and William Krug, who married Amelia Catherine Baley. August Block died of a ruptured appendix March 15, 1864, in Visalia, California. He was buried in the Visalia Cemetery. America Frances then married Abraham Yancey. They operated a hotel in Tollhouse, California, for many years. America Frances died at Tollhouse February 17, 1922. She was buried at the Tollhouse Cemetery. William Krug and Amelia Catherine Baley Krug emigrated to Brazil in 1871 and remained there the rest of their lives. William Krug became a well-known architect in Brazil. Amelia Catherine died in São Paulo, Brazil, March 10, 1910.

As for Jose Manuel Savedra, the guide hired in Albuquerque at the advice of the army and the citizens of that town, little is known about his later life. Despite the low opinions of Savedra expressed by both Whipple and Beale, none of the accounts left by the emigrants blamed him for the attack on the wagon train by the Mojave Indians. Admittedly, he had some difficulties in locating water, but it must be remembered that sources of water in the desert can vary greatly from one year to the next, depending on rainfall. Savedra probably did the best he could under the circumstances; neither Whipple nor Beale had anticipated the hostility of the Mojave Indians. After the return to Albuquerque, Savedra filed a lengthy and detailed affidavit in support of the emigrants' Indian depredation claims.

In spite of the fact that the army established Fort Mojave at Beale's Crossing on the Colorado River to protect emigrants from the Mojave Indians, word of the attack on the Rose-Baley wagon train soon became common knowledge, giving Beale's Wagon Road a bad reputation. Consequently, it was little used by emigrants. Miners from California used portions of it to reach newly discovered gold and silver deposits in northwestern Arizona in the 1860s. In the 1860s and 1870s large numbers of cattle and sheep were driven from New Mexico to California over this road. But it wasn't until the Santa Fe Railroad completed its line from Albuquerque to the West Coast in 1883 that Beale's Wagon Road became a major transcontinental route. The Santa Fe Railroad closely follows much of the road. When the automobile came into popular use, the route was developed into a major east-west highway known as the Old Trails National Highway. Ironically, the route experienced its greatest emigrant use during the 1930s, when, as U.S. Route 66, it was the road of choice for thousands of migrants fleeing the dust bowls of the Midwest for the Promised Land of California. During the 1960s much of Route 66 was incorporated into Interstate 40.

Today, motorists can breeze over Interstate 40 between Albuquerque and Los Angeles in a matter of a few hours, whereas it took members of the Rose-Baley wagon train from nine months to two years to cover the same distance. Such are the marvels of time and modern technology.

Appendix A

Roster of the Rose-Baley Wagon Train of 1858, Leaving from
Van Buren County, Iowa (Ages as of May 1, 1858)

Leonard John Rose — age 31
Amanda Markel Jones Rose — age 25
   Nina Elizabeth Rose — age 3
   Annie Wilhelmina Rose — age 1

Ezra M. Jones — age 55
Elizabeth Burgett Jones — age 54
   Edward Jones — age 18

Alpha Brown — age 45
Mary Baldwin Fox Brown — age 35
   Relief (Liefy) Brown — age 13
   Julia Brown — age 7
   Sophia Frances (Franc) Fox — age 15
   Sarah Estelle (Sallie) Fox — age 13
   Orrin Brown — age 5

Twelve to seventeen young men, employees or grubstakers,
including;

   William C. Stidger — age 19
   William Harper — age 20
   Edward Akey — age 20
   Leander St. Clair (Lee) Griffin — age unknown
   Fred Emerdick — age unknown
   Edward A. Young — age unknown
   Joseph McClellan — age unknown
   Andrew V. Custer — age unknown
   Paul H. Williamson — age unknown
   Richard T. Barnes — age unknown
   Henry George — age unknown

Leaving from Missouri (County Unknown).
  Bentner Family of seven, first names unknown, consisting of:

    Father — age unknown
    Mother — age unknown
    Daughter — age 18
    Daughter — age 15
    Son — age 12
    Two younger children — ages and sex unknown

Leaving from Putnam County, Missouri.

  John Udell — age 62
  Emily Merrill Udell — age 64

Two young employees or grubstakers of the Udells

    John Anspach — age unknown
    Tamerlane Davis — age unknown

  John Lucas Daly — age 49
  Irene Morrow Daly — age 44
    Madeleine Isabelle Adeline Daly — age 22
    Nancy Daly — age 16
    Louisa Daly — age 14
    Adelia Ann Daly — age 12
    John Henry Daly — age 9
    Henry Samuel Daly — age 5
    Joseph P. Daly — age 3

  Isaac Taylor Holland — age 26
  Amanda Melvina Daly Holland — age 27
    Hiram H. Holland — age 4
    Edward Warren Holland — age 3
    Thomas Holland — age 1 (twin)
    John Holland — age 1 (twin)

Leaving from Nodaway County, Missouri.

  Gillum Baley — age 44
  Permelia Eleanor Myers Baley — age 38
    Rebecca Margaret Baley — age 20
    Amelia Catherine Baley — age 19
    America Frances Baley — age 17
    Mary Ann Elizabeth Baley — age 16
    George Washington Baley — age 13
    Eleanor (Ellen) Grafton Baley — age 9

Charles Caleb Baley – age 5
Sonora Berthena (Thene) Baley — age 2 months

William Right Baley — age 39
Nancy Margaret Funderburk Baley — age 38
    Sarah Margaret Baley — age 16
    Nancy Jane Baley — age 15
    Henry Gillum Baley — age 12
    William Washington Baley — age 9
    George Pierce Baley — age 4
    Caleb Baley — age 3
    Benjamin Baxter Baley — age 1
    Mary Patience Baley — born and died en route to California

Joel Hedgpeth — age 49
Jane Hudspeth Hedgpeth — age 50
    Lewis Johnson Hedgpeth — age 20
    Joel Hedgpeth Jr. — age 17
    William Pleasant Hedgpeth — age 14
    Elizabeth Ann Hedgpeth — age 9

Thomas Riley Hedgpeth — age 28
Eliza Jane Elliot Hedgpeth — age 26
    Demetrius (Dee) Hedgpeth — age 7
    James Henry Hedgpeth — age 5
    Calloway Hedgpeth — age 2
    Charles Edward Hedgpeth — age 7 months

Seven or eight young men, employees or grubstakers traveling
with the Baley-Hedgpeth company, including:

    William Krug — age 26
    August Block — age unknown
    William Garton — age unknown
    George Hoffman — age unknown
    John Billings — age 25
    Thomas Billings — age 20
    Wesley Gadsbury — age unknown

APPENDIX B

Copy of Letter from John Udell to His Brothers, Published in the Ashtabula (Ohio) Sentinel, April 7, 1859

Some months ago we gave a little notice of the arrival of our old friend at Albequerque, on his fourth trip to California. By the following extract from a letter to his brothers in this place, it will be seen that he has not finished up his "Life and Travels" yet. He seems to live on in the midst of adventures, more interesting than ever, and, as heretofore, getting through his difficulties with a light heart and full trust n [*sic*] Providence.

Alberquerque, New Mexico, March 5, 1859.

Through the protection and grace of God we are still inhabiting our earthly tenement in this wicked world, and are at present dwelling, I think, in the most wicked part of it. My wife and I are here separated more than one thousand miles from children or relatives, among entire strangers, a large majority of which are black, uncivilized creatures, only in the shape of human-kind, our constitutions worn out and quite feeble with old age, hardship and suffering.

On account of the Mormon difficulties we took the road through Kansas and New Mexico. Our company numbered near 100 persons, 60 of whom were women and children. We pursued our journey through Kansas, and nearly through New Mexico, without any serious interruption, When we cam to this place (Alberquerque) we were advised to take a newly explored route. It was said to be much the nearest, safest and best, and all of the company except myself, immediately concluded to take the new route. I had once suffered extremely in taking a new cut off, when crossing the plains; so I used every reasonable effort in my power to prevent taking it, but to no effect. I was compelled from circumstances to travel on with the company, for protection in a savage country. We had already traveled one thousand miles in an Indian country. We traveled on near five hundred miles farther, before we were molested. When we were within one hundred miles of the Colorado River, we were considerably annoyed by the Cosenenos Indians. Arrows were shot among us, killing some of the company's cattle and one man was dangerously wounded, so that he did not recover for more than two months. . We pursued our journey until within a few miles of the Colorado River, in sight of the mountains in California, and in the bounds of the Mohava Indians, we supposing them to be friendly and kind.

Our cattle were all in good plight. Our hearts beat high with the thought that in a few days the perils of our long and tedious journey would be over. A part of our company had gone on before to the river; and we concluded to leave our wagons and a few of our oldest men, together with the women and children, and let our stock be driven down to the river to water and graze with the others, as we calculated to remain there several days to build a raft to cross on, and recruit our stock. My wife and I being the oldest persons in the company, we remained with the wagons, and our young men went with our stock to the river; consequently we were not in the battle with the Indians which took place at the river after our men had been there two days. On the third day, the 30th of August, 1858, the Mohava Indians, to the number of three or four hundred, (as our men judged,) gathered themselves together in the brush and came upon them in surprise, and began pouring their arrows furiously into the encampment, while some of the men were herding the stock and some were engaged in building a raft. As soon as those who were out heard the alarm in camp, they rushed in to the relief of the men, women, and children, forcing their way through the body of the Indians, — in doing which Mr. Brown, the Captain of the train, was killed. Our men fought the Indians for two hours, (as they supposed,) and it was a close, hard fought battle. One of our men was killed and fourteen wounded, besides a German family of seven persons, supposed to be all killed, as they were some two or three miles distant from the camp, and the body of one was found badly mutilated.—

One of the Indian Chiefs, and about fifty (as was supposed) of their men being killed, they dispersed, so that our company made good their retreat. But the Indians had succeeded, in the meantime, in driving off our stock, amounting to near 400, and had made them swim the river, and they all swam after them, leaving it impossible for us to retake them; and thus our wagons were left teamless, and about fifty women and children not able to walk, in the midst of merciless savages. Death seemed to stare us in the face. It was six hundred miles back to this place, (Albequerque,) where the first white settler lived, and two hundred and forty miles to go forward to white settlers in California. We had nothing to expect but immediate death from the hands of merciless savages, or a more lingering death from starvation, when our provisions should be consumed. We were entirely despondent; no team or means to move ourselves from the spot. But, through the favor of Divine Providence, just at this juncture, aid came. A train was discovered coming from behind us. It proved to be from Iowa, going to California. In it were some of our acquaintances. They, hearing of our misfortunes, concluded to turn back; but their teams were not sufficient to carry anything except our provisions and small children,—all the women and children who could walk at all, had to walk.

In this plight we all started back, and our progress under these circumstances was slow. I had kept a pony with me at the wagons, which the Indians did not get; my wife rode upon it and I walked. We had two blankets for a covering at night, while we slept on the ground in the open air—not having a wagon or tent to go into, for we had left all behind, and those who came to our relief had no room in theirs for us. Thus were we aged and infirm people exposes for many long nights to cold rains, dew and snow,—one of us in the 64th and the other in the 65th year of our age.

But we were not yet released from fear of starvation, for there was not half provision enough in the company to support us back to where we could get any.

In travelling back through the Cosenenos we were again much annoyed, and another of our men so badly wounded that his life was despaired of for many days.

After several days of travel, we met a large train of wagons, cattle, horses and mules, owned by Messr. E. O. and T. O. Smith, brothers, and 40 men, all bound for California. These, after hearing of our misfortunes at the Colorado, also turned back. This to us was another token of Divine Providence, on our behalf; for our provisions were nearly all exhausted, and had we not met with these generous-hearted gentlemen, in all human probability we must have perished before we could have reached a place where we could get relief.

These gentlemen immediately called their men together, whom they had contracted to provision and take through to

California, and put the question to them: 'Now are you willing that we should divide our provisions among these unfortunate people, also to give up our seats in the wagons for heir women and children?' adding at the same time—'We have horses and mules for you to ride, and when our provision is exhausted our cattle shall be butchered to supply us with food'. I think every one voted in the affirmative. The Messrs. Smith were honest and true to their word; for our provisions were soon exhausted, and they butchered their cattle, and we lived on the beef, without other food, for near forty days.

Our company now numbered about 200, nearly one-half women and children. On our return journey, when within six days travel of Albequerque, we came to Zana [Zuñi], an Indian town of friendly Indians, where we remained fourteen days, until some of our men went forward to Albequerque. The Officers of the American Army stationed there and at Santa Fe sent us two wagonloads of provisions, which lasted us through.

We all arrived her on the 13th of November, having been two months and a half on our return trip, and suffered much from frost, snow, cold rains, hunger, and much from anxiety. Here the officers of the army, and American citizens did us no small kindness. They granted us thirty days rations of provisions, and gave us many presents of clothing, and necessaries to make us comfortable.

The county is mountainous, sterile, and many portions of it are entirely barren.—They all live in adobe housed, but they are the most comfortable things you see here. They bring their wood twenty-five miles to supply this large place with fuel, and it is pine and cedar when you get it. It was frozen ice here this winter, from eight to ten inches thick, and the snow was six inches deep for a long time. We have remained here now nearly four months, and our situation is not an enviable one for a Christian, I assure you. I have been laboring in government employ most of the time at $15 per month, and a soldier's ration.

Since I commenced writing this, Lieut. Beal has arrived here, and is on his way to California, with a company of men to improve the new road. He has agreed to take my wife and me through upon his own expense, and we expect to start in three or four days, so we have to try the same rout over again, but we hope we have a force sufficient to protect us from the Indians. At any rate we are thankful to get from her.

Appendix C

United States Court of Claims
Indian Depredation Claim of Leonard J. Rose,
Claimant, No. 2176,

v.

The United States, Defendant

Petition. Filed June 3, 1891

Your petitioner respectfully represents:

On or about April 1, 1858, petitioner left Van Buren County, Iowa, for California, via Albuquerque, New Mexico, with his wife and two children, Mr. and Mrs. Jones, and E. C. Jones, the father, mother, and brother of Mrs. Rose. Also Mr. Brown, wife, and five children; Mr. Bentner(who joined a short time afterward), with wife and five children, and seventeen other hands to drive teams and loose animals.

Mr. Brown was major domo or overseer over train and stock. Besides these there were about sixty immigrants who joined in Kansas, most of whom were women and children. Outfit was all of the best and selected, and consisted of two hundred and forty-seven bulls, oxen, cows, and heifers, one very fine Morgan stallion, one large bay fast-trotting gelding, two young matched Morgan mares, ten other good mares and geldings, mostly mares, two sorrel matched large Kentucky mules, six wagons, one carriage with harness, and other things thereto pertaining, and the wagons were loaded with goods, clothing, provisions, tools, and other outfit for the journey. Train arrived at Albuquerque, New Mexico, without any serious accident or loss of stock. At the advice of the Government officers and citizens of Albuquerque they started from there for California over the new route which Lieutenant Beale had lately explored, on or near the thirty-fifth parallel of latitude. The people of Albuquerque were so anxious that this route should be taken that they paid one hundred and fifty dollars ($150) of the five hundred ($500) paid for a guide.

They left Albuquerque, June thirtieth, eighteen hundred and fifty-eight, after procuring Jose Manuel Savedra as guide and Petro as interpreter. Saw no Indians and had no trouble until they arrived at Peach-tree Springs [Peach Springs] about one hundred and twelve miles east of the

Colorado River. There they saw some Indians of the Cosninos [Hualapai] tribe, who stole a mare from petitioner and a mule from Savedra, and two men pursued them for one day, and while going through a narrow cañon some of the Cosninos Indians shot arrows at them from a high mesa. The next evening Savedra saw some Indians on a mountain side, and by speech and sign induced them to come down. They voluntarily spoke about the mare and mule, and said the Mojaves had stolen them, and they (the Cosninos) had retaken them and would return them. Petitioner treated them kindly and feed them, and when they got to Indian Springs, [White Rock Spring] about twenty-five miles from Peach-tree Springs, about twenty-five Cosninos Indians overtook them with the mare and mule. Petitioner gave them all dinner and supper, and some other things, and about fifteen remained in camp all night. Thirty or forty more joined them in the morning. About noon they began to leave in parties of from three to five. After dinner, three oxen, two heifers, and one steer were found missing, and the men following their trail found four of the cattle killed. From Indian Springs to Savedras Springs [Savedra Spring], forty-five miles east of the Colorado River, nothing of importance occurred, although Indians were constantly watching their movements. Near Savedras Springs, E. C. Jones was shot at with arrows by Cosninos Indians, and two arrows struck him and three arrows struck his horse. One other horse was shot, but both recovered and one other was lost. From Savedras Springs to Colorado Mountain Springs, some cattle were shot, but not seriously, and a mare stolen. No other stock was lost by the Cosninos.

On the west side of the Colorado Mountains, the Mojaves made their appearance and at first were very friendly, but on approaching the Colorado River their numbers increased, and they became very insolent, and killed some of the stock and drove some away, and laughed at any attempt of petitioner or his men to interfere. That day petitioner moved camp to the river bank, and there two Mojave chiefs, with about three hundred warriors, visited him. Petitioner gave them presents and the Indians said they were satisfied, and no more cattle would be stolen, and showed them the road, but petitioner had a strict watch kept.

The next day and the third day that they were on the Colorado River (August 31, 1858), petitioner sent some men out to cut logs for a raft, some to herd and watch the animals, and others staid in camp. There were about thirty men in camp, well armed with rifles, shot-guns, and revolvers.

About 10 A.M. three hundred or more Indians were seen crossing the river above the camp. Petitioner felt frightened, and had the animals herded near camp. After dinner one of the men reported many Indians were near the camp, but hidden by the brush, and one of them had told him a steamboat was coming up the river.

About 2 o'clock P.M. the Indians, perhaps three or four hundred strong, who had surrounded the camp, made an attack, but as petitioner had had some warning they only succeeded in driving off the stock. About twenty or twenty-five Indians wee probably killed.

Some off the oxen were frightened by the Indians up to the wagons, and so saved. There were saved seven oxen, five horses, one wagon and its load, and one carriage. All the other wagons and contents had to be left behind. On returning, petitioner met Messrs. Caves, Jordan, Perkins, Davis, and party on the east of the Colorado Mountains. Petitioner and some of his party arrived in Albuquerque October 24, 1858, with one carriage, and four horses, the cattle and one horse having died

That by reason of the said depredation above set out, petitioner lost the following property purchased and owned by him, viz., the amounts stated being the prices paid therefor by petitioner:

Four thorough-bred short-horn Durham bulls, at $500	$2,000.00
One thorough-bred short-horn Durham heifer	400.00
Nine full-blooded short-horn cows and heifers at $200	1,800.00
Fifty-one graded short-horn cows and heifers, at $100	5,100.00
Thirty-one yoke oxen, at $125	3,875.00
Four two and three-year old steers, at $30	120.00
One hundred and one selected cows and heifers, at $50	5,050.00
One Morgan stallion	2,500.00
Two matched Morgan fillies, at $350	700.00
Seven mares and geldings, at $200	1,400.00
Two matched carriage mules, at $250	500.00
Four wagon covers, etc. 2¼ iron axle and spindle, at 150	600.00
One wagon, covers, etc. thimble skane	120.00
Four axes, $6; scythes and sickles, $3; ropes and halters, $40	49.00
Ox balls and rings, $5; ox whips, $12; dried fruit, $42	59.00
Twenty-four chains, at $3.75; medicine, $79; tools, $84.60	253.60
Indians goods, $233.70; saddles, $112; bells, $5	350.70
Meal, $19; flour in St. Louis, $90; flour at Albuquerque, $140.	249.00
Twenty-four bushels beans, $48; buckskins, $17.50; ferriage, $43	108.50
Ox and horseshoe nails, $21; lariats, $9; three tents, $60	90.00
Wagon grease, $4.90; side meat and hams, $367.25	372.15
Extra bows, $6; chopped rye and wheat, $75	81.00
Thirty sacks corn at Albuquerque, $60; one set harness, $45.	105.00
Bedding and clothing, $300; one Sharp's rifle $30	330.00
Three stoves and utensils, stools, knives and forks	75.00
Brass and tin ware, churns, tubs, irons, etc.	150.00
Tobacco and five gallons brandy (left at Colorado River)	90.00
Sugar, coffee, tea, rice, crackers, lard, vinegar, soap, candles,	

cheese, hominy, salt, citric acid, soda, oysters, preserves,
spices, fish, raisins, figs, canned peaches, and tomatoes, &c.   1,154.81
Paid Savedra as guide and Petro as interpreter   250.00
$27,932.76

From the foregoing account the $43 and $250 paid to
Savedra as guide is deducted   293.00
Total amount claimed $27,639.00

That in the year sworn petition of claimant was transmitted to the Department at Washington, D.C., verified by the affidavits of numerous witnesses; that report thereon was made to Congress, but no appropriation was made to pay any portion of said claim; that in 1873 petitioner refiled his claim with the Interior Department, and on or about June 22, 1875, the Commissioner of Indian Affairs recommended to the Secretary of the Interior allowance of the claim for $13,819.88, being one-half the amount claimed; and on January 5, 1876, said Secretary transmitted such report to Congress; that on October 20, 1886, said Commissioner again reported the claim to the Secretary of the Interior, recommending disallowance thereof upon the sole ground that at the time of said depredation the Indians committing same did not hold treaty relations with the United States, and said report was transmitted to Congress on March 11, 1886.

Therefore your petitioner prays judgment against the United States for the sum of twenty-seven thousand six hundred and thirty-nine 75/100 dollars ($27,639.75).

That no assignment of said claim or any part thereof has been made. The said claimant is justly entitled to the amount herein claimed from the United States, after allowing all just credits and offsets; that petitioner came from Germany when twelve years old and was naturalized in Waterloo, Monroe Co., Ill., and has at all times borne true allegiance to the Government of the United States, and has not in any way voluntarily aided, abetted, or given encouragement to rebellion against the said Government.

L. J. Rose

District of Columbia,
City of Washington,
Leonard J. Rose, having been duly sworn, says that he is the claimant named in the foregoing petition, and that all the statements of fact therein contained are true.

Subscribed and sworn to before me this 22d day of May, A.D. 1891.
[SEAL]

Howard S. Reeside,
Notary Public.

Post-office address of claimant, Los Angeles, California; of attorney for claimant, A.T. Britton, No. 624 F St. N.W., Washington, D.C.

NOTES

CHAPTER I

1. L. J. Rose Jr., *L. J. Rose of Sunny Slope 1827–1899* (San Marino, California: The Huntington Library, 1959), p. 7. L. J. Jr. Rose was better known as Leon Rose.

2. L. J. Rose, "Cross Country Reminiscences," *The Californian* (December, 1892—May, 1893): p. 114.

3. Rose Jr., *L. J. Rose of Sunny Slope*, p. 4.

4. Ibid., p. 5.

5. The Mormon War, or Utah War, of 1857–58 was not a shooting war, although it came perilously close to becoming one. Brigham Young, the spiritual leader of the Mormons, also served as the Utah territorial governor, which is contrary to the American policy of separation of church and state. When President Buchanan receive reports of alleged favoritism of church laws over U.S. laws, he appointed a new governor and other public officials to the territory. Fearing that his newly appointed officials would be met with opposition, he dispatched to Utah a large military force under the command of Colonel Albert Sidney Johnston to force compliance. Governor Young reacted to this challenge by declaring martial law, mobilizing the militia, and recalling all Mormons living in other parts of the West back to Utah to help defend the Mormon homeland. Colonel Johnston's military force was delayed in its march to Utah by winter weather. The delay gave time for tempers to cool and the dispute was settled by negotiation.

    Another factor which might have influenced many emigrants in 1858 to travel another route than the Oregon-California Trail was the Mountain Meadows Massacre (see chap. 10, n. 1), the news of which reached the East in the early spring of that year.

6. Rose Jr., *L. J. Rose of Sunny Slope*, p. 6.

7. John Udell, *Journal Kept During a Trip Across the Plains Containing an Account of the Massacre of a Portion of His Party by the Mojave Indians in 1859* (Jefferson, Ohio: Ashtabula Sentinel Steam Press, 1868; reprint, Los Angeles: N. A. Kovach, 1946). Udell is wrong about the year; it should read 1858 instead of 1859. The journal is typical of

many emigrant journals of this period. He recorded mostly such things as weather and road conditions, location of campsites, availability of water, grass, and firewood, number of miles traveled each day, and the distance of each camp site from the Missouri River at Westport. Except for his ongoing quarrels with L. J. Rose, he reveals little of the interrelationships within the group.

8.   Daly and Holland family records, Tuolumne County Genealogical Society Archives, Sonora, California.

9.   *Miners and Business Men's Directory: For the Year Commencing January 1st, 1856. Embracing a General Directory of the Citizens of Tuolumne, and Portions of Calaveras, Stanislaus and San Joaquin Counties, Together with the Mining Laws of Each District, Description of the Different Camps, and Other Interesting Statistical Matter* (Columbia: Heckendorn and Wilson, 1856; reprint, Donald I. Segerstrom Memorial Fund, 1976).

This interesting directory lists a Thomas Holland, an E. W. Holland, and a John Holland, all living in the Saw Mill Flat district of Tuolumne County, and a J. Daly living in the Chinese Camp district. This J. Daly might have been a relative of John Lucas Daly

10.   Joel Hedgpeth Jr., "A Trip across the Plains 1858–1859," eight page typescript, n.d., of original handwritten copy, Holt-Atherton Department of Special Collections, Mss. 2 H453, University of Pacific Libraries, University of Pacific, Stockton, California.

In this recollection Hedgpeth makes the following statement: "While the four families, first mentioned [the two Baley and he two Hedgpeth families] traveled together alone, Judge Gillum Baley was regarded, by a sort of tacit consent, as the captain or leader of the train." This is further confirmed by John Udell on page 20 of his journal where he states, "I am now enrolled in Mr. Bailey's train."

11.   William Right Baley Family Bible, in possession of author. It gives the birth of Mary Patience Baley as August 22, 1858. This indicates that Nancy Baley was five months pregnant at the beginning of the trip in April of 1858.

12.   *A Memorial and Biographical History of the Counties of Fresno, Tulare, and Kern, California* (Chicago: The Lewis Publishing Company, 1891; reprint, Salem, Massachusetts: Higginson Book Company, 1992), pp. 371–73.

13.   Ann Arnold, *Gleanings on the Hedgpeth Line* (Bakersfield, California: Self published, 1977).

14.   Alexander Majors, *Seventy Years on the Frontier* (Minneapolis: Ross E. Hines, Inc., 1965), p. 106.

It is interesting to note that one of the conditions for employment by the firm of Russell, Majors, and Waddell was that their employees not drink, smoke, or swear. A violation of any of these conditions would result in instant termination. Joel Hedgpeth Sr., being a staunch Methodist, probably had no difficulty in complying with these conditions.

15.   *History of Nodaway County Missouri* (St. Joseph, Missouri: National Historical Company, 1882), p. 203.

  This county history lists Joel Hedgpeth Sr. as settling in Hughes township, Nodaway County, in 1840. It lists Gillum Baley and William Right Baley as settling in Grant township, Nodaway County, in 1842.

16.   *History of Nodaway County Missouri*, pp. 85–86. On days when the weather was unsuitable for work, Joel Hedgpeth Sr. and some of his friends, neighbors, and workers would sit around the fire and study Blackstone and the statutes of Missouri. One member of this group, Robert M. Steward, later became governor of Missouri (1857–61).

17.   The five Baley wagons were Murphy wagons. They were prairie schooners manufactured by Joseph Murphy of St. Louis, Missouri. Rose's prairie schooners, as well as those of other members of the wagon train, were very likely Murphy wagons also. Murphy was known for the care he took in selecting the wood for his wagons. He used only high quality, well-seasoned hardwoods in the construction of his wagons. His vehicles were widely used in the Santa Fe trade because they were sturdy and well built. He built wagons for the U.S. Army during the Mexican War, and later during the Civil War. (See *Overland Journal,* quarterly journal of the Oregon-California Trails Association, Volume 15, Number 3, Autumn 1997), p. 36.

18.   Tom Dean (a descendant of August Block), telephone conversation with author, September 14, 1988.

19.   U.S. Bureau of the Census, Nodaway County, Missouri, 1850. John and Tom Billings were neighbors of Gillum Baley in Nodaway County. The 1850 census listed a Byrd Billings (Census No. 272–279) on the census roll after that of Gillum Baley (Census No. 271–278). In the Byrd Billings household, the census listed a John Billings, age seventeen, and a Tom Billings, age twelve.

CHAPTER 2

1.   The name La Junta was changed to Watrous by the railroad in 1879 to avoid confusion with La Junta, Colorado, on the Mountain Branch. Samuel B. Watrous was an early-day settler in the area and had donated the land for the railroad right of way.

2.   Rose Jr., p. 7.

3.   Hedgpeth, *A Trip Across the Plains.*

4.   Udell, *Journal,* p. 7.

5.   Ibid., p. 18.

6.   Hedgpeth, *A Trip Across the Plains.*

7.   Rose Jr., p. 9.

8. Ibid., p. 8.
9. Ibid., p. 11.

CHAPTER 3

1. William P. Floyd, Typescript of a diary kept on Beale's 1858–1859 Expedition, pencilled original in small notebook, Huntington Library, San Marino, California.

   William P. Floyd was the expedition's physician. He is not to be confused with John B. Floyd, who was secretary of war in the Buchanan administration, 1857–61.

2. Rose used these letters to buttress his Indian depredation suit, filed in the U.S. Court of Claims in 1892, against the U.S. government and the Mojave Indians.

3. Carl Briggs and Clyde Francis Trudell, *Quarterdeck and Saddlehorn: The Story of Edward F. Beale, 1822–1893* (Glendale, California: The Arthur H. Clark Company, 1983), p. 134.

4. In later years Beale could also be addressed as Mr. Ambassador. He was appointed ambassador to Austria by President Grant in 1876.

5. The Whipple journals can be found in the following book: Grant Foreman, ed., *A Pathfinder in the Southwest* (Norman: University of Oklahoma Press, 1941). Aubrey's journals can be found in the following: Ralph B. Bieber, ed., *Exploring Southwestern Trials 1846–1854*, The Southwest Historical Series, Vol. VII (Glendale: The Arthur H. Clark Co, 1938), pp. 353–383.

6. Tom Bahti, *Southwestern Indian Tribes* (Las Vegas, Nevada: K. C. Publications, 1989), p. 63.

   The name is also spelled "Mohave." "Mojave" is the Spanish spelling. This is the spelling most commonly used, such as the Mojave Desert, the Mojave River, Fort Mojave, and the town of Mojave in California. However, it is spelled "Mohave" in the name of the county in Northwestern Arizona, and in some early government documents. I have tried to follow conventional usage. The word is a corruption of the Mojave Indian name for themselves, *Aha-makave*, meaning beside the water.

7. Dennis G. Casebier, *The Mojave Road* (Norco, California: Tales of the Mojave Road Publishing Company, 1975), p. 59. Readers wishing more information on the U.S. Army's camel experiment should read the following: Lewis Burt Lesley, ed., *Uncle Sam's Camels: The Journal of May Humphreys Stacey Supplemented by the Report of Edward Fitzgerald Beale (1857–1858)* (Cambridge, Massachusetts: Harvard University Press, 1929).

8. Edward Fitzgerald Beale, *Wagon Road from Fort Defiance to the Colorado River.* U.S. Thirty-fifth Congress, First Session, House Executive Document No. 124, 1858.

9. Beale had become familiar with the area while serving as superin-
    tendent of Indian affairs (1852–55). Shortly after leaving that post he
    purchased a Mexican land grant near Fort Mojave known as La Liebre
    (the jack rabbit). He later added to the grant by purchasing adjacent
    land grants. He called his ranch the Tejon Ranch because it was
    located near Fort Tejon. It is still known by that name, although it is
    no longer owned by Beale's descendants.

10. To attend the camels, native handlers were brought over from Asia
    Minor with them. Two of the best known of these camel drivers
    were Hadji Ali, better known as Hi Jolly, and George Xaralampo,
    better known as Greek George. Most of these drivers grew home-
    sick and soon returned to their native lands, but Hadji Ali and Greek
    George spent the remainder of their lives in this country. Both
    became naturalized citizens: Hadji Ali under the name of Philip
    Tedro, and Greek George under the name of George Allen. For
    more information on Hadji Ali and Greek George, the reader should
    consult the following book: Bertha S. Dodge, *The Road West: Saga of
    the Thirty-fifth Parallel* (Albuquerque: University of New Mexico
    Press, 1980), pp. 199–201.

11. The commanding officer of the army post in Albuquerque at that
    time was Col. Benjamin Louis Eulalie de Bonneville. Bonneville, a
    Frenchman by birth, came to this country as a boy. He entered the
    U.S. Military Academy at West Point, graduating in 1815 as a second
    lieutenant in the U.S. Army. In 1830, he took a two year leave of
    absence from the army and went West on a trading and exploring
    expedition to the Rocky Mountains. He overstayed his leave but was
    reinstated in the army in spite of this. This gave rise to rumors that he
    had been sent West as a secret agent for the U.S. government to spy
    on the Spanish. A highly exaggerated account of his exploits in the
    West was written by Washington Irving in his book, *The Adventures of
    Captain Bonneville.* He retired from the Army in 1865 as a brevetted
    brigadier general. He left his name in many places in the West, most
    notably, Bonneville Dam and the Bonneville Salt Flats.

    Those who served under Bonneville's command did not find him
    as charming as did Washington Irving. Behind his back, his junior offi-
    cers were known to have referred to Bonneville as "Old Bonny
    Clabber." Chris Emmett, *Fort Union and the Winning of the Southwest*
    (Norman: University of Oklahoma Press, 1956), p. 213.

12. Udell, *Journal,* p. 19.

13. Ibid.

14. Ibid., p. 20. This is further verified by L. J. Rose in a letter to his home-
    town newspaper in Keosauqua, Iowa, written in Albuquerque shortly
    after the disaster at the Colorado River. L. J. Rose, An account (without

title) dated October 28, 1858, Huntington Library, San Marino, California.

In this letter Rose clearly identifies Udell as a member of Gillum Baley's company. He also includes the Dalys and the Hollands in this group. In this account Rose made the following statement:

> "The first company consisted of two parties: Joel Hedgpeth, Thos. Hedgpeth, G. Baily, Wright Baily, J. Holland Baily, John Udell, their families, and probably eighteen hands, forming one party, who had with them one hundred and twenty-five head of oxen and cows: twelve wagons, and fifteen horses. Messers. Bentner, Alpha Brown, E. M. Jones, myself and families, and seventeen hands, the other party, with two hundred and forty-seven head of cattle, and twenty-one horses and mules. We kept our stock separate until our troubles with the Indians began, although we traveled together and camped near each other."

The transcriber got the names "Baley" and "Daly" confused and John Lucas Daly became "J. Holland Baily," a non existing person. This error in transcription has caused confusion in identifying the families of the Rose-Baley wagon train.

15. U.S. Court of Claims, Indian Depredation Division, *Leonard J. Rose v. U.S. Government and the Mojave Indians*, Case No. 2176, RG 123, National Archives, Washington, D.C.

16. The name is also spelled "Saavedra," or "Saevedra." He, himself, spelled it "Savedra" on his affidavit in support of Rose's Indian depredation suit.

17. Grant Foreman, ed., *A Pathfinder in the Southwest* (Norman: University of Oklahoma Press, 1941), pp. 114–15.

18. Ibid., p. 189.

19. David Sloan Stanley, *Personal Memoirs of Major General D. S. Stanley, U.S.A.* (Cambridge, Massachusetts: Harvard University Press, 1917), p. 29.

20. Beale, *Wagon Road from Fort Defiance to the Colorado River*, p. 51.

CHAPTER 4

1. Samuel Gorman, of Dayton, Ohio, was appointed in the spring of 1852 as a missionary to New Mexico by the American Baptist Home Missionary Society. After consultation with the Reverend Henry W. Read at Santa Fe, it was decided to establish a mission at the pueblo of Laguna. Samuel Gorman and his family arrived there on October 5, 1852. Their early difficulties were discouraging, but through the efforts of Indian Agent Henry L. Dodge, they were accepted by the community. Work was continued at Laguna until March 1, 1859, when Gorman was transferred to Santa Fe where he taught and preached until the spring of 1862, at which time he returned to Ohio. Charles

F. Coan, *A History of New Mexico*, vol. I (Chicago and New York: The American Historical Society, Inc., 1925), p. 364.

2. The Spanish spelling is Zuñi with the tilde over the n (ñ), which is pronounced approximately like the "n" in canyon. The author has chosen to use the spelling preferred by the Zuni people, i.e., Zuni, pronounce Zoo-Nee. Their ancient name for themselves is A'shiwi (Ashiwi), signifying "the flesh" and apparently bespeaking their own personal selves, a people distinct from all others. Bertha P. Dutton, *Friendly People, The Zuñi Indians* (Santa Fe, New Mexico: Museum of New Mexico Press, 1963), p. 10.

3. The highway builders (U.S. Route 66, and Interstate 40) chose not to follow Beale's Wagon Road over the Continental Divide at this point; instead they elected to follow the route of the Santa Fe Railroad, which crosses the Zuni Mountains at a lower elevation through Campbell Pass. It then veers northwest through Grants, and Gallup, New Mexico, thus bypassing El Morro National Monument and the pueblo of Zuni. The railroad and I-40 rejoin Beale's Wagon Road in the vicinity of Holbrook, Arizona.

4. For more information on Inscription Rock and El Morro National Monument, the reader should consult John M. Slater, *El Morro Inscription Rock, New Mexico* (Los Angeles: The Plantin Press, 1961).

5. Slater states in his book on El Morro and Inscription Rock that, "Ironically enough, the greatest single act of damage to the rock took place after the establishment of the Monument. About 1924 an attempt was made to cleanse the rock of countless worthless signatures by rubbing them out with sandstone. In the course of this ill-advised project many valuable inscriptions were erased, and the beautiful sandstone surface was so disfigured as to draw questions, from the most casual visitor, as to what happened." Slater, pp. 49–50. Among the "worthless signatures" erased was that of the famed Archbishop Jean Baptiste Lamy, the central character in Willa Cather's novel, *Death Comes for the Archbishop*. Slater, p. 46.

6. Bertha P. Dutton, *Friendly People: The Zuñi Indians* (Santa Fe: Museum of New Mexico Press, 1963) p. 25. Old records show that the Zuni population in 1860 was approximately 1,560. The population had formerly been much higher, but smallpox and other whiteman's diseases had taken a heavy toll of the Zuni.

7. Hedgpeth, *A Trip Across the Plains*. The presence of albinos among the Zuni Indians seems to have excited the imagination of early American visitors to Zuni. Some speculated that these albinos might be descendants of a colony of Welsh who supposedly were planted in America in the twelfth century by Prince Madoc of Wales. Some even thought that they detected similarities between the two languages. Actually, the

Zuni language is not closely related to any other language, Indian or European. There is no reference to Welsh or any other white ancestors in Zuni legend or folklore.

8. Udell, *Journal*, p. 26.

9. Edith Allen Milner, "Recollections of Edith Allen Milner From Her Mother's Talks to Her About the Emigrant Trip Across the Plains in 1858." Eight page typescript, n.d., Powers Family Papers, Nut Tree, California. In this paper Mrs. Milner states that her mother picked up some beautiful petrified wood specimens at Lithodendron Creek on the outward journey in 1858.

10. Udell, *Journal*, p. 28.

11. Register Rock No. 4 is in Canyon Diablo near Leupp, Arizona. It is located on private property and permission is required before entering the area. There are other rocks engraved with many names in and near the canyon.

12. Hedgpeth, *A Trip Across the Plains*.

CHAPTER 5

1. Udell, *Journal*, p. 32.

2. Ibid.

3. Much of the territory traveled by the Rose-Baley wagon train in 1858 had not yet been fully explored, and many of its geographical features were still unnamed. The emigrants yielded to the temptation to name such features after themselves or after other members of their group. Udell, for example, named two of the canyons that they passed through "Udell's Canyons." The spring where Thomas Hedgpeth killed a bear was called "Hedgpeth Springs" by some of the emigrants, while others referred to it as "Bear Springs." Hedgpeth Springs is the only one of several names bestowed by this emigrant train which is still in use. The only maps that these emigrants had with them were copies of Whipple's maps and reports from his 1853–54 expedition, as Beale had not yet published his report or his maps at the time that the Rose-Baley wagon train passed through.

4. These so-called monsoons should not be confused with the monsoons that bring copious rainfall to parts of Asia, Africa, and other places in the world. The monsoons of Arizona and other southwest states are caused by masses of cool, moisture-laden air from the Pacific Ocean and the Gulf of California drifting northeastward and colliding with the hot dry air over the southwest deserts. This results in numerous thunderstorms during the months of July and August. These thundershowers are both unpredictable and unreliable; they may bring heavy rainfall in one area while another area only a few miles away may receive no rain at all. Arizona, like most of the south-

western states, receives the bulk of its rainfall during the winter months.

5. The Indians referred to by the emigrants as "Cosninos," or "Coseneñoes," as Udell called them, were the Hualapai, also spelled "Walapai" or "Hualpai." The name means "Pine Nut People" in their native tongue. They are members of the Yuman language group. They occupied and continue to occupy a large section of northwestern Arizona south of the Grand Canyon and between Peach Springs on the east and the Black Mountains on the west. On the south they are bordered by the Yavapai. The Hualapai practiced a limited amount of agriculture, but depended mostly on hunting and seed gathering for their sustenance. At the time the Rose-Baley wagon train passed through their territory, these Indians had experienced very little contact with whites. They were not considered warlike, but would fight to protect their territory.

6. L. J. Rose, An account (without title) dated October 28, 1858. This is an account of the battle written for his home town newspaper in Keosauqua, Iowa, upon the return of the emigrants to Albuquerque after they had been attacked by Mojave Indians at the Colorado River and is in the Huntington Library, San Marino, California. Rose's account also appears as appendix 4 of Robert Glass Cleland's book, *Cattle on a Thousand Hills* (San Marino: The Huntington Library, 1951), L. J. Rose, "Massacre on the Colorado," pp. 306–315. It does not appear in later editions.

7. To guard against future incidents like this, the members of the Rose-Baley wagon train adopted the habit of placing one arm around the spoke of a wagon wheel whenever the wagon train would stop for a rest at night, so that they would be awakened by the turning wagon wheel and not inadvertently be left behind. Kate Heath, "A Child's Journey Through Arizona and New Mexico," *The California* (January 1881), 24–18.

8. Udell, *Journal*, p. 41.

9. Boys' Pass near Kingman, Arizona, was so named by Beale during his 1857 expedition because it was discovered by the three teenagers in his party: May Humphreys Stacey, J. Hampton Porter, and Joseph Bell. Beale called them, "My boys, May, Ham and Joe." The pass is now called Bog Pass.

10. Rose Jr., p. 18.

CHAPTER 6

1. William C. Sturtevant, ed., *Handbook of North American Indians*, vol. 10, *Southwest*, ed. Alfonso Ortiz (Washington, D.C.: Smithsonian Institute, 1983), p. 56.

2. Foreman, ed., *A Pathfinder in the Southwest*, p. 237.

3. A. L. Kroeber, *Handbook of California Indians* (Washington, D.C.: Government Printing Office, 1925), p. 752.

4. Ibid., p. 752.

5. Sturtevant, p. 62.

6. Udell, *Journal*, p. 44.

7. It is ironic that the area where the emigrants were building a road out of the canyon later became one of the most productive gold mining camps in Arizona. It was called "Goldroad." Although several members of this wagon train had experience in mining gold during the California gold rush, none reported finding any traces of gold in this area. Perhaps it was because they were so preoccupied with finding a way to get their wagons out of the canyon that their sights and senses were not attuned to the presence of gold.

8. Actually, had the emigrants been successful in crossing the Colorado River at this location (Beale's Crossing), they would have been in the extreme southern tip of present-day Nevada near Laughlin, and about six miles east of the present California-Nevada border. Nevada at that time was still part of Utah Territory and its border with California had not yet been clearly defined. The southern part of the California-Nevada border runs on a southeast diagonal line from the center of Lake Tahoe to a point where it strikes the Colorado River about fifteen miles north of Needles, California.

9. Even after getting across the Colorado River and through Mojave territory, the emigrants would still have faced approximately one hundred and seventy-five miles of very difficult travel before reaching the first white settlement in California at San Bernardino. Most of this distance is through the Mojave Desert, one of the most arid places in North America. Their Indian problems wouldn't have all been behind them either, as this area was then inhabited by the Pah-Ute Indians. Although not considered by white travelers to be as fierce or as treacherous as the Mojave or Hualapai appeared to be, the Pah-Utes nevertheless had been known to commit depredations on whites passing through their territory.

    For most emigrants, just getting to the California border brought great joy and excitement even if they were yet some distance from their intended destination.

10. Rose Jr., p. 22.

11. Ibid., p. 23.

12. Ibid., p. 24

13. Hedgpeth, *A Trip Across the Plains*.

14. Rose Jr., p. 24.

15. J. W. Cheney, "The Story of an Emigrant Train," *Annals of Iowa*, No. 2 (July): 82–97. State Historical Society of Iowa, Iowa City, Iowa.

16. Hedgpeth, *A Trip Across the Plains.*

17. The emigrants believed that the Mojave chief shot during the battle was the second of the two chiefs who visited them in camp just prior to the battle. Savedra, in his affidavit in support of Rose's Indian depredation suit, identifies the chief as "Jose" and he identifies the first chief who visited them as "Cai-rook." This might be the same Jose that Whipple described as one of the great Mojave chiefs that he was introduced to in 1854. Whipple stated that a sub-chief called Cai-rook served as a guide for his party, and conducted them around a mountain spur which intersects the Colorado Valley between the territory of the Chemehuevis and that of the Mojave. (Grant Foreman, *A Pathfinder in the Southwest,* pp. 224–47.) If the Jose and the Cai-rook described by Whipple were the same two Mojave chiefs who visited the emigrants before the battle, it would explain why the second chief was so much more elaborately dressed than the first chief who visited the camp. Jose would have been a great chief while Cai-rook was only a sub chief.

18. Rose Jr., p. 26. Rose credits the slaying of the Mojave chief to the Missouri Preacher, but claims to have forgotten his name. Since John Udell was also a lay preacher (Baptist) from Missouri, this has caused some confusion as to the true identity of the Missouri Preacher who shot the Mojave chief and saved the emigrants. Some people have thought that Udell was the Missouri Preacher. Udell, according to his journal, (pp. 44–45), was back at the mountain camp and not at the scene of the battle at the Colorado River. There is no record that Udell ever made such a claim. Therefore, the Missouri Preacher who shot the Mojave chief could not have been John Udell! Since Gillum Baley was the only preacher from Missouri at the battle, he must have been the Missouri Preacher.

Joel Hedgpeth Jr. in *A Trip Across the Plains* stated: "Toward the close of the conflict Judge Baley (Uncle Gillum, we called him), seeing a prominent looking Indian, who seemed to be directing and urging on the others, leveled on him with his rifle and brought him to the ground. Soon after the savages ceased yelling and went away." The story of the slaying of the Indian chief by Gillum Baley has been a tale handed down by family tradition in the Baley and Hedgpeth families.

19. Rose Jr., p. 26.

20. Hedgpeth, *A Trip Across the Plains.*

21. Rose Jr., p. 26.

22. Another option for the emigrants would have been to follow the Colorado south to Fort Yuma. This would have been a detour of more than two hundred miles and through territory occupied by unfriendly Chemehuevi and Yuma Indians. This option was ruled out because the emigrants wanted no more contact with hostile Indians.

23. This is exactly what happened to Jedediah S. Smith when he crossed the Colorado River near the Mojave Villages on his second trip to California in 1827. On the first trip, the year before, he had been treated in a very friendly manner by the Mojave Indians. Remembering this, he decided to cross the Colorado River at the same location again on his second trip. Again, the Mojaves appeared friendly, even helping the explorers in making boats out of cane grass for crossing the river. When Smith and eight of his men were almost across the river, the Mojaves suddenly and without warning attacked the remaining ten men on the bank as they were preparing to cross the river. These unfortunate men were clubbed and stabbed to death while Smith and his companions watched helplessly and horror-stricken from the other bank of the river. Only the fact that Smith and his eight men were armed with rifles enabled them to escape.

24. Hedgpeth, *A Trip Across the Plains.*

CHAPTER 7

1. Udell, *Journal*, p. 45.
2. Calvin "Cal" Davis and James H. Jordan were from Iowaville in northern Van Buren County, Iowa, while John Bradford Cave and Robert Perkins were from Bonaparte, in the southern part of the county. The four families did not leave together but joined up on the way, along with several other families including Udell's friend, John Hamilton, and two or three unnamed families. Udell did not state where he knew John Hamilton from; it could have been from Putnam County, Missouri, or from one of the neighboring counties in Missouri or Iowa. The best known of this group was James H. Jordan. Jordan was a well-known Indian trader and a close personal friend of Black Hawk, the great chief of the Sauk Indians who led his tribe and the Fox Indians in a war against the whites known as the Black Hawk War.
3. Truxton (Truxtun) Canyon was named by Beale, either for his grandfather, Commodore Thomas Truxtun, or for Beale's son, Truxtun Beale, or perhaps for both.
4. U.S. Court of Claims, Baley v. U.S. Government.
5. Edith Allen Milner, "Covered Wagon Experiences," n.d., Arizona Historical Society, Tucson.
6. She actually named her son Edward Oliver Allen. She substituted her father's first name, Oliver, in place of Owen. Nevertheless, her son's initials were E. O., just like in E. O. Smith.
7. Udell, *Journal*, p. 52.
8. Ibid., p. 53.
9. The Butterfield Overland Mail, under the direction of John Butterfield, began mail and passenger service between St. Louis,

Missouri, and San Francisco, California, in September of 1858 over a variant of the Southern Route. The emigrants probably heard about it while they were in Albuquerque. Another contract, for mail service only, was made with the Central Overland Mail; this carrier was to begin service in October of 1858. The terms of the contract called for the mail to be carried between Kansas City, Missouri, and Stockton, California, once every sixty days. The carrier was to use Beale's Wagon Road between Albuquerque and the Colorado River, and to use existing roads for other sections of the route. This mail service had to be abandoned before it ever really got started because of hostilities with the Navajo and Mojave Indians.

10. The emigrants obviously confused Mount Floyd with Picacho Butte, which lies a few miles to the south. Mount Floyd has the appearance of both a sharp peak and a butte, depending on the direction from which one approaches it. The name "Picacho" means sharp peak in Spanish, and seems to be a generic term for almost any sharp peak in territory once ruled by the Spanish. William C. Barnes, in *Arizona Place Names*, lists fourteen different locations in Arizona with the word "Picacho" as part of their place name.

11. U.S. Department of War, Army Continental Commands, Letters Received by the Department of New Mexico, "Emigrants to Commander, Fort Defiance, Picacho, Territory of New Mexico, September 22, 1858," Letter B 70-DNMex, RG 393, National Archives.

12. Udell, *Journal*, pp. 55–56.

13. Ibid., p. 57.

14. Ibid., p. 58.

15. The Navajo War of 1858 started on July 11, 1858, when a Navajo Indian who had been loitering around Fort Defiance for some unknown reason shot an arrow into the back of a Negro, causing his death. The victim happened to be the personal servant of Major W. T. H. Brooks, the post commander. The Major demanded the Navajos surrender the culprit responsible, but they refused. This so angered Major Brooks that he issued an ultimatum to the Navajos: Turn over the murderer within twenty days or face punitive action. The Navajos then tried to pull a fast one on the Americans. They killed a Mexican and turned over his body to the army as that of the accused. The ruse was discovered when some of the Americans at the fort recognized the body as that of a local Mexican. This further infuriated the army. A punitive force of 300 men, under the command of Lieutenant Colonel D. S. Miles, took the field on September 9, 1858. They attacked the Navajos at Canyon de Chelly, killing six warriors and capturing a few women and children. Two American soldiers also were killed. The dispute was settled by negotiations, but the war

revealed a weakness in government policy. This weakness was the fact that the U.S. government treated each Indian tribe as a separate sovereign nation and considered any treaty negotiated with any chief or group of chiefs as binding on the entire tribe. Most tribes had no central government or governing body that could speak for or bind the whole tribe.

Problems with the Navajos continued as more and more white men encroached upon their territory. In 1863, General Carleton and Kit Carson rounded up a large portion of the tribe and brutally marched them to Bosque Redondo [Fort Sumner], New Mexico, in what would become known to Navajos as the Long Walk. This was one of the most shameful and disgraceful episodes of the white man's dealings with Indians in the settlement of the West.

16. U.S. Department of War, Army Continental Commands, Letters Received by the Department of New Mexico, "Major E. Backus to Lieutenant L. W. O'Bannon, October 12, 1858," Letter B 70-DNMex, RG 393, National Archives.

17. U.S. Department of War, Army Continental Commands, Letters Sent by the Department of New Mexico, "Colonel B. L. E. Bonneville to Lieutenant Colonel L. Thomas, A. A. G., Headquarters of the Army, New York, November 6, 1858," RG 393, M1072, roll 2, National Archives.

CHAPTER 8

1. Edward Warren Holland, Autobiography, eight page typescript, n.d., original in Tulare Public Library, Genealogy Department, Tulare, California.

2. Harvey K. S. O'Melveny later came to Southern California and settled near L. J. Rose. O'Melveny became a successful attorney and later served as county judge of Los Angeles County. He advised and represented Rose locally in the early phases of Rose's Indian depredation suit against the U.S. government.

3. U.S. Court of Claims, *Baley v. U.S. Government*. Affidavit of Gillum and William Right Baley signed before Judge Kirby Benedict, Chief Justice of the Territory of New Mexico Supreme Court, in Albuquerque, November 19, 1858.

4. Heath, pp. 14–18. Kate Heath was the pen name for Julia Brown, daughter of Alpha and Mary Brown, and a member of the Rose-Baley wagon train. It was not unusual for women in those days to use pen names when writing articles for publication.

5. Milner, "Covered Wagon Experiences."

6. It is unknown which company John McCord was with. His name is not mentioned in any of the emigrants' statements or accounts. He

inscribed his name on Inscription Rock at El Morro, as "J. McCord, Ohio, July 30, 1858." The date would indicate that he was a member of the Cave company from Iowa; they camped at Inscription Rock on July 29–30, 1858.

7.   *The Santa Fe Gazette*, December 4, 1858. The Huntington Library, San Marino, California.

8.   Udell, *Journal*, pp. 62–63.

9.   Ibid., p. 63

CHAPTER 9

1.   Edward F. Beale, *Wagon Road from Fort Defiance to the Colorado River*.

2.   *Weekly Alta California* "Supplement," Report by "Yesar," dated May 3, 1859, Hayden Files, Arizona Historical Society, Tucson, Arizona.

     Rasey Biven, who, under the pen name "Yesar," was a correspondent for the *Weekly Alta California* newspaper, accompanied Lieutenant Colonel William Hoffman's punitive expedition to punish the Mojave Indians for their attack on the Rose-Baley wagon train. His reports were published from time to time in a supplemental edition of this newspaper. Biven interviewed William Garton, one of the former employees of the Baley company, at Beale's camp for his road workers near the Colorado River. He also interviewed John Udell and Joel Hedgpeth in another camp near Fort Mojave, giving further documentation that Beale brought the Udell and the Joel Hedgpeth families to California with him on his road-building expedition in the spring of 1859. No new information was brought out in either of these interviews.

3.   Floyd, Typescript of a Diary, p. 26.

4.   Edward F. Beale, Beale Journal, Entries from March 1–May 4, 1859, Photocopy of handwritten original, no pagination, Beale Family Papers, Decatur House Papers, Library of Congress.

5.   Floyd, Typescript of a Diary, p. 27.

6.   Jack Beale Smith, *Kerlin's Well: A Unique Site on the Beale Wagon Road near Seligman, Arizona* (Flagstaff, Arizona: Tales of the Beale Road Publishing Company, 1986), pp. 8–9.

     The engraving might have been done by P. (Peachy) Gilmer Breckinridge, one of the young men that Beale brought with him from the East on his 1859 road building expedition. Although only a youth of twenty at the time, Breckinridge had already mastered the skill of tombstone engraving, and had brought all the necessary tools with him. The only other places besides Inscription Rock where he is known to have used his professional skill, according to Jack Beale Smith, a student of the Beale Road, were at Kerlin's Well and at Law Springs.

Breckinridge did not endear himself to Beale when he wandered off alone from camp and got lost during the Fort Smith to Albuquerque phase of the expedition. Nearly two days were spent in searching for Breckinridge before he was found. He had wandered nearly forty miles from camp before he was discovered. "So much for these greenhorn annoyances," Beale recorded in his journal. Breckinridge had friends in high government circles who had insisted that Beale take the inexperienced youth with him on the expedition. Breckinridge was a distant relative of Vice President John C. Breckinridge (second cousin once removed). P. Gilmer Breckinridge was killed on May 24, 1864, while fighting for the Confederate cause in a skirmish at Kennon's Landing (known as Wilson's Wharf on the Union side) in Virginia.

7. Beale, Journal.
8. Ibid.
9. Ibid.
10. Floyd, Typescript of a Diary, p. 19.
11. Beale, Journal.
12. Udell, *Journal*, p. 71.
13. Casebier, *The Mojave Road,* p. 92.
14. Hedgpeth, *A Trip Across the Plains.*
15. Beale, Journal.
16. William Hoffman, 1807–84, graduated from West Point in 1829. Lieutenant Colonel Hoffman served as commissary general of prisons for the Union during the Civil War. His tightfisted fiscal policies resulted in much suffering for Confederates confined in Union prisons.
17. Beale, Journal. Beale was equally critical of the peace treaty that Lieutenant Colonel Hoffman concluded with the Mojave Nation because he thought that Hoffman had been too easy on the Mojaves. Beale believed that the emigrants should have been avenged before any peace treaty was signed with them. In a letter to his wife dated May 17, 1859, (Beale Family Papers, Decatur House Papers, Library of Congress), he wrote, "Within twenty steps of the place where Hoffman made his treaty, we saw sticking in the rough bark of the trees the golden hair of a child, one of the Bentner children, whose brains the bloody savages had knocked out."

In general, the treaty required that the Mojaves permit an army post to be constructed in their territory and that they permit emigrants to pass through their country unmolested. They were further required to turn over to Hoffman three of those warriors who were engaged in the attack on the emigrants the previous year. To guarantee future good conduct, the Mojaves were required to hand over one hostage from each of the six bands. No attempt was made by Hoffman to recover any of the property taken from the emigrants or its equivalent value.

Neither did he attempt to identify or punish those Indians responsible for the murder of the Bentner family. The Mojaves denied responsibility for the attack on the emigrants and tried to blame it on the Chemehuevis and the Hualapais. Peter Odens, *Fire Over Yuma* (Yuma, Arizona: Southwest Printers, 1966), p. 22.

Because of language difficulties it is doubtful that the Mojaves understood much of what was in the treaty. Hoffman made his statements in English which were translated into Spanish by Captain Henry S. Burton. Jose Maria, a Diegueño Indian who spoke Spanish, then translated the message into the Yuma language. Pascual, a Quechan Indian, made the final translation into Mojave. Some meaning might have been lost in the translation, but if the Mojaves didn't understand all the semantics, there was one thing they did understand—the overwhelming firepower of Hoffman's soldiers. Consequently, they signed their Xs to the treaty with little argument

18. Lewis Addison Armistead, 1816–63. Armistead was expelled from West Point for hitting a fellow cadet over the head with a plate. He earned a commission during the Mexican War, and remained in the army until he resigned in 1861 to join the Confederate Army, where he rose to the rank of brigadier general. The cadet that he hit over the head with a plate at West Point, Jubal Early, also served in the Confederate Army where he attained the rank of lieutenant general.

At the battle of Gettysburg, Armistead was mortally wounded while leading Pickett's famous charge against Union positions on Cemetery Ridge. Armistead's brigade is reported to have made the deepest penetration of Union lines during Pickett's unsuccessful charge. A monument was later erected on the spot where Armistead fell. The inscription on the monument refers to the spot as "The High Tide of the Confederacy."

19. Casebier, *The Mojave Road*, p. 95.

20. Arthur Woodward, "The Founding of Fort Mojave," *Pony Express Courier* (May 1937), pp. 4–5.

21. An excellent account of Lieutenant Colonel Hoffman's Colorado River Expedition is given in Dennis G. Casebier's *The Mojave Road*, pp. 81–94. See also, Philip J. Avillo Jr., "Fort Mojave: Outpost on the Upper Colorado," *The Journal of Arizona History* (Summer 1970), pp. 77–99. Also see, Leslie Gene Hunter, "The Mojave Expedition of 1858–59," *Arizona and the West* (Summer 1979), pp. 237–144.

22. Records of the Adjutant General, Letters Received, "Beale to Hoffman, May 13, 1859, Hoffman to Beale, May 14, 1859," RG 94, M567, roll 597, National Archives.

Beale wrote a long letter to Hoffman complaining of the theft. Hoffman denied that his men committed the theft, stating that his men couldn't possibly have stolen such a large amount of supplies without their officers knowing about it.

A court martial was held at Fort Yuma, and the charged soldiers were found not guilty of opening the caches. Secretary Floyd dissented from the findings of the court, stating in a letter to Beale and in general orders, that the enlisted men's actions were criminal and the officers who permitted the opening of the supply caches were "reprehensible" in their conduct. Floyd ordered that the troops involved pay for the stolen property out of their company funds or from their own rations.

Dennis G. Casebier, *Fort Pah-Ute, California* (Norco, California: Tales of the Mojave Road Publishing Company, 1974), *passim.*

23. *Des Moines Register,* September 6, 1964, "Time Wins a Victory in Southeast Iowa," by James L. F. Wilt, Iowa Clipping File 2, State Historical Society of Iowa, Capitol Complex, Des Moines, Iowa.

24. Milner, "Covered Wagon Experiences."

25. The Bascom Affair was the result of an incident which took place in Southern Arizona on January 17, 1861. On that date two parties of Western Apaches raided the ranch of John Ward and abducted Ward's twelve-year-old stepson, Felix. They also drove off some of Ward's cattle. Ward reported the incident to army authorities at Fort Buchanan, blaming the theft and abduction on the Chiricahua branch of Apaches headed by Cochise. Contrary to other Apache tribes, Cochise up to that time had advocated a policy of friendship and cooperation with the Americans. Other Apache chiefs criticized him for this. The matter was assigned to Lieutenant George N. Bascom for investigation and follow-up. Lieutenant Bascom was a brash young officer new to the frontier and without any previous experience dealing with Indians. Bascom, with a detail of fifty-four soldiers, set out for the vicinity of Apache Pass to recover the boy and the property. Word was sent to Cochise that Bascom wished to parley with him. Cochise and a few of his warriors, including several of his close relatives, came into the army camp to talk to the lieutenant. Bascom accused Cochise and his Chiricahuas of committing the abduction and theft. Cochise denied any knowledge of the depredations, but promised that he would look into the matter and do his best to get the Ward boy released and the property returned, but that it would take a few days. Although Cochise was chief only of the Chiricahua branch of the Apaches, he had wide influence with other Apache tribes. This wasn't good enough for Lieutenant Bascom. He declared that Cochise and his entourage would be detained until the boy and the property were returned. On hearing this Cochise grew angry and bolted from camp. Several shots were fired by the soldiers and one of the Indians was killed and Cochise himself was slightly wounded. Six of his braves

were captured and made prisoners. Cochise retaliated by capturing
three Americans from one of the Butterfield Stage stations. Cochise
offered to exchange them for the six warriors being held hostage by
the army, but Bascom refused the offer. Just what happened next is
unclear, but the three Americans were found murdered. Bascom, in
retaliation, hanged the six Apaches, including Cochise's brother and
nephew. Cochise then declared war against the Americans, and from
that day on he waged an unrelenting battle against them.

    Lieutenant George N. Bascom, 1836–1862, West Point Class of
1858, was killed at the Battle of Valverde in February of 1862 while
fighting on the side of the Union. While his courage was never questioned, his judgment in the Bascom Affair certainly could be.
Heitman, *Historical Register*, I, p. 197. Felix Ward, the boy who was
abducted by the Indians, in later years became scout and interpreter
for the Americans during the Geronimo wars under the name of
Mickey Free.

26.   There are no records of walnuts having ever grown along the banks
of the Gila River, or even in that vicinity. They must have been carried down to the Gila River by one of its tributary streams in central
or northern Arizona were black walnuts are known to grow. Edith
Allen Milner in her manuscript *Covered Wagon Experiences*, stated, "The
nuts that Mama [Sallie Fox] found at Gila Bend near Yuma, she picked
up, put them in her apron pocket and said that she was going to take
them to her Uncle Si's ranch [Josiah Allison] and have him plant them
for her."

27.   Dan W. Messersmith, *The History of Mohave County to 1912* (Kingman,
Arizona: Mohave County Historical Society, 1991), p. 178. For an
account of the ordeals of the Oatman family, see: Royal B. Stratton,
Captivity of the Oatman Girls (New York: Carlton & Porter, 1857;
reprint, Alexandria, Virginia: Time Life Books, *Classics of the Old West*,
1982).

28.   Milner, "Covered Wagon Experiences."

29.   Ibid.

30.   Milner, "Recollections."

31.   Ibid.

32.   Milner, "Covered Wagon Experiences."

33.   The Nut Tree Amusement Park has closed since this was written, and
its future remains uncertain. However, Sallie's dress and other artifacts
which were at the Harbison House at the Nut Tree are now at the
Solano County Museum in Vacaville, California.

34.   Paul E. Vandor, *History of Fresno County, California, with Biographical
Sketches*, (Los Angeles: Historical Records Co., 1919). vol. 2, pp.
2387–2388.

35. Ibid. Vandor, in his biographical sketch of America Frances Baley Yancey, gives the date of the double marriages as September 9, 1859, and the place of marriage as New Mexico, while en route to California. This information probably came from Frances herself, who was still alive in 1919 when Vandor published his *History of Fresno County*. George Hiatt in an unpublished, undated genealogy of the Baley family, located at the Fresno City and County Historical Society, Kearney Park, Fresno, California, gives the place of marriage as "A Presbyterian mission sixty miles from Albuquerque." This location would place it near Laguna, New Mexico, where Reverend Gorman ran a Baptist mission. Hiatt could have been mistaken in the denomination of the mission, or it is possible that there could have been a Presbyterian mission in the vicinity of Laguna. The Presbyterians were very active in New Mexico during this period.

36. The religious preferences of the two bridegrooms is unknown. August Block died in 1864, only five years into the marriage. He is buried in Visalia Cemetery, Visalia, California, in the Protestant section of the cemetery. His widow, America Frances, then married Abraham Yancey; both were active members of the Methodist Episcopal Church, South. William Krug, and his wife, Amelia Catherine, emigrated to Brazil, a predominately Catholic country, in 1871, and remained there the rest of their lives. It is unknown what their religious affiliation was.

37. *Fresno Morning Republican*, February 9, 1930, column by Ernestine Winchell.

38. The Elisha Cotton Winchell family was also living in the old abandoned fort at this time. The two families became good friends. Elisha Cotton Winchell later became Fresno County's first superintendent of public schools, and opened the first public school in Fresno County in one of the rooms of the fort. He hired Gillum Baley's eldest daughter, Rebecca, as the county's first school teacher.

Elisha Cotton Winchell's son, Lilbourne Alsip Winchell, wrote a history of Fresno County entitled, *History of Fresno County and the San Joaquin Valley, Narrative and Biographical* (Fresno, California: A.H. Cawston, Publisher, 1933). Lillbourne Alsip's wife, Ernestine Winchell, was a journalist for the *Fresno Morning Republican*. From 1922 until 1932 she wrote a column in that paper each Sunday, entitled "Fresno Memories," in which she wrote about the early history of Fresno City and the county. Gillum Baley and members of his family were the subjects of several of these articles.

Fort Miller was reactivated during the Civil War and manned by the California Volunteers. After the Civil War it was again deactivated and the land and buildings sold at public auction. The site is now covered by the waters of Lake Millerton. The blockhouse was saved and later reconstructed at Roeding Park in Fresno. It has recently been moved again, to the Table Mountain Casino at Friant, California.

39.   Holland, Autobiography.

CHAPTER 10

1.   The incident involved a group of approximately one hundred and fifty emigrants from Arkansas who were traveling the Mormon Trail from Salt Lake City to southern California in the summer of 1857 and became involved in a bitter dispute with some of the local Mormons living in southern Utah. At Mountain Meadows, a well-known rest stop on the trail, the emigrant train was attacked by Indians and a group of whites belonging to the southern Utah militia. Some of the whites held offices in the local Mormon Church as well as being officers in the militia. One hundred and twenty members of the wagon train were brutally murdered, and their bodies buried in shallow graves that were later dug up by wolves or Indians. Sixteen young children were spared, temporarily adopted by local southern Utah families, and later released to their relatives by the territorial government. Some of the emigrant's property was reportedly taken by the Indians; much of it was gathered up and sold at public auction by southern Utah Mormon officials.

The only person ever brought to trial for these atrocities was John D. Lee, a major in the Mormon militia and a member in good standing of the Mormon Church at the time of the incident. He was tried twice. The first trial ended in acquittal, but he was convicted in the second trial and sentenced to death by hanging or by firing squad, as specified by Utah law. He chose the firing squad. Many people, including some Mormons, believed that Lee was made a scapegoat to protect higher ranking members of the church. For more details the reader should consult Juanita Brooks, *The Mountain Meadows Massacre* (Normon: The University of Oklahoma Press, 1962).

2.   Melvin T. Smith, "Colorado River Exploration and the Mormon War," *Utah Historical Quarterly* (Winter 1970), pp. 207–23.

3.   Brooks, *The Mountain Meadows Massacre*, pp. 31–59.

4.   A.L. Kroeber and C.B. Kroeber, "Narrative of Chooksa homar, Episode 2, First Conflict with Americans" in *A Mohave War Reminiscence, 1854–1880.* University of California Publication in Anthropology, vol. 10 (Berkeley: University of California Press, 1973), 11–14.

5.   *U.S. Statutes at Large* 10, 1852, 979.

6.   U.S. Court of Claims, *Rose v. U.S.*

7.   Ibid.

8.   Ibid.

9. Ibid.

10. Ibid.

11. Ibid.

12. The amount of Rose's original claim was $27,932.76. He deducted $293, his share of the guide's fee, when he filed his petition with the court of claims in 1891. He probably did this on the advice of his attorney, as the guide's fee was not a chargeable loss since he would have had to pay this even if he were not attacked by Indians.

13. U.S. Court of Claims, *Rose v. U.S.*

CHAPTER 11

1. Sonoma County Recorder, *Udell-Anderson,* Marriage Book C, p. 104.

2. There is some confusion about John Udell's date of death. According to a descendant, Melvin Bliven, the generally accepted date of death for John Udell is June 30, 1874. Bliven stated that this date was copied from the John Udell family Bible by John Udell Jr., and from his copy by J. L. Udell in 1897. His headstone gives his date of death as July 1, 1873, and his age at the time of death as 80 years and 3 days. If correct, this would make his date of birth June 28, 1793. In his journal entry for June 22, 1858, he stated, "This is my sixty-third birthday," that would make his date of birth June 22, 1795. He is consistent with the June 22 date of birth in all of his writings. John Udell was an intelligent and articulate individual; one would have to believe that he knew his date of birth. Errors in dates of birth and death on headstones are not uncommon.

3. Annie R. Mitchell of the Tulare County Historical Society, undated letter to author.

4. Tulare County Recorder, *Hedgpeth-Enloe*, Marriage Book A, p. 40.

5. U.S. Court of Claims, *Hedgpeth v. U.S.*. In his deposition in the Hedgpeth Indian depredation suit, Gillum Baley was asked the following questions in direct examination:

> Q. Were you acquainted with Joel Hedgpeth, the deceased, during his lifetime?
> A. Yes Sir, I was.
> Q. Do you know that he is dead?
> A. I do because I saw him die.
> Q. When and where did he die?
> A. He died in Millerton, Fresno County California. He died about the year 1874.

6. The Department of Interior removed all the remaining graves from Fort Miller to Winchell Cove in Millerton State Park in 1944, but by then many of the grave sites were unidentifiable, including that of Joel

Hedgpeth. All the graves of military personnel had been removed to the Presidio in San Francisco many years before.

7.   *The Annual Minutes of the Missouri Conference of the Methodist Episcopal Church, South, for the Year 1887*, Missouri West Conference Archives, Central Methodist College, Fayette, Missouri, pp. 42–43.

8.   *The Annual Minutes of the Missouri Conference of the Methodist Episcopal Church, South, for the Year 1917*, Missouri West Conference Archives, Central Methodist College, Fayette, Missouri, p. 113.

9.   *The Annual Minutes of the Los Angeles Conference of the Methodist Episcopal Church, South, for the Year 1913*, General Commission on Archives and History, The United Methodist Church, Madison, New Jersey, pp. 109–11;

10.   J. C. Simmons, *The History of Southern Methodism on the Pacific Coast* (Nashville, Tennessee: Southern Methodist Publishing House, 1886), p. 336. See also, Joel W. Hedgpeth, "Grandfather Joel," a short biography of Joel Hedgpeth Jr. contained in a manuscript along with other personal papers, Santa Rose, California, copy in possession of author.

11.   J.M. Guinn, *History of the State of California, and Bio-Graphical Records of Coast Counties, California* (Chicago: The Chapman Publishing Co., 1904), biographical sketch of E. O. Smith, pp. 353–54.

12.   *San Jose Mercury*, March 12, 1892, "Edward O. Smith, A Memorial Sketch." E. O. Smith left two of his men in Texas (he had previously made arrangements with them to raise horses on shares). Seeing the conditions that existed in Texas at that time, he had but little hope of ever reaping any return from his investment. Seven years later, however, to his great surprise, his horses were delivered to him in Decatur, Illinois.

13.   *Fresno Morning Republican*, "The Flood at Bailey Flat" by Ernestine Winchell, April 6, 1924.

14.   *Memorial and Biographical History of the Counties of Fresno, Tulare, and Kern, California*, Biographical sketch for Gillum Baley, pp. 370–73.

15.   Phonetic spelling was used by most people in those days. Since there is no W sound in the name Right, William Right Baley always spelled his name Right, never Wright. He sometimes signed his name W. R. Baley. This has caused much confusion to descendants and historians accustomed to Right being spelled Wright They have trouble figuring out what the R stands for. On his headstone the name is "W. R. Baley." To his friends and relatives he was always called Right, never William or Bill.

16.   Udell, *Journal*, p. 59. "Nov. 1. To-day I joined Mr. Ezra Bucknam and Miss Adaline Daily in the sacred bonds of Matrimony."

17.   Hart Ralph Tambs, "The Life of Madeleine Isabelle Adeline Daly Bucknam, 1836–1913" Fifteen page handwritten, unpublished biography

[1990], Hart Ralph Tambs Family Papers, Tuolumne County Genealogical Society, Sonora, California.

18. Tulare County Recorder, *Divorce, Bucknam v. Bucknam,* Tulare County Suit No. 106. The divorce was granted June 21, 1880.

19. Tulare County Recorder, *Bucknam-Ketcham,* Marriage Book B, p. 448.

20. A newspaper account of the accident appeared in the *Tuolumne Independent,* Sonora, California, November 29, 1913.

21. Holland, Autobiography.

22. Page 157, Dwelling No. 399, Family No. 399.

23. Ibid.

24. Rose Jr., pp 52–60.

25. Ibid., p. 59.

26. Ibid., p. 133.

27. Rose Jr., p. 219. L. J. Rose's son and biographer, L. J. (Leon) Rose Jr., stated that although his father's investments were unsuccessful, he still possessed valuable holdings, and had he been patient and waited out the financial crisis, Leon believed that his father would have weathered the storm and emerged triumphant. However, little was known about mental depression in those days.

28. Los Angeles County Registrar-Recorder/County Clerk, Certificate of Vital Records (Death), *Elizabeth Burgett Jones,* Local Registered No. 728.

    This certificate of death for Elizabeth Burgett Jones lists her date of birth as February 2, 1804, and her place of birth as the State of New York. Her age at the time of death is given as 105 years and 24 days. Not surprisingly, the cause of death is listed as "senility."

29. *Fresno Bee,* December 3, 1947.

BIBLIOGRAPHY

UNPUBLISHED

Beale, Edward F. Beale Journal. Entries from March 1—May 4, 1859. Photocopy of handwritten original, no pagination. Beale Family Papers, Decatur House Papers. Library of Congress.

Floyd, William P. Typescript of a Diary Kept on Beale's 1858–1859 Expedition. Pencilled original in small notebook. Huntington Library, San Marino, California.

Hedgpeth, Joel Jr. "A Trip Across the Plains 1858–1859." Eight page typescript, n.d., of original handwritten copy. Holt-Atherton Department of Special Collections, Mss. H453, University of Pacific Libraries, University of Pacific, Stockton, California.

Holland, Edward Warren. Autobiography. Eight page typescript, n.d. Original in Tulare Public Library, Genealogy Department, Tulare, California.

Milner, Edith Allen. "Covered Wagon Experiences." n.d. Arizona Historical Society, Tucson, Arizona.

_____. "Recollections of Edith Allen Milner From Her Mother's Talks to Her About the Emigrant Trip Across the Plains in 1858–1859." Robert Powers Family Papers, Nut Tree, California.

Tambs, Hart Ralph. "The Life of Madeleine Isabelle Adeline Daly Bucknam, 1836–1913." Fifteen page handwritten, unpublished biography (1990). Hart Ralph Tambs Family Papers, Tuolumne County Genealogical Society, Sonora, California.

PUBLISHED

Annual Minutes of the Los Angeles Conference of the Methodist Episcopal Church, South, for the Year 1913. General Commission on Archives and History, The United Methodist Church, Madison, New Jersey.

Annual Minutes of the Missouri Conference of the Methodist Episcopal Church, South, for the Year 1887. Missouri West Conference Archives, Central Methodist College, Fayette, Missouri.

Annual Minutes of the Missouri Conference of the Methodist Episcopal Church, South, for the Year 1917. Missouri West Conference Archives, Central Methodist College, Fayette, Missouri.

Arnold, Ann. *Gleanings on the Hedgpeth Line*. Bakersfield, California: Self
    published, 1977. Family History Center, United States/Canada
    [Canada?] fiche area, 6055–227, RN0108478. Salt Lake City, Utah.
Avillo, Phillip J. Jr., "Fort Mojave: Outpost on the Upper Colorado." *The
    Journal of Arizona History* (Summer 1970): 77–100.
Bahti, Tom. *Southwestern Indian Tribes*. Las Vegas, Nevada: K. C. Publications,
    1989.
Baley, William Right. Family Bible, in possession of author.
Barnes, William C. *Arizona Place Names*. Revised and enlarged by Byrd H.
    Granger. Tucson: University of Arizona Press, 1960.
Bonsal, Stephen. *Edward Fitzgerald Beale: A Pioneer in the Path of Empire,
    1822–1903*. New York and London: Putnam's Sons, 1912.
Briggs, Carl, and Clyde Francis Trudell. *Quarterdeck and Saddlehorn: The Story
    of Edward F. Beale, 1822–1893*. Glendale, California: The Arthur H. Clark
    Company, 1983.
Brooks, Juanita. *The Mountain Meadows Massacre*. Norman: University of
    Oklahoma Press, 1962.
Casebier, Dennis G. *The Mojave Road*. Norco, California: Tales of the Mojave
    Road Publishing Co., 1975.
————. *Fort Pah-Ute, California*. Norco, California: Tales of the Mojave
    Road Publishing Co., 1974.
Cheney, J. W. "The Story of an Emigrant Train." *Annals of Iowa*, No. 2 (July
    1915): 82–97.
Coan, Charles F. *A History of New Mexico*. Vol. I. Chicago and New York:
    The American Historical Society, Inc., 1925.
Crampton, Charles Gregory. *The Zunis of Cibola*. Salt Lake City: University
    of Utah Press, 1977.
Dodge, Bertha S. *The Road West: Saga of the Thirty-fifth Parallel*. Albuquerque,
    New Mexico: University of New Mexico Press, 1980.
Dunlop, Richard. *Great Trails of the West*. Nashville & New York: Abingdon
    Press, 1971.
Dutton, Bertha P. *Friendly People, the Zuñi Indians*. Santa Fe, New Mexico:
    Museum of New Mexico Press, 1963.
Emmett, Chris. *Fort Union and the Winning of the Southwest*. Norman:
    University of Oklahoma Press, 1956.
Foreman, Grant, ed. *A Pathfinder in the Southwest*, Norman: University of
    Oklahoma Press, 1941.
Fresno City and County Historical Society Archives, Kearney Park, Fresno,
    California, Baley family records.
Guinn, J. M. *History of the State of California, and Bio-Graphical Records of Coast
    Counties, California*. Chicago: The Chapman Publishing Company, 1904.
Heath, Kate. "A Child's Journey Through Arizona and New Mexico." *The
    Californian*, January 1881, p. 18.

History of Nodaway County Missouri. St. Joseph, Missouri: National Historical Company, 1882.

Hunter, Leslie Gene. "The Mojave Expedition of 1858–1859." *Arizona and the West* (Summer 1979): 137–144.

Jones, Dana H. *L. J. Rose and the Founding of Rosemead*. [published where?] First Bank of Rosemead, 1953.

Kroeber, A. L. *Handbook of California Indians*. Washington, D.C.: Government Printing Office, 1925.

Kroeber, A. L., and C. B. Kroeber. "Narrative of Chooksa homar. Episode 2, First Conflict with Americans." *A Mohave War Reminiscence, 1854–1880*. University of California Publication in Anthropology, vol. 10, Berkeley, California: University of California Press, 1973.

Lesley, Lewis Burt, ed. *Uncle Sam's Camels: The Journal of May Humphreys Stacey Supplemented by the Report of Edward Fitzgerald Beale (1857–1858)*. Cambridge, Massachusetts: Harvard University Press, 1929.

Los Angeles County Registrar-Recorder/County Clerk. Certificate of Vital Records (Death). *Elizabeth Burgett Jones*. Local Registered No. 728.

Majors, Alexander. *Seventy Years on the Frontier*. Edited by Colonel Prentiss Ingraham. Minneapolis: Ross E. Haines, Inc., 1965.

Memorial and Biographical History of the Counties of Fresno, Tulare, and Kern, California. Chicago: The Lewis Publishing Company, 1891. Reprint, Salem, Massachusetts: Higginson Book Company, 1992.

Messersmith, Dan W. The History of Mohave County to 1912. Kingman, Arizona: Mohave County Historical Society, 1991.

Mitchell, Annie R. Tulare County Historical Society. Undated letter to author.

Miners and Business Men's Directory: For the Year Commencing January 1st, 1956. Embracing a General Directory of the Citizens of Tuolumne, and Portions of Calaveras, Stanislaus and San Joaquin Counties, Together with the Mining Laws of Each District; Description of the Different Camps, and Other Interesting Statistical Matter. Columbia: Heckendorn and Wilson, 1856. Reprint, Donald I. Segerstrom Memorial Fund, 1976.

Odens, Peter. *Fire over Yuma: Tales from the Lower Colorado*. Yuma, Arizona: Southwest Printers, 1966.

Past and Present of Nodaway County Missouri, vol. 1. Indianapolis, Indiana: B. F. Bowen and Company, 1910.

Rose, L. J. An account (without title) dated October 28, 1858, published in Keosauqua, Iowa, newspaper, Huntington Library, San Marino, California.

———. "Massacre on the Colorado." Appendix 4, in *The Cattle on a Thousand Hills*, by Robert Glass Cleland. San Marino: The Huntington Library, 1951.

Rose, L. J. Appendix IV, "Massacre on the Colorado," in *The Cattle on a Thousand Hills* by Robert Glass Cleland. San Marino: The Huntington Library, 1951.

———. "Cross Country Reminiscences." *The Californian* (December, 1892–May, 1893): 114–22.

Rose, L. J. Jr. *L. J. Rose of Sunny Slope 1827–1899*. San Marino, California: The Huntington Library, 1959.

Simmons, J. C. *The History of Southern Methodism on the Pacific Coast.* Nashville, Tennessee: Southern Methodist Publishing House, 1886.

Slater, John M. *El Morro Inscription Rock, New Mexico*. Los Angeles: The Plantin Press, 1961.

Smith, Alson Jesse. *Men Against the Mountains: Jedediah Smith and the Southwest Expedition of 1826–1829.* New York: The John Day Company, 1965.

Smith, Jack Beale. *John Udell: The Rest of the Story.* Flagstaff, Arizona: Tales of the Beale Road Publishing Company, 1986.

———. *Kerlins Well: A Unique Site on the Beale Wagon Road Near Seligmon, Arizona.* Flagstaff, Arizona; Tales of the Beale Wagon Road. Publishing Company 1986.

Smith, Melvin T. "Colorado River Exploration and the Mormon War." *Utah Historical Quarterly* (Winter 1970): 207–223.

Sonoma County Recorder. *Udell-Anderson* in Marriage Book C. p.104.

Stanley, David Sloan. *Personal Memoirs of Major General D. S. Stanley, U.S.A.* Cambridge, Massachusetts: Harvard University Press, 1917.

Stratton, Royal B. *Captivity of the Oatman Girls.* New York: Carlton & Porter, 1858. Reprint, Alexandria, Virginia: Time-Life Books, Inc., 1982.

Sturtevant, William C., ed. *Handbook of North American Indians.* Vol. 10, *Southwest*. Edited by Alfonso Ortiz. Washington, D.C.: Smithsonian Institute, 1983.

Thompson, Gerald. *Edward F. Beale and the American West.* Albuquerque: University of New Mexico Press, 1983.

Tompkins, Rose Ann. "Early Beale Road Emigrants." Paper presented at the Oregon-California Trails Association Symposium, Casa Grande, Arizona, June 1990.

Tulare County Recorder. *Hedgpeth—Enloe*, Marriage Book A, p. 40. *Bucknam—Ketcham*, Marriage Book B, p. 448. *Divorce, Bucknam v. Bucknam*, Tulare County Suit No. 106.

Tuolumne County Genealogical Society Archives, Sonora, California, Daly and Holland family records.

Udell, John. *Journal Kept During a Trip Across the Plains Containing an Account of the Massacre of a Portion of His Party by the Mojave Indians in 1859.* Jefferson, Ohio: Ashtabula Sentinel Steam Press, 1868. Reprint, Los Angeles, California: N. A. Kovach, 1946.

———. Letter to the *Ashtabula [Ohio] Sentinel*, April 7, 1859.

Vandor, Paul E. *History of Fresno County, California, with Biographical Sketches.* Vol 2. Los Angeles: Historical Records Co., 1919.

Winchell, Ernestine. "Fresno Memories." *Fresno Morning Republican,* April 6, 1924; November 29, 1925; September 29, 1927; February 9, 1930.

Winchell, Lilbourne Alsip. *History of Fresno County and the San Joaquin Valley, Narrative and Biographical.* Fresno, California: A. H. Cawston, Publisher, 1933.

Woodward, Arthur. "The Founding of Fort Mohave." *Pony Express Courier,* (May 1937): 4–5.

NEWSPAPERS

Daily Missouri Republican, December 29, 1858.

Des Moines Register, September 6, 1964.

Fresno Bee, December 3, 1947.

Fresno Daily Expositor, November 12–13, 1895.

Fresno Morning Republican, November 12, 1895; March 7, 1900; December 9, 1906; April 6, 1924; February 9; 1930.

Fresno Weekly Expositor, November 23, 1881.

Keosauqua [Iowa] Republican, November 23, 1858.

Los Angeles Star, November 18, 1858.

San Bernardino Sun Telegram, October 9, 1960.

Santa Fe Gazette, October 16, 1858; December 16, 1858.

San Jose Mercury, March 12, 1892.

Tuolumne [Sonora, California] Independent, December 15, 1877; January 15, 1887; September 17, 1892; October 15, 1892; November 29, 1913.

Union [Sonora, California] Democrat, September 17, 1892; September 24, 1892.

Weekly Alta California "Supplement," May 3, 1859.

GOVERNMENT DOCUMENTS

Beale, Edward Fitzgerald. *Wagon Road from Fort Defiance to the Colorado River.* U.S. Thirty-fifth Congress, First session. House Executive Document No. 124, 1858.

————. *Wagon Road from Fort Smith to the Colorado River.* Thirty-sixth Congress, First Session. House Executive Document No. 42, 1860.

Bureau of the Census, Fresno County, California, 1860, 1870.

————, Tulare County, California, 1860, 1870.

————, Tuolumne County, California, 1860, 1870, 1880.

————, Van Buren County, Iowa, 1850, 1860.

————, Nodaway County, Missouri, 1850.

Records of the Adjutant General. Letters Received. "Beale to Hoffman, May 13, 1859. Hoffman to Beale, May 14, 1859." RG 94. M567, roll 597. National Archives.

U.S. Court of Claims, Indian Depredation Division. *Gillum Baley, as Surviving Partner of Gillum Baley and William R. Baley, Deceased, Late Co-Partner, U.S. Government and the Mohave Indians*. Case No. 8214. RG 123. National Archives.

———. *William P. Hedgpeth, Administrator of the Estate of Joel Hedgpeth v. U.S. Government and the Mohave Indians*. Case No. 8373. RG 123. National Archives.

———. *Leonard J. Rose v. U.S. Government and the Mohave Indians*. Case No. 2176. RG 123. National Archives.

U.S. Department of War, Army Continental Commands. Letters Received by the Department of New Mexico. "Major E. Backus to Lieutenant L. W. O'Bannon, October 12, 1858." "Emigrants to Commander, Fort Defiance, Picacho, Territory of New Mexico, September 22, 1858." Letter B 70-DNMex. RG 393. National Archives.

———. Letters Sent by the Department of New Mexico. "Colonel B. L. E. Bonneville to Lieutenant Colonel L. Thomas, A.A.G., Headquarters of the Army, New York, November 6, 1858." RG 393. Vol. 10, pp. 286–87. M1072, roll 2. National Archives.

INDEX